From Two Republics to One Divided

A book in the series

Latin America Otherwise: Languages, Empires, Nations

Series editors:

Walter D. Mignolo, Duke University

Irene Silverblatt, Duke University

FROM TWO REPUBLICS

TO ONE DIVIDED

Contradictions of Postcolonial Nationmaking

in Andean Peru

MARK THURNER

Duke University Press   Durham and London

2nd printing, 2006
© 1997 Duke University Press
All rights reserved
Printed in the United States of America on acid-free paper ∞
Designed by Katy Giebenhain
Typeset in Caslon by Tseng Information Systems, Inc.
Library of Congress Cataloging-in-Publication Data appear
on the last printed page of this book.

CONTENTS

ABOUT THE SERIES

atin America Otherwise: Languages, Empires, Nations is a critical series. It aims to explore the emergence and consequences of concepts used to define "Latin America" while at the same time exploring the broad interplay of political, economic, and cultural practices that have shaped Latin American worlds. Latin America, at the crossroads of competing imperial designs and local responses, has been construed as a geocultural and geopolitical entity since the nineteenth century. This series provides a starting point to redefine Latin America as a configuration of political, linguistic, cultural, and economic intersections that demand a continuous reappraisal of the role of the Americas in history, and of the ongoing process of globalization and the relocation of people and cultures that have characterized Latin America's experience. Latin America Otherwise: Languages, Empires, Nations is a forum that confronts established geocultural constructions, that rethinks area studies and disciplinary boundaries, that assesses convictions of the academy and of public policy, and that, correspondingly, demands that the practices through which we produce knowledge and understanding about and from Latin America be subject to rigorous and critical scrutiny.

From Two Republics to One Divided studies a range of predicaments that haunted the making (and unmaking) of the nineteenth-century Peruvian nation-state. These predicaments, as Mark Thurner demonstrates, were rooted in the contradiction between the cultural politics of Spain's colonial enterprise and the camouflaged cultural politics of the Peruvian liberal state. The Peruvian Republic's ideology of statecraft denied ethnic categories any role in government: "Indian" did not officially exist. Nevertheless, in the practice of government, the Republic had to take those categories into account. Reflecting on postcolonial theory, Thurner is able to carve analytical space for the unimagined of both Republican historiography and of Republican politics. Because he envisions the transformation of the Viceroyalty of Peru into a modern nation-state from a local perspective, Thurner is uniquely able to amplify these analytical predicaments: he can assess peasant engagement with elite Republican political worlds as he recasts disciplinary methodologies. He does so with a critical use of anthropology, history, and literary theory. *From Two Republics to One Divided* speaks across centuries, disciplines, and locations to all students of postcolonial dilemmas.

Walter D. Mignolo, Duke University
Irene Silverblatt, Duke University

PREFACE

The questions I ask in this book were first raised in graduate seminars in anthropology and history at the University of Wisconsin–Madison. In anthropology, Frank Salomon and Ann Stoler (now at Michigan) were my mentors, while in history Steven Feierman (now at Penn), Florencia Mallon, and Steve Stern were significant teachers. Despite this advance preparation, the unpredictable, lived-in experience of doing research in Peru in those earth-shattering years of 1989–90 was decisive (probably in more ways than I suspect) in shaping what this study has become. As the Berlin Wall came tumbling down in Europe, the wall of an ultraorthodox Maoism was going up in Peru. At the same time, the Peruvian Left was falling in disarray, and the scholar-hero of that Left had just died, at a tragically young age, of brain cancer. As the coffin of Alberto Flores Galindo was carried out of the Casona of San Marcos University and enveloped in the flurry of red flags (of PUM, the United Mariateguist Party) and masked *diablada* dancers, the Peruvian Left seemed to go with him. The world seemed upside down, out of joint.

My project was disjointed, too. Originally designed with a significant ethnographic and oral history dimension, I was soon obliged to discard the field component when the (until then) largely silent war in and around Huaylas-Ancash escalated in 1989 (it has since subsided). A series of political assassinations, nightly bombings, power outages, armed attacks and counterattacks in several peasant communities, and the temporary presence of counterinsurgency patrols combined to produce a pervasive sense of fear and suspicion during the months I spent in Huaraz, now largely confining myself to the archives. Lima was by no means peaceful either. Car bombings and gunfire were not uncommon in our neighborhood. Legitimate strikes and marches, as well as the Shining Path's so-called armed strikes, often elicited the repressive response of military and anticrowd forces in the streets adjacent to the archives in downtown Lima.

Somewhat to my surprise, reading in the archives was rarely alienating from the current political and social climate. Reading often heightened my sense of what was happening in the streets or in the hills, particularly when tear gas wafted into the reading room of the National Library as a protesting crowd was herded into waiting personnel carriers in the street below, or when the National Archive's unpaid staff decided to stage a lockout. Still, nineteenth-century documentation rarely approximated the thick, lived-in intensity of street or country life, particularly when it came to the subaltern majorities. With the ethnographic angle removed, the now exclusively "archival" project invariably ran up against the representational limits of the Creole imagination and a weak national state. The postcolonial, liberal negation of the Indian, which was also, apparently, characteristic of the Mexican experience, had combined with the pale and disrupted functioning of republican courts (when compared to their efficient Bourbon predecessors) to produce an archive nearly devoid of ethnographic content. In search of some trace of negated Andean political culture, I turned to the voluminous colonial record. By deepening the diachronic dimension to include the colonial period, shifts in the elite political imagination and, indeed, in what the state bureaucracies were concerned to document, became increasingly clear. Aided by this longer perspective, the postcolonial predicament and the colonial contradictions of Peru's abiding "national question" came more clearly into view.

In Peru, Rodrigo Montoya first pointed me in the direction of Huaylas-Ancash in that most memorable summer of 1986. Over an earthy and at once exquisite Andean meal prepared in the charming Lima way, Rodrigo piqued a regional interest and problematic subsequently reconfirmed by the late Alberto Flores Galindo, by Nelson Manrique and Christine Hünefeldt, and most decidedly by Manuel Burga. Had Manuel not welcomed me at the Instituto de Apoyo Agrario and shared his enthusiasm for the project, it might never have gotten off the ground. I also owe more than I can say to staff and colleagues at Lima's Instituto de Estudios Peruanos (IEP). The offices and courtyard of IEP provided an appropriate place for intellectual work and debate, as well as a home away from home. Carlos Contreras and Luís Miguel Glave deserve special recognition for tolerating my eighteenth-month intrusion in the Sección de Historia. I also thank Rafael Varón, likewise of IEP, for his generosity with documentary microfilms and transcriptions concerning colonial Huaraz.

In Huaraz, the Archivo Departamental de Ancash (ADA), most of which had never been worked in detail by scholars, was central to my research. In 1989 several important local archival collections were consolidated under the new administration of the ADA, ostensibly a departmental branch of the Archivo General de la Nación (AGN). The invaluable Archivo Notarial Valerio (formerly the Notaría Alvarado), along with several other notarial and local governmental archives, was handed over to the ADA's director. Piled in a sufficiently large but dimly lit depository, housed in a corner of the

Municipal Market of Huaraz, these archives were only remedially inventoried and stacked in precarious piles as I worked through them in 1989–90. Thus, citations given for individual documents may no longer correspond to the actual organization of the archive, which has been in considerable flux. In addition, several documents cited by earlier scholars who saw the Notaría Alvarado collection were undoubtedly lost in the process of transfer to the new archive, if not before. Sadly, I must also report that the ADA was bombed in 1992, although it appears that the collection remains intact.

I could not have done research in the ADA without the steadfast guidance and friendly support of Florencio Quito and Yolanda Auqui. Florencio and Yolanda are to be commended for their unfailing dedication to a little-known archive, despite dismal administration and an absolute lack of funds. To Yolanda especially, without whose help I could not have made the necessary photocopies, I extend heartfelt thanks. I hope that this book will eventually provide some small recompense for their unrecognized labors *a favor de la historia andina.* But there is another debt here that cannot be repaid, one that is owed to all who left some trace of their lives in those paper bundles. I am under no delusion about why they are there: the words attributed to them have been recorded for other purposes. Perhaps it is this sense of debts unpaid that urges me to redeploy those words as much as possible without, I hope, overtaxing readers.

Back in Lima, two Ancash expatriates and colleagues who have devoted much of their lives to the history of Huaylas-Ancash shared lively conversation and compared notes, for which I am most grateful: Manuel Reina Loli and César Augusto Alba Herrera. I also benefitted immensely from the insights and researches of William Stein, whose detailed study of the Atusparia insurgency must inform any serious work on the period. I could not have located the relevant material at the Archivo Histórico Militar (AHM) in Lima without the tireless assistance and warm hospitality of the highly competent Elía Lazarte. Irma García, director of the Sala de Investigaciones of the Biblioteca Nacional del Perú, kindly granted access to reserved documentary collections. Also at the Biblioteca Nacional, special thanks to "Mifu" for his great work in the microfilm department. At the AGN, the reading room staff was very helpful despite the almost unimaginably restrictive and exploitative conditions under which they worked (and struck). Special thanks goes also to the microfilm department at the AGN for going the extra mile when grisly budget cuts made things look very grim indeed. Mario Ormeño, *huaracino* and then director of the Archivo Histórico Arzobispal de Lima, assisted in locating obscure documents and in general facilitated my research there.

For providing the opportunity to teach a graduate seminar on Andean peasants in Peruvian history, and for his warm conversation, I thank Franklin Pease of the history program at the Pontifícia Universidad Católica del Perú. I must express gratitude to Félix Denegri for receiving me in his impressive private library and letting me search to my heart's content. I also owe much to the late Guillermo Mayer, for his hospitality and dignity, and to Elizabeth Mayer for letting me ride that old bicycle to Denegri's library. More personal debts are with Félix Oliva, for being here, and with Rick and Flaca, and also Karen, for being there.

My heartfelt gratitude goes out to María and especially to Liduvina, who at different times provided wonderful childcare for Olga. Beyond making this book possible, they made life in Lima enjoyable even in the hardest and darkest of times. Still, Olga managed to interrupt my work whenever she could, for which I am immensely grateful. Alejandra, whom I also met that memorable summer of '86 in Lima, shared the emotional extremes of living and doing archival research during Peru's time of fear. Our lives, our dreams, and our work get caught up somehow in this eerie yet seductive place which is like no other: Lima.

In Brooklyn, where most of this manuscript was first fashioned, there is a park called Prospect. The elitist, nineteenth-century urban commons has become that rare, late twentieth-century refuge for imagining community. I may not have finished the dissertation on which this book is based were it not for that park and the times shared in it. Across the East River in Manhattan, the Social Science Research Council was largely responsible for making my research in Peru possible, for which I am most grateful. SSRC/ACLS dissertation support, generously provided by the William and Flora Hewlett Foundation and the Andrew W. Mellon Foundation, was especially critical since it allowed me to work in a region of Peru that was otherwise off-limits to U.S. nationals. At the University of Florida, where I refinished most of the manuscript, I have contracted many personal debts with my new community of colleagues and friends, some of whom have read all or parts of this book.

I am grateful to Cambridge University Press for permission to use in this book material previously published in my article " 'Republicanos' and 'la Comunidad de Peruanos': Unimagined Political Communities in Postcolonial Andean Peru," *Journal of Latin American Studies* 27 (1995), pp. 291–318.

Except where otherwise noted, all translations in this book from Spanish sources are my own.

My sincere thanks to Valerie Millholland of Duke University Press for her keen and decisive interest in this book, to Jean Brady and the Duke

team for taking care over its production, and to freelance copyeditor Charles
Purrenhage for trying to fix my prose. I am also grateful to Walter Mignolo
and Irene Silverblatt, editors of Duke's new "Latin America Otherwise"
series, for wanting to include my book on their list.

Finally, I thank readers Paul Gootenberg, Brooke Larson, and Joanne
Rappaport for their unflinching support and insightful criticism.

Lima
7 March 1996

PERU Huaylas-Ancash and major towns

From Two Republics to One Divided

CHAPTER 1

Historicizing the Postcolonial Andean Predicament

This regional history of Huaylas-Ancash plots critical shifts in the discourse and practice of state-peasantry relations during Peru's long nineteenth-century transition from dual colonial to unitary postcolonial forms of nationhood. Although unreplicable, Peru's troubled transition from pluriethnic colony of castes toward unitary postcolony of citizens was an early moment in the universally ambivalent trajectory broadly characteristic of our age. To wit: in the world history of European colonialism and postcolonial nationmaking, the New World is old and the Old World new. And if the first wave of European colonialism washed up on American shores long before it reached high tide in late-nineteenth- and twentieth-century Asia and Africa, then the irreversible cultural and political conundrums of colonialism's aftermath were perhaps nowhere more unanticipated, and deeply contradictory, than in South America's pluriethnic Andean region.[1]

Writing "in an anthropological spirit" on the origin and spread of nationalism, Benedict Anderson made an underappreciated move that in effect shifts the historical relationship between so-called old European nations and the new postcolonial states.[2] Since, Anderson argued, the modern invention of nationhood was everywhere as fundamentally cultural (in Clifford Geertz's sense) as religion or kinship, one could sidestep the then regnant notion of nationalism as mere political ideology and approach nations as the cultural inventions of "print capitalism," as "imagined political communities" of intermediate scale wherein citizens were territorially bound by emerging concepts of sovereignty. This new style and scale of community was distinct from the face-to-face communities of the peasant village or small town, and it superseded the boundless, plurinational religious ecumenisms of the medieval (and early colonial?) world. The historical origins of this modern nation and its nationalism were traceable to the workings of absolutist dynasties and the rise of printing and national vernaculars, which served as narrative media for imagining the social space and "simultaneous time" of unseen national cohorts.[3] Like Eric Hobsbawm[4] and other critical scholars, Anderson proposed that nations and their nationalisms are of modern invention; contrary to "organicist" or "primordialist" readings, no "old nations" in this sense of the term could have existed before the late eighteenth century.[5] Thus the Latin American republics are relatively old "by the standard of nationhood"[6]—indeed, even "pioneering" in that they were the front line of anticolonial republican nationalism, thereby anticipating anticolonial nationalist movements in the colonized Old World.[7] In light of this reformulation, Geertz's insightful summation of the postcolonial predicament of Asian and African "new states" as, to paraphrase, not quite the present without the past, nor the past in the present, may be rephrased for the Americas: Latin America's republics were "old" like some European nations, but they were also postcolonial like the African and Asian "new states" of the twentieth century.[8]

Latin American nations are also relatively "old" because Spain's colonial rule in the Americas both predated and endured longer than most extra-Iberian European colonialisms in interior Africa and Asia. In the colonial core regions of Mesoamerica and the South American Andes, the antiquity of Iberian colonialism was deepened by the greater antiquity of densely peopled precolonial states and societies. The worn phrase of "old societies and new states" which Geertz summoned to describe postcolonial Asian and African predicaments,[9] may also be applied to the core regions of ancient American civilization—despite the early demographic collapse of the indigenous population which, in the Peruvian case, did not begin to recover until the late eighteenth and nineteenth centuries.[10]

Anderson's useful phrase "old empires, new nations" is perhaps a more precise reformulation of the state/society equation in nuclear Spanish America, since it captures the colonial predicament of much of the region.[11] In this regard, Anderson noted, after Gerhard Masur, "the striking fact that 'each of the new South American republics had been a [colonial] administrative unit from the sixteenth to the eighteenth century.' In this respect they foreshadow the new states of Africa and parts of Asia in the mid-twentieth century."[12] As in Africa and parts of Asia, postcolonial American nations inherited the political boundaries of colonial administrative units, in this case because "the very vastness of the Spanish American empire, the enormous variety of its soils and climates, and, above all, the immense difficulty of communications in a preindustrial age, tended to give these units a self-contained character."[13]

But by what "hegemonic trick" were colonial administrative units—
which were inscribed across the fragments of precolonial polities—to
be imagined as bounded and sovereign nations? Anderson's provocative,
Habermasian thesis concerning the role of the elite public sphere spread
by print capitalism and vernacular understandings gets us part of the way
there, as do his sparkling hypotheses about the nationalist mutation of colonial spaces and the perambulations of Creole officials.[14] But what becomes
clear with local and regional historical analysis is that the colonial legacy of
administrative frontiers was rather less significant for postcolonial nationmaking than were the hierarchical, discontinuous, and internal boundaries
of ethnic caste, color, class, gender, and corporation (to mention only these)
bequeathed by the centuries of Spanish rule.

In Andean Peru, as elsewhere in Spanish America, the postcolonial history of nationmaking was haunted by an earlier history of colonial state
formation which, in the ambivalent fashion diagnostic of postcolonial
nationalist predicaments everywhere, it was condemned both to negate
and reclaim.[15] Despite critical differences, Peru—like other old postcolonial
nations of the New World South—may be seen to share this predicament
with the new postcolonial nations of the Old World South. In all cases,
this predicament meant that the postcolonial nation and its history had to
be constructed—albeit in very different ways and to different degrees—by
"contesting colonial rule and [at the same time] protecting its flanks from
the subalterns."[16]

The Postcolonial Creole Predicament

In contrast to most textbook versions of the advent of European nation-
states, Anderson follows John Lynch (and other historians of Latin
America) in asserting that the Latin American republics were not the political by-products of middle-class struggles against an aristocratic ruling class.
Instead, they were states created from above by landed colonial elites who
sought to break free from a decadent metropolis whose representatives still
monopolized political and economic privilege in the colonies. But discon-
tented Creole elites were at the same time spurred to independence "by the
fear of 'lower class' political mobilizations: to wit, Indian or Negro-slave
uprisings."[17] In short, "the perennial contradiction of the [Creole] position
[was to be] forever caught between the intrusive authority of the European
metropolis and the explosive discontent of the native masses."[18] In practice,
this contradiction meant that "the great challenge facing [Creole patriots]
was to obtain independence without unleashing a revolution."[19] One social
result of this contradiction was, as Lynch observed in his monumental study

of Spanish American Independence, that after Spanish rule the *caudillo-*ridden Latin American republics could look rather more like militarized *haciendas,* or landed estates, than liberal societies.[20]

In the northern Andes (Venezuela, Colombia) the Creole liberator Simón Bolívar first had to put down the popular uprisings of loyalist black *pardos* and, later, the backland *llaneros*—although subsequently he wisely struck an alliance with "the hordes" that had once sworn death to the Creoles. Bolívar's dictatorial and patrician style of republicanism reflected a widely felt social distrust of popular democracy among Creoles.[21] In Peru, things could be worse: "memories of the great *jacquerie* led by Tupac Amaru [II in 1780] were still fresh" in the minds of the Creole elite.[22] Andean Indians sometimes supported loyalist forces in the fight against the "foreign" troops of José de San Martín of Argentina (who fought his way up the coast from Chile) and Bolívar (who marched down the Andean Cordillera from Venezuela and Colombia).[23] Perhaps a majority of Creole elites in Viceregal Lima could be persuaded to support the decrepit Bourbon monarchy, not least because they feared the consequences of widespread Indian unrest more than they reviled Spanish tutelage.[24]

But, as Anderson is wont to show, the aspirations of the Creole movements for independence in South America went beyond mere reaction against popular mobilizations. The desire of regional elites to wield greater control over the indigenous and mixed-blood castes could and did merge with commercial and state-building interests. These desires and interests could also blend with the rising Creole patriotic impulse that sought to rid the Americas of "the tyranny of the Spanish stepmother" so as to be free to self-govern their adopted "native land."[25]

Contrary to Creole nationalist historiography, Creole claims to this modern nativism conferred by place of birth did not make them the natural allies of indigenous elites in an epic, anti-imperialist, Pan-American struggle against the despised Europeans. Indeed, the Creole nationalist identification with America presented inevitable and transparent contradictions—of which Bolívar himself was well aware—given the historically deeper claims to native status made by rival Andean or Indian elites and their communities. As Bolívar confessed: "Americans by birth and Europeans by law, we [Creoles] find ourselves engaged in a dual conflict, disputing with the natives for titles of ownership, and at the same time struggling to maintain ourselves in the country of our birth against the opposition of the [Spanish] invaders. Thus our position is most extraordinary and complicated."[26] This complicated Creole predicament was to be exacerbated by the colonial heritage of the state.

Of Colonial Fragments

As "the anthropologist among historians" Bernard S. Cohn noted for the case of the British in India, "one of the first problems confronting a colonial power after establishing *de facto* or *de jure* sovereignty over a new territory is to set up procedures for settling disputes arising within the dominated society, and to establish a whole range of rights in relation to property and obligations of individuals and groups to one another and to the [colonial] state."[27] Key to the Spanish resolution of this colonial problem was the late sixteenth-century juridical invention of the colonized "Indian nation" and its "republic of Indians" juxtaposed, in binary fashion, to the colonial "Spanish nation" and its "republic of Spaniards." Although this flatly imperial designation did violence to the ethnic diversity enveloped within then current notions of nation and republic, the juri-political classifications nevertheless did create the necessary institutional "locale of contestation"[28] wherein the colonial cultural politics of "national" identity could be played out. In Peru as elsewhere in the New World, Spain's dual-nation system of colonial rule also interstitialized in problematic ways the proliferating castes (*castas*) of mixed-blood or uncertain descent.

The colonial policy of legal-political segregation by "nation" and "republic" was made imaginable by virtue of the transnational imperial arch, or "head," of state provided by the ecumenical Catholic Crown of Spain. The Creole nationalist project that tore off what was left of this arch was, in contrast, partly inspired by the universalist, "enlightened liberal" ideal that "true" nationhood (and economic progress) could be achieved only if the "despotism" inherent in Spain's colonial particularism were abolished. Decolonization (or abolition) of the colonized Indian republic and the ambivalent banishment of the colonial Spanish republic (of which Creole nationalists were, and ethnically remained, members) would allow formerly oppressed Indians to be gradually "enlightened" and "civilized" so that they could "join the rest of the free citizens" of Peru in the semisacred unity of the independent nation of citizens. Thus—following the illusory logic of the liberal utopia envisaged by Bolívar and his associates—where two republics and their interstitial castes had once languished under the crushing weight of Spanish despotism, one free and united republic of national citizens would emerge.

For Creole liberals the "Republic" in the postcolonial Republic of Peru could not be the same as the "republic" in the colonial republic of Indians or republic of Spaniards. In his essays on nations and nationalism, Eric Hobsbawm noted that only after 1884 did the official Spanish notion of "nation" (*nación*) take on the connotation of "the inhabitants" or "people" (*pueblo*) under one "government" (*gobierno*) or "state" (*estado*).[29] It was not until the 1920s that the rewritten formula of ethnicity = people = nation was combined with the modern doctrine of the so-called natural desire for statehood to produce the contemporary, quasi-ethnic notion of the nation-state, which is sometimes identified (in Eurocentric fashion) as "the German model." But prior to the European liberal age of the middle to late nineteenth century, and emerging during the post-Enlightenment Age of Revolution of the late eighteenth and early nineteenth centuries, "nation" carried an almost exclusively political meaning. It was then that the modern nation was increasingly thought of as "the body of citizens whose collective sovereignty constituted them a state which was their political expression."[30] This nation was a novelty unencumbered by history and above ethnicity, and it was opposed to earlier, pre-Enlightenment usages that linked "nation" to ancestral lineage and, by instantiation, to local ethnic corporation. It was this novel, parahistorical concept of the nation—as a body of citizens whose expression was the territorial state—that infused the imagination of the "Creole pioneers" who founded independent republics in early nineteenth-century South America.[31]

During most of Spanish America's long colonial period, quite different notions of nation and republic were in circulation. Official colonial usage designated "nation" as an ethnic-ancestral "collection of inhabitants" associated with a "kingdom" or place (not the same as late nineteenth-century notions of "race"), while the "republic" was often understood to be that nation's legitimate body of public governance as well as its "commonweal of interests" (*causa pública*).[32] As mentioned, state discourse and fiscal classificatory schemes designated subjects of Spanish descent (including the "American Spaniards," or Creoles) and those of Indian descent, respectively, as members of the Spanish nation (colonizer) or the Indian nation (colonized). In Spanish legal theory, which buttressed a local form of colonial indirect rule, each nation's republic was granted distinct but unequal privileges and obligations to the Crown.

Like the postcolonial Republic of Peru, the overarching dual republics of the colonial period were more fictional and juridical than they were actual and social/ethnic, but one contention of the present book is that these imagined constructs had real historical consequences. The imperial legal architecture of state that classified the colonized as an Indian nation, juxtaposed in subordinate fashion to the Spanish nation, had its real historical manifestation in the local making of particular *pueblos* or *repúblicas de indios*. In the late sixteenth and early seventeenth centuries, diverse and far-flung Andean ethnic communities and polities were "reduced," or resettled, in gridlike "Christian towns" (*pueblos*) where they would "live in republic," thereby acquiring the virtues of Christian civility and "good government." As post-Conquest fragmentation of far-flung Andean polities advanced in the wake of Spanish colonialism, the *república* or *pueblo de indios* emerged by the middle of the crisis-ridden seventeenth century as the new focal point of Indian political, religious, and juridical culture.[33] Unlike the inward-looking, "closed corporate communities" of twentieth-century anthropology, the Indian republics of colonial Huaylas were hybrid imbrications, grids made plastic by Andean political and cultural dynamics. The complex historical formation of these new, but in many ways enduring, political communities during the Toledan (1568–80) and post-Toledan periods (1580–1700) of the Habsburg era challenges two notions: (a) that Andean social formations were "paralyzed" or wholly "destructured" by the trauma of the Conquest, and (b) that Indian identity was formed in violent opposition to Spanish domination.[34] Although the imperial project of republic formation had missionizing, tributary, segregationist, and civilizing goals, the reconstituted Indian political communities worked these new jural identities in particularly Andean ways. Much of the cultural and political work was done by the Indian *cabildos,* or town councils, of chiefs and elders, who represented the community assembly (*república*) of the *pueblo.* Thus the locally contested colonial site of the Indian republic became a "locus of enunciation"[35] for subaltern or tributary politics wherein an "Indian republican" identity could be catholic in its heterodoxy. In short, the local, guild-based Indian republics were the building blocks and staging grounds for everyday forms of colonial state formation in the Andean hinterlands.

The local Indian republics of Huaylas, however, were formed in the midst of an acute demographic crisis surpassed only by the post-Conquest collapse of the indigenous populations of the Caribbean and central Mexico.[36] After the initial shock of the Conquest, the crisis in Huaylas was most severe in the poorly understood seventeenth century. By the early decades of the eighteenth century, the population crisis had culminated in the ruin of many ethnic chiefs, or *kurakas* (often called *caciques* by the Spanish), who were obliged to meet the tribute obligations of deceased and absent Indian peasants. Chiefs were forced to sell Indian lands to pay their tributary debts, and as a result much Indian land was alienated or parceled. By the end of the eighteenth century the authority of colonial chiefs was itself under siege. The reforms of the Bourbon state, combined with the protests of Indian community leaders against illegitimate *caciques* who failed to protect Indian interests, would seriously erode the authority of chiefship in Huaylas. Out of this crisis emerged the Toledan *alcaldes de indios,* rotating village headmen, or *varayoc* (staff-holders), who assumed official tribute-collection duties and community political representation in the proto-Independence period (1812–21). The intermediary role of the *alcaldes* would subsequently become critical to postcolonial rule and republican politics in the Andean hinterlands.

Bourbon Spain's strained and belated effort to reinvigorate the imagined social boundaries of colonial rule in the late eighteenth century generated "basic tensions of empire."[37] By the 1780s the fictitious social boundary between Indians and Spaniards was blurred and routinely trespassed. In Huaylas the unsanctioned product of this trespass, the interstitial *mestizos* (persons of mixed Indian and Spanish descent) and the Indian *cholos* (urban plebeians), were by the time of Independence (1821–24) nearly as numerous as the "Indian nation." The internal fragmentation and crisis of the local Indian republics, combined with the inevitable trespass of the castes, would undermine colonial social (if not juridical) dualism, thereby anticipating postcolonial transfigurations.

With this deep past of colonial political history, postcolonial nation-making in Andean Peru could not be the wished-for tabula rasa of enlightened Creole invention but, instead, a dense and multilayered entanglement of colonial ethnic "republican" politics past and postcolonial national "republican" politics present.

Fissures in the Creole Nation

Creole nationalist imagining in Latin America was not entirely confined to the modernist, "enlightened liberal" negation of the colonial past. Although all postcolonial or ex-colonial nationalisms (old and new, Latin American, Asian, African) must discursively negate (and then selectively forget) certain aspects of their colonial past—preferably by violent means, and if not by these, then by hegemonic discursive tricks, as well as by tangible reforms of the state—they are also obliged to find some ingenious way to recover and appropriate the precolonial past for national history. In New Spain, Creole patriots like Servando Teresa de Mier and Carlos María de Bustamante laid imaginative claim to an invented tradition that linked the Aztec Empire with the new nation of "Anáhuac," thereby endowing the Mexican Republic with the deep national history it needed to divorce the colonial interruption.[38] Creole Peru, however, may have hesitated at this latter, nationmaking task of inventing an integral national history with precolonial roots.[39] Despite the steady trickle of Creole indigenist rhetoric that adorned early nineteenth-century pamphlets and literary pieces,[40] David Brading has argued that "the Creole elite of Lima . . . failed to generate myths or images which might have articulated the identity of Peru as successor of Tawantinsuyu."[41] Why were Peruvian Creoles unable to appropriate fully the legacy of the Inkas?[42]

The reason, as John Rowe and subsequent Andeanist scholars have noted, was that certain segments of the subordinate but rival Andean elite, represented by the *kuraka* class of indigenous and *mestizo* nobles and merchants reproduced under colonial indirect rule (a class which was strongest in Cuzco and in the surrounding provinces of the central-south altiplano), laid a stronger and demonstrably threatening claim to that legacy.[43] Claims to Inka descent were made by an insurgent segment of the Indian (and half-Indian) nobility, and these claims lent nationalist legitimacy to the great Andean insurrection of the 1780s. This remarkable insurrection was not exactly the "precursor to Independence" that Creole nationalist historiography would later proclaim. It was led by such provincial chiefly merchants and would-be "Inka kings" as José Gabriel Condorcanqui Thupa Amaro (Tupac Amaru II), Tomás Katari, and Julián Apasa (alias Tupac Katari).[44] Although the insurrection of the 1780s presented a multiethnic front supported by many *mestizos* and highland Creoles (some of whom dabbled in forms of neo-Inkaism), by the early decades of the nineteenth century many Creole elites harbored dark memories of Indian peasant masses, under the loose command of the *kurakas*, sacking and burning Creole estates, and sacrificing whites to the "Earth Mother" in the name of the "Inka king."[45] This haunting memory meant that the Inkas would be timidly resurrected by Creoles as the nation's antiquity, its distant, "classical" past.

There was an additional ideological dissonance between insurgent segments of the subordinate Andean elite and the Creole patriots. The rebels of the 1780s — Indian and *mestizo* chiefs and their sometime allies among the Creoles — were for the most part not republicans in the contemporary sense of "antimonarchists," nor were they, at least in any overt form, separatists fighting for independent sovereignty. Like the *comuneros* of New Granada, who proclaimed "¡Viva el Rey y muera el mal gobierno!"[46] they sought to revive the broken, early colonial pact that Peru was imagined to have engaged, in jural terms, long ago. Peru, with its restored Inka dynasty, would recover its place among the many semi-independent principalities once united under the Catholic monarch of Spain.[47] Making such claims in the 1780s was heretical and dangerous, but it would not have been in 1550.

Yet the claims of the dissident Andean *kurakas* were not unlike the arguments of contemporary Creole nationalists like Mier, Viscardo, and Francisco de Miranda — albeit with the critical difference that the latter proposed Creoles as the rightful heirs to the Aztec and Inka dynasties.[48] Such an American dynastic project was still imaginable in the late eighteenth century (its last gasp may have been in the hushed designs of San Martín). Yet with Bolívar's coming in the late 1810s and early 1820s—by which time, given events in Europe, the collapse of the Spanish Empire had become inevitable, and the political authority of the Andean *kuraka* class had been severely repressed—the American monarchist project was eclipsed by Creole republicanism.[49]

The eclipse of both 1780s "Inka nationalism" and subsequent Creole versions of it (for example, Gabriel Aguilar's aborted conspiracy of 1805) is critical to any understanding of the troubled genesis of Peru's postcolonial nationhood. For Bolívar and the self-styled, Bonapartist republicanism he trafficked in, "America had no useable history," whether European or Indian, colonial or precolonial. For America was on the one hand "separated both culturally and geographically from Europe" and, on the other, "inhabited by peoples whose cultural inheritance had been obliterated by conquest."[50] For many nineteenth-century Creole patriots the appeal of monarchy was fading fast. Only the "true republics" of the liberal type emerging in the North Atlantic would prosper in the modern age. And for Bolívar, "no Indian could be the bearer of a significant past or the spiritual leader, however fictionalized, of a republican future. For the most part Bolívar thought of Indians [with the exception of the romanticized 'untamed Araucanians' of Chile], when at all, as an essentially docile, unpoliticizable mass that 'wishes only for rest and solitude.' "[51]

Bolívar appears to have viewed what remained of the Indian nobility of Peru with similar contempt. They had been complicit in Spain's "despotic" rule. As a degenerate aristocracy, they could not be the vehicles of an "enlightened" political project. Indeed, when Bolívar arrived in the old Inka capital of Cuzco in 1825, he promptly declared the abolition of all colonial titles of nobility, including those of the chiefs or *caciques,* who would be replaced by appointed republican officials. Without any usable past, then, Creole republicanism would largely look to the future (and thus to artifice or modernism) as the wellspring of Latin American nationhood—and not, as much as was possible, to the Iberian or Andean past. In short, *Bolívar no andaba buscando un inca.*[52] He sought the liberal's tabula rasa from which to begin anew.

When Peruvian Creoles did turn their imaginative attention to the Andean heritage (which was rare), they routinely juxtaposed the once great but ostensibly vanished civilization of the Inka against the degenerate and inferior "Indian race" that surrounded them. In the eighteenth and nineteenth centuries — and, alas, even today[53] — Peruvian and foreign elites held a measure of fashionable awe and fascination for the "lost golden age" of the Inka, while at the same time they felt obliged to belittle the "fallen" or "degenerate" contemporary Indian as unworthy of serious study or reflection, except perhaps in the racialist and "anti-conquest"[54] modes of nineteenth-century travel writing. Brading notes that already by the mid-eighteenth century such critical observers as Antonio de Ulloa and La Condomine "had marveled at the difference between the degraded character of contemporary natives and the elevated images of the Incas as portrayed [in Garcilaso de la Vega]."[55] The rhetorical strategy of drawing critical contrasts between Inka achievements and Spanish colonialism was employed not only by "enlightened" Spanish critics but also by such earlier, "utopian" Andean authors as Guaman Poma de Ayala.[56] Anthony Pagden notes similar motifs in Mexican discourse, where the disassociation of degraded Indians from once great Aztec nobles yielded contradictions in nationalist rhetoric that could be surmounted only by acrobatic associations of the distant Aztec past with the Creole present — associations, moreover, that seemed more socially viable in Mexico than in Peru.

Of course, binding antiquity (Greek, Roman, Aztec, or Inka) to the national present was and is a common trope of nationalist historiography and literature both in Europe and the Americas. Thus, eighteenth-century Mexicans like the exiled Jesuit Francisco Clavigero could argue that

> the Indians present miserable condition was . . . merely the consequence of the life they had been compelled to live since the Conquest. Would you ever believe . . . from the condition of the modern Greeks, that such a people could have produced a Plato or a Pericles? After two hundred years of destruction and persecution and slavery, of flight and change of religion, of government . . . what trace could remain of their ancient customs?[57]

The apparent gulf between the native past and the native present was tactically deployed by patriotic Creoles like Mier, Bustamante, and Viscardo to justify the Creole cause of independence. By citing the present "degraded" condition of the Indian as living proof of the cruel exploitation and "despotism" of Spanish rule, they could stake out the moral high ground for rebellion. But in the post-Independence period Creole liberals would continue to blame the Spanish for having "frozen" the Indians in a kind of primordial stupor which, they now rationalized, in effect rendered them incapable of assuming the responsibilities and privileges of full citizenship in the Peruvian Republic.

By the mid-nineteenth century, the Anglo-American historian William Prescott, who was widely read in Peru, would blame Indian "degeneration" in Peru and Mexico not only on Spanish colonialism but, more profoundly, on the abiding "oriental despotism" of the precolonial Inka and Aztec states. This deep, indigenous despotism, Prescott argued, had the broad and continuing effect of squelching individual ambition and, therefore, progress.[58] Such views of "Inka despotism" were common among Creoles by the late nineteenth century, when the racialist and positivist transformation of "enlightened liberalism" was nearly complete in elite circles.[59]

But whether one blamed Spanish or Inka despotism was largely immaterial. All such views shared the notion that the contemporary Indian in his present state had little or nothing to contribute to the progress of modern civilization. In short, contemporary Indians had no history, no contemporaneity.[60] They were simply, and irremediably, hung over. It is not difficult to fathom why the most worthy object of ethnological study in nineteenth-century Peru was the archaeological ruin (antiquarianism), not contemporary Indian society (ethnography).[61] No link between the Inka past and the Indian present was discernible: Indians had been cut off from their history, suspended or frozen in time by the Spanish Conquest. That twentieth-century indigenist literary traditions in Peru should admire past Inka greatness while betraying contempt for contemporary Indians was not, by any means, inconsistent with the trope.[62] The contemporary Indian remained unimagined, dehistoricized.

Historicizing the Subaltern Nineteenth Century

To plot the dim and fragmentary "realm of peasant politics" in the Andean hinterlands of nineteenth-century Peru is—to invert Benedict Anderson's felicitous phrase[63]—to historically imagine *unimagined communities* largely "incomprehensible from the standpoint of bourgeois politics" and unassimilable to the liberal imagination.[64] With some momentary exceptions, the postcolonial national community imagined by Peru's nation-founding Creole elite consigned the Andean peasant majority (and its history) to perdition.[65] But they (and it) would not disappear.

This book does not claim to "recover the subaltern" voice of postcolonial Andean Peru from the dustbin of history but, rather, to render imaginable and historical what was once anathema and anachronic in the Creole political imaginary and its nationalist historiography. The task has demanded methodological descent from elite or canonical texts, where subaltern historical agency is routinely elided, to the petty archives of local courts and public notaries where Andean peasant declarations were more likely to be registered. But the nineteenth-century archival sources on peasant political discourse and practice in Peru are fragmentary, standardized, often counter-insurgent and, when compared to the mountains of colonial documentation, ethnographically thin. During my researches, I came to realize (albeit belatedly) that much of this ethnographic thinness was owing precisely to the nature of the postcolonial archive, which holds the residue of the liberal state's ideological negation of what it understood to be colonial, or "despotic," forms of difference. The local ethnic machinery of indirect rule, for example, was of some interest to the tributary colonial state, but unsavory to the postcolonial liberal state of would-be citizens. That is why, in this case at least, colonial inspectors made better ethnographers than postcolonial bureaucrats. To recognize and record ethnic categories or local difference was in most contexts contrary to the liberal-republican discursive framework of the postcolonial state.

Nevertheless, nineteenth-century archives are still rather more abundant and vocally diverse than the "literary" texts of the period. The archives hold the transcultured, translated, and transcribed verbal testimony of illiterate peasants who were called as witnesses in petty civil and criminal cases; the fingerprinted or shakily signed petitions of semiliterate peasant authorities; the town notary's endlessly repetitious register of land transactions; the dusty files of official and unofficial correspondence between small-time functionaries and their superiors in the ministries of the capital; and those well-worn ledgers of provincial tax collectors and inspectors which escaped the rebel's torch. In short: the petty debris of the local state apparatus, the refuse of "everyday forms of state formation."[66]

My descent into the petty archive of the unimagined, in order to write the history of what was not historical, carries with it that irresolvable, late twentieth-century tension between the ethnographic impulse of politically committed, "bottom-up" social history and the literary-critical desire to dissemble the power-laden textuality of the archive in which "subaltern voices" were fashioned and inserted.[67] The attendant textual tension between streams of narration and thickets of critical reading is also unresolved and, dear reader, must leave its mark on this book. Although the task is less to narrate the "native point of view" than to unpack the shifting "discursive framework" and "grammar of politics" that encoded the archive of state–peasantry relations, the grammatical framework of the archive is also always referenced in practice.[68] Historical subjectivity and agency thus reenter via the back door (or, to use another metaphor, were always already under the rug).

Inscribing this archive's textuality, local scribes were prescribed to follow formulas. Indigenous peasants, speaking in Spanish or in their native Quechua through an appointed translator,[69] formulated declarations in idioms "that the magistrate would most clearly understand and be receptive to." In short, the local ledger of state–peasantry relations was "a complex negotiation, perhaps actually spoken by a participant but just as likely chosen from a dictionary of official values and prejudices."[70] As I read them, such codified sources resist the ethnologist's pursuit of the authentic native, but they are also not easily reduced to the Foucauldian "capillaries" of an omniscient hegemony.[71] Nor are the "elementary aspects" of the peasant politics encoded in the local archive of state–peasantry relations readily grasped as mere "negation" of elite "keywords" and prejudices, as Ranajit Guha has suggested in another context.[72] Instead, these local sources suggest a negotiated selection of terms and positions within dominant— but shifting and vicariously interpreted—discursive frameworks. Ambiguity and slippage are thus made possible, and these internal (intertextual) possibilities are sometimes exploited for their political potential.

In its pursuit of the shifting political practices and discourses of Andean peasant subalternity under late colonial and postcolonial rule, this book moves in the interstices of history and anthropology and, more specifically, between Anglo-American anthropology's subdisciplines of ethnohistory and ethnography as they have been historically practiced in the Andean field. Andean ethnohistory has—with some notable exceptions— largely been defined by a now classical and rigorous tradition of archival research in the formidable early colonial archive that represents the European encounter with Andean societies. One consequence of this perhaps inevitable definition was that Andean ethnohistory came to be understood as being about the scholarly recovery of protocolonial or pre-Hispanic Andean societies and polities. Modern Andean ethnography, on the other hand, developed as the fieldwork counterpart to ethnohistory, and by the 1970s it was largely devoted to the symbolic and ecological analysis of contemporary indigenous communities.[73] Reacting against the acculturation and modernization paradigms of 1950s–60s rural sociology and applied anthropology, Andeanist ethnographers of the 1970s (many of whom, incidentally, were advised by ethnohistorians) took to the field in search of "the Andean," defined as resistant cultural traits and practices previously documented in the "ethnohistorical record." In short, the relatively flat protocolonial or early colonial "ethnohistorical" past became the cultural yardstick of the ethnographic present.

This juxtaposed phase in the development of ethnohistory and ethnography in the Andean field left a critical gap in historical coverage, however, which would not be bridged (and then only fleetingly) until the 1980s. At its widest, the gap in coverage extended from the seventeenth through the nineteenth centuries. The nineteenth century was the least studied and perhaps the most misunderstood. In the 1950s, George Kubler wrote that the Andean nineteenth century was "for all practical purposes . . . an ethnohistorical blank."[74] The very same statement was made at academic conferences in the early 1990s. Moreover, the gap was not filled by (proper) historians, who until the late 1980s also considered the nineteenth century to be a historiographical "dark age."[75]

The subdisciplinary schizophrenia in the field of Andean anthropology fitted with the wider disciplinary pattern of history and anthropology in the West. Anthropology's post-Enlightenment divergence from history was complicit with the colonial history of power/knowledge, which had sentenced the former to "the field"—to the colonized periphery where the "primitive" could be studied. Once in the field of colonial cultural production, ethnologists studied the present of peoples whose history had been displaced by the Western colonial present. "Native" history became the "archaic" or "lost"—the appropriate object of antiquarianism, archaeology, and the museum.[76]

In the case of Andeanist ethnography, there were particular conceptual consequences of this general colonial displacement of native history. Without rigorous historical research on the Andean experience of the intervening centuries of colonial and postcolonial rule, the only native past that working ethnographers could access (and dutifully cite in the obligatory "historical background chapter" of ethnographies) was the early colonial archive consulted in the construction of an "ethnohistorical present," albeit "with the more obvious results of colonial rule lopped off."[77]

The disciplinary predicament of Andean anthropology has nurtured, and been nurtured by, twentieth-century popular and nationalist images of "the Andean" (*lo andino*) as essentially continuous with the precolonial Inka. In these politically useful discourses of authenticity in continuity, Andean peoples could have no meaningful post-Conquest history, only the negation of, or resistance to, that history. Between Tawantinsuyo (the Inka realm) and the ethnographic present, what was "Andean" was the essentially unchanged, or unsoiled. Indeed, to qualify as "Andean" it had to be the same, for if it had changed that was surely because of the polluting or degrading effects of Westernization.

This book is far less concerned with the ethnohistorical and ethnographic chronicle of "the Andean" than it is with shifting Andean predicaments under postcolonial rule. Still, my reading of "anthropological subjects" his-

torically engaged with their political worlds is deeply indebted to the pro-
ductive tension between history and anthropology which now "reverberates
among the fragments" of much Latin Americanist, Africanist, and Asian-
ist scholarship and which has been an active if sometimes quiet current in
Andean studies since at least the early 1980s.[78] Such work makes it possible to recognize post-Conquest (e.g., colonial and postcolonial) historicity
among Andean peoples, to imagine what was unimagined in the nineteenth
century and uninterrogated for much of the twentieth: the fractured contemporaneity of Andean cultural and political practice.[79] In this reading,
Andean identities emerge in grounded, blurred shades of gray, rather than
in the too crisp black-and-white portraits lifted from the distant ethnohistorical past or the not-quite-contemporary ethnographic present.

The Postcolonial Andean Predicament

From this in-between and grayish position we may approach and historicize
the postcolonial Andean predicament and outline the problem of this book.
Although the independence movement rallied diverse support in Peru —
most notably from the *montoneras* (mounted insurgents) of the central highlands, including Huaylas, which fought alongside the continental forces of
the Creole *libertadores*[80] — the particular timing and manner of national independence (1821–24) were largely imposed by the international armies of
San Martín, Bolívar, and Antonio José de Sucre.[81] It was not a "Peruvian"
but rather the "Argentine" (Argentina did not yet exist) José de San Martín
who in 1821 enacted the secular nationalist baptismal of Indians as "Peruvians." He did not bother to ask them first. For San Martín as well as Bolívar, such an inquest would have been absurd. In their eyes akin to children,
the "disgraced" Indians were not yet rational, which was to say political,
subjects. Making them so was one of the rhetorical justifications for Independence.

But how might "Peruvian" be read by the "Indian" majority? The question is not as transparent as some scholars, including Anderson, have
supposed. Analysis of local legal-political discourse reveals unanticipated,
subaltern translations of Creole nationalist discourse. "Ex-Indians," or
"Peruvians," in Huaylas would interpret the republican national project in
ways that San Martín and Peruvian Creole elites had not imagined.

In theory, as Tristan Platt recognized for Bolivia, and Heraclio Bonilla
and Karen Spalding for Peru,[82] the Creole citizenmaking project which renamed "Indians" as "Peruvians" logically implied the negation or displacement of the separate *derechos,* or colonial "privileges," and status derived
from membership in the colonial Indian republic, in favor of the unitary

civil model of liberal nationhood under the Peruvian Republic. As in the Bolivian case of Chayanta described by Platt, the nineteenth-century history of Huaylas-Ancash, viewed from above, can be read as an unfinished chapter in the (neocolonial) Creole reconquest of colonial Andean space. As Platt noted for Bolivia,

> the homeland desired by . . . Creoles could only be secured to the extent that they were successful in realising their national project. This involved increasing their control over land and surpluses in areas populated by Indians, forcing Indian landholdings on to the market. . . . [Moreover,] an ideological [stake in] homeland [was made] in the [Creole-*mestizo*] control of writing as an instrument of administration, and with it a claim to a monopoly on civilization.[83]

There are striking parallels between this Bolivian experience and the Peruvian one presented here, despite the many critical divergencies in the historical trajectories of the two regions and states.[84] Nineteenth-century Huaylas-Ancash and Chayanta were both battlegrounds for "the secular confrontation by which enlightened liberalism attempted to dismantle [the] Andean-colonial inheritance, in the name of a historicism oriented toward universal progress through the expansion of private property, capital accumulation, and free trade."[85] Central to this postcolonial confrontation with the "Andean-colonial heritage" were the divisive issues of local Indian authorities, tribute, and community lands, and it is for this reason that these aspects are given so much attention in the chapters that follow. Once free to govern "in their native land" Creole nationbuilders would gradually dislodge native claims to the special entitlements of land and local political office that the Habsburg colonial state had conferred upon Indian communities and their authorities in exchange for loyalty and tribute.[86] As Platt demonstrated, and as the present book confirms, the Creole drive to dislodge colonial native claims involved rather more than images and identities: the postcolonial state's fiscal solvency as well as access to land and labor were at stake.[87]

When possible, Andean peasants and their authorities in Huaylas-Ancash engaged and worked the state to minimize or buffer the disenfranchisement that followed from insertion in the overarching, but still relatively weak, and fragmented structures of the liberalizing national state. The working contours of this engagement (and disengagement) with the state would mark the modern history of Peru's troubled nationmaking process. The long nationbuilding scramble of the nineteenth century would be circuitous and interrupted, its path crooked, not least because the Creole elite itself was never monolithic in its national ideology or politics. Indeed, it may be more accurate to say that Peruvian elites were forever divided in the camps of one or another regional *caudillo,* and that this chronic situation of division allowed peasant subalterns more room to move within the fissures. Moreover, the illiberal factionalism of the *caudillo*-ridden, postcolonial state meant that "enlightened liberalism" would never be hegemonic, nor orthodox.

Despite the "ethnocidal" impulse of Creole "enlightened liberalism"— which in theory sought to atomize Andean ethnic communities so as to make propertied citizen taxpayers of their individual male members[88]—the postcolonial state necessarily reproduced selected aspects of colonial administration. The ambivalent administrative practice of the weak postcolonial state would in turn be vicariously interpreted by subalterns, albeit within the flexible republican discursive framework that dominated nineteenth-century statecraft in the Americas.

By the late nineteenth century the Andean peasantry of Huaylas-Ancash and its subaltern *alcalde* authorities, or *varayoc* (staff-holders, village headmen), signed historically informed readings of what the republican framework meant, declaring themselves to be "the true citizens of the nation." They also demonstrated agency by holding the erosive, liberal reforms of the postcolonial state in check and by taking a militant, nationalist stance in the Peruvian civil war of 1884–85 and in the Atusparia uprising of 1885, which together constituted the domestic social climax of the international War of the Pacific (1879–83). For reasons of race, class, and political opportunism, however, Andean peasant aspirations were repressed and willfully misread by many Peruvian elites as the backward demands and irrational fury of "the savage horde."

In early twentieth-century Peru, Andean peasant energies would not be mobilized and "normalized" within an inclusive national project directed from above by the Creole-*mestizo* elite, such as that, for example, initiated in postrevolutionary Mexico.[89] Instead, Peru skidded into the twentieth century as an "aristocratic republic" governed by positivist patricians, albeit without the benefit of the forced-march centralization process of Porfirian Mexico (but, rather, with the broken legacy of "fictitious prosperity" under the "guano state").[90] In the agrarian hinterland, Ancash Prefect Anselmo Huapaya now found it necessary to reenact Simón Bolívar's 1825 decree which had abolished the colonial *caciques* in favor of petty state officials. In 1904 Huapaya declared that "the *indígenas*" of Ancash must (once again) obey "only those authorities recognized by the [Peruvian] Constitution." The prefect could justify his abolition of the *alcalde* posts by misrepresenting

Andean leaders (as Bolívar had) as despots who were "the worst exploiters of their kind." In doing so, he revived the hallowed rhetorical tools of colonialism. In moments of colonial crisis such as the 1560s and 1780s, rebellious Andean chiefs were branded by their detractors as ruthless *caciques,* thereby justifying their convenient removal. Now Prefect Huapaya warned the Ministry of Government that "they and their Indians formed an independent state" within his department and, as such, posed a direct challenge to the national authorities.[91] For Huapaya, the nation had not yet reached Ancash.

But Huapaya's word was not the last. His immediate successor, Prefect Eulogio Saldías, defied Lima's Ministry of Government and reversed his predecessor's prefectural decree, arguing that the *alcaldes* (*varayoc*) were actually "a venerated custom" that kept the otherwise wary Indians "within reach of the authorities."[92] For the prudent Prefect Saldías, the *alcaldes* were the indispensable instruments of republican rule in the Andean provinces of Ancash.

But Prefects Huapaya and Saldías were both wrong (or, more charitably, both right). The Indian *republicanos* and their village authorities, the *alcaldes,* did not make an independent state in Huaylas-Ancash or anywhere else in Peru, but neither were they always disposed to the whims of provincial officialdom. Their ambivalent predicament vis-à-vis the Peruvian nation-state was to be separate in their integration, outside in their belonging. It is the contradictory making of this tense postcolonial predicament, whose legacy stretches far across the twentieth century, that this book plots.

CHAPTER 2

Unimagined Communities

The Indian nation having been made equal to the Spanish [nation] . . . it was not possible to diminish the prerogatives and privileges they enjoy[.] [A]ll individuals . . . should enter into the tax system according to their means and without exception or privilege. . . . [A]nd [it was thought] that to immediately subject the Indian to equality with the Spaniard in all the taxes that are required . . . and in the mode and form in which they are collected[,] was risky and likely to disturb the peace in the provinces, since this is the slow work of example and enlightenment. . . . It was if not impossible then [a] very prolonged and tardy [process], and the urgency of the moment did not afford us the luxury of waiting. —Junta of the General Tribunal, Lima, 1812[1]

[T]he [repartition] lands now belong to the patria, since dominion had already been acquired by the comunidad de peruanos. . . . In any case she [the chief] should reinstate the excessive usufruct rents that she still holds over various lands of the comunidad . . . which rightfully correspond to the Hacienda Pública. — Manuel Jesús Barreto and María Francisca, peruanos, to the Primary Claims Court judge of Huaraz, 1823[2]

[A]t the repartition-land indigenous rate we affirm our right [of possession] in that [plot] which corresponds to us . . . as Indians who pay the state's income with the status of originarios republicanos. . . . As republicanos [who fulfill] all . . . services [to the Republic], Your Excellency should . . . uphold the present legislation of 1828 and 1829 that protects [us] the indios originarios. — José María Chacpi and Manuel Aniceto, indígenas contribuyentes of Ecash Waranka, Carhuaz, to the Primary Claims Court judge of Huaraz, 1846[3]

Between Dual Colonial and Unitary
Postcolonial Nationhoods

During the Peninsular War of 1808–14 a historic episode of liberal consti-
tutionalism in Spain would help shift the terms of political discourse in the
Americas. In the interregnum of Bourbon succession subsequent to Napoleon's occupation of Iberia, Joseph Bonaparte was installed on the Spanish throne and the young Bourbon monarch Ferdinand VII went into exile.
Meanwhile, Spanish resistance to the French army was driven south, and
after 1810 a Cortes, or parliament, of liberal patricians was summoned to
Cadiz in the monarch's absence. Across the Atlantic, many American jun-
tas proclaimed their support for Ferdinand VII, thereby "using the mask of
Ferdinand" to assume de facto independence from occupied Spain.[4]

In a liberal gesture intended, perhaps, to counter the unrest brewing in
the American colonies, the Cortes de Cadiz included in its assembly forty-
nine representatives of "the Indies," nine of whom hailed from Peru.[5] The
liberal parliament proclaimed the abolition of tribute for the *castas,* or non-
Indian castes, of New Spain and, subsequently, that of *"yndios y castas* in
the rest of America," thereby "elevating the Indian nation to equality with
the Spanish nation." Along with the abolition of tribute, the Spanish parliament stipulated that Indians would now meet the same obligations as
"Spaniards" (Creoles as well as Iberians, or *peninsulares*). That is to say,
Indians would be made subject to the same "obligations" and "taxes" and
would "cease to partake in any special privileges as Indians." To the Indians would also be extended "la gracia de repartimiento de tierras"—that is,
individual title to the *topos,* or usufruct plots, within the *tierras de repartición*
(Crown lands which had been assigned to Indian chiefs and their communities since the late sixteenth century for the purpose of redistribution among
tribute-paying Indian households). The non-Indian castes, however, were
not blessed with this "grace."[6]

In theory, this was the first in a series of nineteenth-century liberal ex-
periments on the Peruvian scene, and its fate was foreseeable. The new
Indian *contribución,* which was to replace the *tributo,* was in fact uncollectable, and the royal coffers in Lima plummeted to depths that alarmed colonial administrators. At the same time, royal battalions stationed in Upper
Peru (Bolivia) were in desperate need of funds to keep down the Creole
independence movement in La Paz, and viceregal Lima simply could not
carry on its administrative functions without the substantial revenue gar-
nered from the Indian tribute. To save the day, "the Indians of the principal
provinces of the kingdom" came forward and "spontaneously volunteered"
to continue making their tribute payments to the Crown.[7] Facing bank-

ruptcy and the threat of insurgency, the voluntary tribute "of the *pueblos* and *ayllus*" was accepted and rationalized by Lima's Junta General de Tribunales as a "noble" gesture of "love and loyalty to the *madre patria*, and to our unlucky monarch, Don Fernando VII." In recognition of such a "generous offer" the junta decreed in 1812 that "for now all the privileges that the Laws [of the Indies] grant them in the quality of their nature [as Indians of these kingdoms] be continued, and that they not be required to satisfy the taxes and obligations expected of other citizens." In addition, the junta informed the intendants of the interior provinces that "the appointed tribute collectors are to be extinguished, and that from now on tribute shall be collected by the *alcaldes* and *mandones* of the *pueblos*."[8]

The frequently despised *cacique* tribute collectors of the late colonial intendancies (usually *mestizos*) had been appointed in many cases during the 1780s and 1790s to replace the legitimate hereditary chiefs, or *kurakas*.[9] Replacement of these neo-*caciques* in 1812 with the local Andean authorities (*alcaldes* and *mandones*), who were elected village headmen, was in part a response to Indian concerns about losing the privileges ceded to them "por calidad de su naturaleza" (i.e., as Indians). These privileges were by no means vague, and they included contingent access to the public commons and distributed community lands ceded to Indians and protected by the Crown. The junta's hasty acceptance of the "generous offer" betrayed both the great fiscal pressure of the moment and the perceived threat of social disorder. The liberal dystopia had begun.

This episode was only the beginning of Peru's nineteenth-century saga of coerced expediency on the critical issue of Indian tribute and taxation, and the linked issues of ethnic or caste classification, and civil status. This fiscal expediency was rationalized then, as it was time and again over the course of the century, by taking rhetorical recourse to the discursive motifs of enlightened liberalism *a lo criollo*.[10] In 1812, when it became clear that the new status of Indians as citizen taxpayers would cause a sizable fiscal deficit, the voluntary desire "of the *pueblos* and *ayllus*" to pay the royal tribute was quickly rationalized. Indians, the discourse went, were not ready to be suddenly granted equal footing with Spaniards. Such a radical change of status required "the slow work of example and . . . enlightenment to uproot [the Indian] from his ancient practices and customs and his tenacious adhesion . . . to the example of his elders. . . . [T]he urgency of the moment did not afford the luxury of waiting, and in the meantime produces a situation in which the Indian pays neither the tribute nor the taxes of citizens." However, since the term "tribute" was incompatible with the "dignity of the Spanish citizen," it would (in the meantime) be stricken from official discourse. The "odious tribute" would be rechristened, in enlightened liberal fashion, the "provisional and . . . voluntary contribution."[11]

By 1814, however, Napoleon's invasion had been repelled and the Bourbon dynasty restored. Ferdinand VII quickly reversed the liberal constitution of 1812, thereby annulling the decrees of the Cortes relative to the American colonies. On 15 October 1815, broadsides were posted in Lima reestablishing the king's royal tribute while preserving, in the enlightened spirit of the age, the "more dignified" term of *contribución*. Although the days of Spanish rule in Peru were counting down, the life of the "contribution" would be strangely renewed.

On the eve of José de San Martín's liberating invasion of the Peruvian coast, conspiring members of the *nación española* in Huaylas petitioned the intendant of Tarma for recognition of what they believed to be their right to establish *alcaldes ordinarios de españoles*. They requested permission to establish their own local government because the still reigning *alcaldes ordinarios de indios* (inherited from Huaraz's sixteenth-century foundation as a colonial "Indian republic") were, according to the petitioners, incapable of "controlling crime, theft, disorder, and filth" in the populous *pueblos* of the Callejón de Huaylas, or Huaylas Valley—*pueblos* which, by the early nineteenth century, had been transformed from colonial *repúblicas de indios* into largely *mestizo* and Spanish towns of artisans, farmers, merchants, and petty officials.[12]

Since the late eighteenth century, this group of "Spaniards" in Huaraz—there were numerous "American Spaniards," or Creoles, among them—had repeatedly petitioned the subdelegate of Huaylas in Huaraz for the right to elect "alcaldes de españoles para que esté mejor gobernada su República." On these occasions, however, their petitions had been rejected and their persons persecuted "for their pretensions." In 1797, for example, the subdelegate of Huaylas had this uppity "Spanish" group of "revoltosos" which sought to establish the Spanish *alcaldía* brought before his court. The subdelegate was dismayed to have to declare: "It has come to my attention that a few townsmen of the *pueblo* of Huaraz, acting with arrogance and unabashed impunity, have been maneuvering and influencing their neighbors to sign a petition requesting Spanish *alcaldes*. . . . It is public knowledge that they do this despotically, and that their pretensions are none other than to fuel their rebellious and abusive tempers."[13] In 1820, however—and now on the verge of extinction—the colonial intendant of Tarma approved a resubmission of the very same petition, thereby recognizing the new Spanish *alcaldes,* "but with the condition that said Spanish *alcaldes* do not exercise jurisdiction over the Indians, *since they are governed by those of their own Nation in those aspects addressed by the laws of Peru*" (my emphasis).[14]

But the "Spaniards" of Huaraz would have precious little time in which to exercise this local self-rule under a segregated *alcalde* system of district and municipal government which disallowed direct jurisdiction over the Indian *alcaldes* and their "nation." For in a matter of months (in some other regions of Peru, five or more years) Spanish colonialism's half-fictional ethnopolitical duality would be precariously bridged by the half-fictional unitary administrative apparatus of the new Peruvian Republic. Once postcolonial rule was established in Huaylas (1821–24), the republican *gobernadores* (governors) with their *tenientes* (lieutenant governors) and *jueces de paz* (justices of the peace), complete with their staffs and pointed, black top hats, emblems of republican authority,[15] exercised what the would-be Spanish *alcaldes* of 1820 could not: direct jurisdiction over the Indian *alcalde* authorities and their now officially dissolved "nation." The parallel but asymmetric political hierarchies of the colonial period were to be subsumed under the juridically uniform Peruvian Republic. Although this shift had been clinched with the demise of the intermediary colonial chiefs in the late eighteenth century, and the conditions for it had been forming since the late seventeenth when the dual colonial nations of Indians and Spaniards began to be seriously blurred,[16] the postcolonial drive for legal-political uniformity as the basis for united nationhood generated profound shifts in the practice, discourse, and mediation of state–peasantry relations.

The foundational liberal-nationalist decrees are by now familiar to historians, but their consequences, which are often taken for granted, are not. In 1821 San Martín abolished the "shameful exaction that, with the name of tribute, was imposed by tyranny as a sign of lordship." But in Peru, unbeknownst to the Argentine foreigner San Martín and, it would seem, to several generations of historians, the *tributo* was for ten years now (for the same liberal reasons San Martín cited in his abolition) officially renamed *la contribución.* In his more noted decree, San Martín declared that all "Indians" or "naturals" would henceforth be known as "Peruvians."[17] But in postcolonial Huaylas at least, San Martín's proclamation seems to have been taken rather more literally and exclusively than the Liberator had anticipated. In Huaylas, "peruanos" was originally applied to Indian commoners (now dubbed "ex-indios") and not to citizens at large. In 1824 Indians were declared the private owners of their usufruct parcels in the colonial repartition lands (*tierras de repartición*), now rebaptized *tierras de la República* or *tierras del Estado,* but actually it was the so-called nationalist-conservative Congress of

1828 that passed the decisive legislation on Indian land tenure and literate propertied citizenship. Finally, in 1825, Simón Bolívar abolished "the title and authority of the *caciques*," adding that henceforth "the local authorities will exercise the functions of the extinguished *caciques*."[18] This last decree was notable for its effects, but it was already the prevalent practice in Huaylas since 1812, and the foundations for it had been firmly laid by 1783.

It is not, as was once the fashion to claim, that these dictatorial decrees and the politico-military events that accompanied them were non-events, meant nothing to the Andean majorities. The problem, rather, is that they could mean several things at once, some of them rather unanticipated by their architects. In Huaylas, the decrees of the Independence era left clearly discernible (albeit crooked) tracks in the surviving notarial records of the postcolonial period. Following these crooked tracks leads us down unexpected paths of inquiry.

Postcolonial Republicanism and the "Comunidad de Peruanos"

In September of 1820 Gregoria Gonzáles, whose full name was Gregoria Palma Gonzáles y Rimaycochachin,[19] heiress to the early colonial *kurakas* of Waranka Ychoc Huaraz (the Gonzáles-Cochachin lineage) and identified as "cacica deste pueblo de Huaras" and "repartidora de tierras" in the *parcialidad*, or *waranka* (ethnic tributary collectivity), of Ychoc, won a civil decision against a landless "yndio arrendatario" (Indian tenant farmer) by the name of Manuel Jesús Barreto.[20] Barreto allegedly owed the chief "12 mule loads of wheat," payment of which, Doña Gregoria claimed, she would apply toward fulfilling her *waranka*'s tribute obligations to the colonial state. According to the *cacica* (female chief) and the judge presiding over the case, Barreto was not a legitimate member of her *waranka* of *originarios* (local natives) but, rather, a *forastero* (outsider) from "another *parcialidad*" who merely rented "repartition lands" from the *cacica*. It was not uncommon in late colonial Huaraz for *kurakas* to rent vacant repartition lands to *forasteros* and then use the rents to meet the tribute payments of deceased or absent *originarios*.

Since the colonial judge ruled that Barreto was not of Gregoria's *parcialidad*, or *waranka*, Barreto had "no right to the *topo* that the king concedes to those of his class" and, thus, his "contract" with the *cacica* was entirely "voluntary." In short, he had no basis for claiming that he had been charged excessive usufruct rents, and he was ordered to pay up. When Barreto could not pay, he was quickly thrown into debtor's prison—in this case, the textile sweatshop known as the Obraje Santo Toribio, the routine destination of local Indian convicts since the late sixteenth century. But on 31 October 1820 Barreto returned to protest his incarceration by citing the "publicada y jurada Constitución Política de la Monarquía Española" of 1812 which expressly protected him from being jailed for petty indebtedness.[21] Barreto was released on the condition that he pay his debts and promise not to re-occupy the chiefly repartition lands of Marcac.

In December of 1821 the official paper trail continued, only now with the block letters "PERÚ INDEPENDIENTE" and the new national emblem boldly stamped over the royal seal of Ferdinand VII which still decorated the legal paper, or *papel sellado,* of the strapped Republic. Doña Gregoria now appeared as a "citizen of this *pueblo* . . . having corresponded to my ancestors and relatives, by reason of chiefship (*cacicazgo*), some lands named Marcac," demanding that the *peruano* Barreto, who with his mother had reoccupied the repartition lands of Marcac, be made to pay what Gregoria claimed he still owed her.

In April of 1823 Doña Gregoria appeared in legal script once again, this time as "ex-Cacica de la Parcialidad de Ichoc de esta Ciudad de Huaraz," asking for five years of back rents for "usurped lands" that Barreto still occupied with his mother. Once again the hapless Barretos were thrown into debtor's prison. Two months later, the "vecina" Gregoria pressed her case when the new "Alcalde y Gobernador Ynterino" of Huaraz reduced Barreto's debt to twenty mule loads of wheat, or only two years' rent. According to the insistent Doña Gregoria, Barreto still had not paid what was her due. She explained to the newly constituted authority that

> I filed suit with the authorities of the Spanish government, and favor-able sentence was passed; I also repaired to [the *mariscal* and president of Huaylas] Señor Luzurriaga[22] and presented the proceedings, and he dispatched the corresponding provisional decrees; but certain quick maneuverings made things difficult until said provisional sentence was hidden from me, and only with great sacrifice was I able to recover the documents, having had to pay various bribes.

The countertestimony offered by the hapless "Peruvians" Manuel Jesús Barreto and his widowed mother, María Francisca, nicely illustrates the de-ployment or, as Doña Gregoria put it, the "certain quick maneuverings," of the new republican rhetoric. For their part, the Barretos declared

> that we were residing on a small plot of the repartition lands of this community in the Estancia of Marcac through the [authority of] pre-vious *caciques;* that our rents began to rise with the *cacica* Gregoria

Gonzáles; that we had complained of the excessive rents to the previous [colonial] government, but with the favors that [the *cacica*] commanded she was able to compel us to pay the said excesses; that we were released [from these obligations] when the division of our liberating army took the plaza [of Huaraz]; and that afterward we presented ourselves before the Señor Presidente Don Toribio Luzurriaga, and he relieved us of the unjust charges of the *cacica*, ordering that henceforth we pay [our tribute to] the *patria*, which we can verify with the attached receipts.

The Barretos argued further that

the [repartition] lands now belong to the *patria*, since dominion had already been acquired by the *comunidad de peruanos*, and in virtue of this, the presidency adjudicated half of the lands to Ventura Tamasa for her service, and they say that the other half was given to said *cacica* [Doña Gregoria], but we don't know what her services [to the *patria*] were. In any case she should first reinstate the excessive usufructs that she still holds over various lands of the community; and it is with these excessive claims that she has demanded that we be made to pay her unjust charges, which we were relieved of by your predecessor Señor Luzurriaga, and which today [Doña] Gregoria revives. . . . [T]he enclosed receipts and Article 61 of the Code [make it clear that] the aforementioned Gregoria has transgressed the law with respect to the fact that she wants to adjudicate for herself the usufructs that correspond to the national treasury (Hacienda Pública).[23]

Subsequent statements made by the Barretos expanded on the liberal theme of "*cacique* despotism," which was contrasted with the patriotic nature of the *peruanos'* cause. For the Barretos, the patriotic "community of Peruvians" did not include "despotic" Indian chiefs like the "tyrannical" Doña Gregoria. The republican overtones (in the antidynastic sense that was then gaining currency in Peru) of the Barretos' imagined, yet face-to-face, Indian peasant "community of Peruvians" are unmistakable. The Barretos' usage of "Peruvian" and "the Peruvian community" is, in fact, surprisingly confirmed by other Huaylas briefs dating from the early Republican period. Literally, *peruano* was used to mean common *indio* (or, more precisely, *ex-indio*) in post-Independence Huaylas. It seems that local elites had not yet included themselves in this new "national" category (they preferred the highbrow *ciudadano* or *vecino*). Nor did the Barretos' "community of Peruvians" have much in common with the national community imagined in the salons of Lima. Perhaps this is why the Barretos' (i.e., their lawyer's) politically astute claims had no bearing on the outcome of the case, which was decided, in legalistic fashion, on the merits of past decisions, especially since the only evidence the Barretos could produce was, in the words of the judge, "a few insignificant receipts." Those past decisions established that the Barretos had not met their contractual obligations to the *cacica* as landlord (not in the capacity of chief). The heart of the matter was that the Barretos could not prove that Manuel Jesús was descended from colonial *tributarios originarios* (the desperate widow, perhaps trying to hit two birds with one stone, claimed that Manuel's father had been a "tributario contribuyente"), which was the indispensable prerequisite for *contribuyente originario* status (and rights) under the Peruvian Republic. The chief's version — that Barreto did not belong to her *parcialidad*, but "voluntarily" rented her lands as a *forastero,* and that the rent she collected had helped her meet the tribute obligations of her dominion — was more persuasive to the court.[24]

María Francisca petitioned for the last time in December 1823, arguing that her deceased husband had indeed possessed the repartition plot, or *topo,* for more than eighty years. However, she lamented, the documents that could prove this had, in fact, been lost. She closed the case with this pitiful plea: "that I, being a poor Peruvian, will have to pay this exaggerated sum all because of the carelessness of the lawyer who has lost the receipts . . ." Having heard enough of this, the judge closed the case, upholding past decisions against the Barretos and ordering them once and for all to "guardar un perpetuo silencio."

The Politics of Indian *Republicanos: ¿Un Perpetuo Silencio?*

After 1826 it was more usual for Indian commoners to represent themselves before the courts not as *peruanos,* but as *republicanos* (often in combination with the fiscal modifiers *originario* and/or *contribuyente*). In official state discourse about postcolonial ex-Indians, however, the terms "indios" and "peruanos" were superseded by the more fashionable "indígenas." "Indígena" was, since Bolívar, the progressive choice, but the motivations for its use were then clearly nationalist (the negation of the colonial "indio" and the "nation of Indians") and, later, subtly racialist. The national invention of the "indigenous" subject would become clearer in the late nineteenth century, when such useful phrases as "our indigenous race" or "the indigenous race of Peru" appear with frequency.[25] The new term was also useful as postcolonial fiscal classifier. But as the Huaylas archival record clearly documents, *republicano,* unlike *indígena,* was a multiplicious colonial identity, albeit one with significant postcolonial resonance. This resonance may be attributed to the wide-reaching and ambivalent semantic domain of the term and to its ability to articulate local politics, both discursively and in practice, with national politics, whether colonial or postcolonial.

Colonial Spanish parlance of state could recognize the active, tribute-paying members of the colonized *repúblicas de indios* as *republicanos* (as well as by the better-known fiscal label of *originarios*, or native-borns). I have argued elsewhere that it was in the colonized Indian republics that the notion of *indios republicanos* began to take on local meaning.[26] But why Indian *republicanos* in 1846? The short answer is that the postcolonial reinvention of the late colonial "indigenous contribution," or tributary head-tax (1826–54), elicited this de jure identity to resolve disputed claims to usufruct parcels ceded to "indigenous contributors" by the republican state. To answer the question in the local ways in which it was deployed, however, we have to sample the bulky record of some rather petty civil lawsuits, most of them inter-Indian, that were generated in Huaylas as a result of the compromised privatization law passed by the Constitutional Congress of 1828.

In Carhuaz in 1846–48 the Chacpis (heirs to an Indian tributary whose name was Tomás Aquino) challenged the *mestizo* Villanueva, whose Indian wife had inherited repartition lands from her family, the Motas.[27] The Chacpis, citing an *escritura imperfecta* (an unauthorized, locally manufactured document) argued that the Motas "had ceased being the possessors of said repartition land in 1818." The Chacpis submitted documents which proved that in 1818 their forebear, the Indian Tomás Aquino, had in fact been a duly documented *originario* and *tributario* and, just as important, an active *republicano* of the "Guaranga de Ecas" (Ecash Waranka). In the late colonial period, Aquino had faithfully "served the republic" (i.e., his local moiety or tributary *waranka*) as well as "Our Lord of Souls and Our Lady the Virgin of Rosario" (local patron saints) and so, in virtue of this, and because he paid his tribute, and because the "judges and justices of His Majesty" protected him as a tributary, he had dutifully earned the *republicano*'s right to a *topo* (usufruct plot) in the repartition lands assigned to his local *pachaca* (the *ayllu* tributary unit within the encompassing *waranka*).[28]

Similarly, on 12 and 16 May 1846, José María Chacpi and Manuel Aniceto, identified as *indígenas contribuyentes* by the court, declared before the judge that "at the repartition-land indigenous rate we affirm our right in that which corresponds to us . . . as Indians who pay the state's income with the status of *originarios republicanos*. . . . As *republicanos* [who fulfill] all . . . services [to the Republic], Your Excellency should . . . uphold the present legislation of 1828 and 1829 that protects [us] the *indios originarios*." This and similar Indian testimony provide clues to the transfiguration of colonial *republicano* notions of identity and legitimacy in the postcolonial context. The "right" here was the right of possession, and "that which corresponds to us" was precisely the usufruct parcel granted under colonial law in the repartition lands and under early republican law in "the lands of the Republic." As the documentation on Tomás Aquino makes clear, in colonial Huaylas to be a good Indian *republicano* meant several things: to serve the local *república*, which could mean the *ayllu* or *pachaca*, the home *waranka*, and the *pueblo* (usually reduced *warankas*, or half-*warankas*, i.e., *pichka-pachacas*) of which these formed part; to serve the local patron saints of the *pueblo* and *waranka*; and to pay the royal tribute to the king. In postcolonial republican Peru, to be an *originario republicano* implied, among other things, dutiful fulfillment of one's *tasa* or "contribution" to the *patria*, assumption of community posts, and labor brigade service both in community *minka* and stipulated public works projects (both of the latter forms of collective labor could conveniently be called "la república" in Huaylas).[29]

It is significant to note that this case was decided in favor of the Chacpis. Such *republicano* arguments could work and were recognized in the legal forum. Further cases initiated by Indians as a consequence of the Law of 1828 illustrate the transformed republican conditions under which colonial Indian land rights and *republicano* identity claims were redeployed by postcolonial peasant villagers.

The 1849–54 case of Manuel Resurrección, officially identified as an "indíjena de Chuquibamba" in the District of Yungay (then "Ancachs"), vs. Juan de Mato over the subdivision of colonial repartition lands inherited from their common father, Pedro Pablo, betrays those domestic conflicts within and among Indian households which entered the legal record as a consequence of the Law of 1828.[30] Manuel Resurrección's was an exemplary case of too many heirs for too little land. Resurrección explained to the judge:

> I have four sons of contributing status [who are] named in the tax-collection receipts [that I have presented]. They pay their contribution heavily, without possessing even one handbreadth of state lands (*tierras del Estado*); for this reason, and being right and just, I repair to Your Excellency persuaded that your rectitude will remedy this ill. My motive in calling your attention to this case is not to try to exempt my sons from the contribution, but rather that they fulfill it in the class of *forasteros sin tierras* at the corresponding quota or, in the contrary case, that they be adjudicated the *topos mostrencos* that are now unduly pos-

sessed by Estefana Sarmiento. . . . [A]s descendants of *originarios con tierras* those lands correspond to my sons, and to corroborate this you may consult the district governor, who will prove that the lands that Estefana possesses belonged to the predecessors of my sons.

The root of the problem had to do with Andean partible inheritance and how the Law of 1828 froze more fluid processes of peasant-household demographic differentiation into a more rigid property regime under which it was more difficult for expanding households to reconsolidate *topos* as demand for new lands arose. This critical land problem was the result of insufficient "tierras de la República" or "tierras del Estado" in nineteenth-century Huaylas—a direct consequence of the shrinkage of Indian lands and populations during the colonial period, and of subsequent population increase.[31] It was now possible to "sell out" of an extended family by alienating one's slice of the inherited plot, leaving the rest of the family in a more precarious subsistence balance, especially if the household in question had several young men coming of age as contributors, as was the case with the Resurrección family. Often, young men or *arrimados* (dependents) wishing to start out on their own would not receive new *topos* as *originarios*—there were none to go around—and would, perhaps, take on *forastero* or *mostrenco* status with its lower fee, or *tasa*, which could, if land were available under the postcolonial fiscal regime, bring access to precarious, noninheritable plots or *topos mostrencos* (the Resurrección case is inconclusive on this point). More likely, they would go on paying as *originarios* without receiving a usufruct plot of their own but, rather, working on their father's or family plots. Dependents often maintained *originario* status in the hope that they might later, upon their father's death, claim his or another plot as their rightful inheritance.

But rival heirs who married and then claimed private possession pursuant to the Law of 1828 could dash such hopes. This was the case of Resurrección's rival, Juan de Mato, who argued that he had inherited his plot in colonial times when Indians were not yet owners of their plots, holding them instead in inheritable usufruct. But in 1828 Juan de Mato had become absolute owner, and therefore the Resurrección sons could not dispossess him of his property just because they also claimed inheritance rights as *originarios*. He explained to the justice of the peace in an oral hearing (*juicio verbal*) that

before he died, his grandfather Pedro Pablo distributed to his sons and even his daughters the lands he obtained purely by occupation, and belonging to the state; currently these heirs are in possession of said lands. . . . This partition [by inheritance] was carried out [at a time] when no Indian held any property rights in state lands [in 1818]; and being in possession of his *topo* for more than fifty years [I am now] absolute owner by ministry of the Law of 27 March 1828.

The language of the Estéban Ramírez case of 1851–53 in Caraz is perhaps the most striking of the petty litigations pursuant to the Law of 1828. The Ramírez case, like the Resurrección dispute, betrays the by now common problem of too many heirs for too little *república* land. Such disputes — which often followed gender lines drawn between sons and daughters staking rival claims of private dominion to the precarious inheritance left by their *originario tributario* fathers — revealed both the promise and plague of the ambivalent postcolonial "land-for-contribution" compact.

Don Estéban, identified as yet another *indígena contribuyente*, this time of the *Parcialidad de Llactas* in Caraz, argued that

> my possession . . . was given me by my legitimate father . . . in the days of Spanish government . . . and [I] have been peacefully making my contributions to the treasury, and suffering . . . in the services of the republic . . . as is public knowledge. . . . [But] the greediness of my sisters in wanting to divide in partible inheritance a precarious possession that was at that time a royal right granted to every Indian — having been transmitted to me by my [father] under the expired government, and on these grounds I also passed the [said lands] to one of my sons who is now a contributor — have caused me great harm.[32]

Don Estéban argued that the justice of the peace had committed an infraction against the literacy clause of the Law of 1828 when he allowed one of Estéban's sister's husbands to alienate one of his plots

> when they could not read or write, but principally were not even republicans, and secondly because both have other lands in another *parcialidad* of their husbands, one in Allauca and the other in the Estancia of Guaya. . . . And it has been many years since they left the dominion of our common father.

Don Estéban also stated that it was he who had taken care of his father until his death, and not his sisters, and that he therefore had more right to the lands. (This last argument followed from the Andean custom of ultimogeniture; that is, the last sibling, whose duty it is to care for the elderly parents, inherits the house and houseplots as a reward.) Finally, Don Estéban declared that his sisters had no right to intervene in his lands, because

(a) he had contributing sons and (b) the rights to repartition lands were precarious and were passed on directly to the sons.

What did Estéban Ramírez mean when he said his sisters and their spouses "principally were not even republicans"? He meant that they now belonged to a distinct *parcialidad* or *ayllu;* that is to say, following patrilocal residence rules, the sisters now belonged to the "republic of the *ayllu*" (his words) of their husbands' fathers. On the other hand, Don Estéban detailed his dutiful fulfillment of obligations to his own "republic," or local descent community, all of which was presented to support his claim to the status (*gremio*) of *republicano originario* of the *parcialidad* of Llactas. Estéban had "served the republic" without the least repugnance for the "impositions of my status" as *originario*. He had held the post of tribute collector for four years, and later *mayordomo* of the patron saint, and then captain (deputy sheriff); he had been *alcalde mayor de campo*, or *varayoc* authority, of the *pueblo* of Caraz, standard-bearer in processions of the saint, and census-taker and scribe for five years, as well as chapel crier, and he had fulfilled other minor offices and services.

The then current *recaudador de contribuciones* (local tax collector) for the *parcialidad* of Llactas, Manuel Blas, supported Don Estéban's declarations. Blas confirmed that "Estéban Ramírez and his son Marcelo Ramírez are contributors to the state treasury and republicans disposed to fulfilling all services." He explained that the sisters resided in a distinct *parcialidad* outside his, and that "they had no rights in this *pachaca* to the parcels of the Republic, nor did they serve in the days of their parents." In the latter instance, Blas's use of "Republic" meant not the local "republic of the *ayllu*" but rather the "tierras de la República" (i.e., the colonial "tierras de repartición" which were now state or national lands).

Finally, Don Estéban made it very clear to the prefect what he thought his rights and prerogatives in the case were:

> The repartition lands correspond to the state; and we are their possessors by virtue of paying the departmental treasury, which is a branch of the Hacienda Pública [national treasury]; that all indigenous contributors assigned lands pay our semester rates; and for these reasons I have not alienated my lands even though I know how to read and write and even though the law of the sovereign Congress [of 1828] has granted me that right, considering that I have a large family and a son who is now a contributor, and who does not have his respective repartition plot.

Taken together with other peasant litigation from the early Republican period, the arguments presented by Estéban Ramírez and the Chacpis open up the political worlds of taxpaying nineteenth-century "indigenes." To be a good *republicano* had a local meaning that included the fulfillment of civic, religious, and economic obligations to the local ethnic polity or community. But the semantic and political reach of this nineteenth-century "Indian republicanism" did not end there. The local republic was articulated with the national Republic via the "contribution" to the national treasury of the *patria* and via *la república* public works labor. Thus, to be a good republican of the village community meant to take on with dignity all the obligations of local civic and religious service without remuneration (indeed, usually at a loss). To be a good republican in the broader, national sense of taxpaying republican indigene, meant to pay the contribution to the state treasury (and not to the ethnic chief, as in the colonial period). In return for this state contribution, Indians expected protection of their precarious access to a usufruct right inherited from their colonial forebears.

The notion here was distinct from the colonial land-for-tribute "pact of reciprocity" noted by Tristan Platt for highland Bolivia.[33] Colonial access to repartition lands was mediated by the *kurakas, principales,* and colonial magistrates, and it ultimately rested with the sovereign authority of the king of Spain. The postcolonial compact was mediated by local collectors — agents of the *alcaldes* and the *alcaldes* themselves — and, significantly, by a series of petty *misti* (non-Indian) officials who subordinated the local Indian authorities to themselves in what was, at least in theory, a two-tiered but unitary hierarchy. Another decisive difference in this republican hand, as we have seen, was the divisive card played by the so-called Law of 1828.

The Law of 1828 was actually enacted in part as a response to reports of rapid and exploitative alienation of Indian lands following the liberal Bolivarian decrees.[34] Paradoxically, in Huaylas-Ancash the most immediate consequence of this law appears not to have been heightened grabbing of Indian lands by *mestizos* and whites, but rather the accentuation of inter-Indian disputes over the inheritance of partitioned, quasi-privatized plots within the "tierras de la República" of each community. These petty conflicts did sometimes involve sales or alienation of lands to *mestizo* affines and, in some cases, sales to corrupt officials and landlords. In such cases, the literacy clause of the 1828 law was invoked, although not always with success.

The bottom line of the literacy clause of the Law of 1828 (which was extended until 1854) and of the early republican fiscal-classificatory system which made Indian *republicano* politics necessary was the importance of the *contribución indígena* to the state treasury. As Manuel del Río noted in his 1849 *Memoria* (Annual Report) as Peru's minister of state finance:

> The Law of 27 March 1828, which declared *indígenas* owners of the lands they possessed, far from improving their condition is actually reducing them to a more deplorable state, and is causing a decline in contributions. . . . If we allow the unrestrained alienation of [indigenous] lands, dominion will be transferred to the other castes, and *indígenas* will become simple proletarians, and we will be unable to impose the tax that today they pay, and thus the treasury will suffer a decline.[35]

The unrestrained alienation of the colonial repartition lands — now known in Huaylas as the "tierras de la República" or "tierras del Estado" — would have precipitated a dangerous decline in state revenues. The postcolonial Peruvian state would not make the same mistake that the liberal parliament of Cadiz had in 1812, prompting the junta in Lima to reverse policy in 1813 and reinstitute the tribute as a "voluntary contribution." As Heraclio Bonilla and other historians of Peru's state finances have observed, only in the 1850s would revenues from guano exports make abolition of the contribution an acceptable option.

Although in theory the Law of 1828 privatized Indian and *mestizo* holdings in the colonial repartition lands, it forbade alienation in cases where the new owner was not proven to be literate in Spanish. Many Indians, it seems, would not have availed themselves of the opportunity even if they qualified. Estéban Ramírez, literate and theoretically propertied, was one Indian *republicano* who had good reason not to sell his parcel, for he endangered the transgenerational livelihood of his lineage and extended family by doing so. But the literacy clause did exclude the vast majority of peasants from full claim to those rights and responsibilities which, in liberal republican ideology, were deemed to follow from propertied citizenship. In this case, the useful slippage between tributary subject and propertied citizen generated a subaltern form of Indian citizenship wrapped up in the hybrid notion of *republicano*.

The Uneven Mediation of *Alcalde* Authorities

The tax registers (*matrículas de contribuyentes*) of the postcolonial period suggest an increasingly direct, albeit clientist, penetration of Andean peasant society by non-Indian petty state officials in the 1830s and 1840s.[36] In accordance with republican ideals, tribute was now to be paid directly to the *patria* (via the necessary petty officials) and not to the ethnic chief. By the early 1820s, as Bolívar had dictated, the remaining chiefs were officially removed as tribute collectors in Huaylas, and local *misti* authorities replaced them. The new local authorities included the departmental prefect, the provincial subprefect, and the district governor-collectors (*gobernadores recaudadores*—similar to the appointed *mestizo* governors and royal tribute collectors, or neo-*caciques*, of the intendancy regime) and their lieutenant governors. The departmental *apoderado fiscal*, or treasurer, with a direct link to the Ministry of Finance in Lima, kept the books.

The tax registers themselves were based on, but not identical to, the late colonial *padrones* (ecclesiastical censuses) and were put together by the treasurer with the local help of the subprefects and parish priests, who supplied the *libros de bautismo*, or baptismal records, used to determine descent (fully indigenous or not) and age. As George Kubler noted, the postcolonial taxation system was "more diversified and inclusive than Colonial tribute, which affected only the Indian[s]." In theory, the new registers "covered all taxpayers"[37]—albeit under two covers. The postcolonial "nation," as textually and numerically represented in the tax registers, was until 1854 divided into the fiscal categories of *indígenas* (indigenous) and *castas* (nonindigenous). Although historians (echoing the liberal critics of the day) have considered the early republican contribution to be little more than a "neocolonial" continuation of the colonial tribute system, it was actually rather different in important ways. The postcolonial system was hybrid, at once universal (republican) and particular (colonial) in its approach to taxation, and its classificatory language had also shifted in important ways. "Indios" had been displaced by "indígenas," while "blancos" or "viracochas" (Quechua term for "whites" which was sometimes used in colonial censuses, or *padrones*) was uncomfortably merged—fiscal officials noted the awkwardness of the category—with "mestizos" and other mixed bloods of the colonial "castas" category, which, however, was not homogenous but rather differentiated by occupation, type of tax, and level of income. In short, a new, more inclusive (for *mestizos*) binary opposition was established.[38]

The postcolonial *contribución indígena* (1826–54) was to be paid, on the lowest level, to the lieutenant governor or his local *comisionados* (commissioned agents), then to the district governor, who passed it on to the subprefect where, in theory, the peso stopped; the subprefect was in effect responsible for meeting the provincial quotas. The subprefect subtracted his salary as a percentage cut (4 to 6 percent), or *premio*, from the projected revenues. The subprefects were to turn in the cash as well as any unredeemed receipts to the treasurer of the department. The *contribuyente*, or taxpayer, was given a receipt upon payment and—if he or she could prove *originario* descent, and if lands were available (frequently they were not)—access to a plot of land in the "tierras de la República" (colonial repartition lands claimed and renamed by the republican state) was granted. In some cases *topos mostrencos*, or *forastero* plots, were granted in state lands, although not in usufruct.

In displacing the colonial chiefs declared defunct by Bolívar, petty state officials developed webs of clientage and modes of coercion that could reach deep into postcolonial Indian communities.[39] During the Independence Wars (1820–24), secular contributions as well as ecclesial tithes were apparently collected by military-political officers and their assistants, some of whom were militant clergy, and most of the proceeds were directed to the war effort. However, later documentation suggests that the webs of petty clientage used by the departmental state relied increasingly upon the Indian *alcaldes* or *varayoc* at the district and subdistrict levels to collect the contribution, purvey public works or *la república* labor, and carry out police functions.

These functions were not new. The first Indian *alcalde* posts, although not identical to the *alcaldes ordinarios* and *pedáneos* of the postcolonial era, were instituted in the early colonial period of the Toledan reforms (1560s–70s). The *alcalde* posts, which were one- or two-year rotations filled by election, were created to check the power of hereditary chiefs (Andean *kurakas*), to serve as the agents of parish priests, and in general to provide the key police and service functions necessary for (neo-Mediterranean) civil society in the "Indian republic." In practice, the early colonial *alcaldes* of Huaylas often were literate, were chosen by consensus and prestige, served the interests of chiefs, and usually were drawn from the lesser noble class, known to the Spaniards as *principales* or *camachicos*. The early seventeenth-century line drawings attributed to Don Felipe Guaman Poma de Ayala suggest that the *alcalde ordinario* was typically more Andean, or peasant, in extraction and dress than the more Hispanized and socially distinguished chiefs.[40] But with the decline and separation of hereditary chiefly functions in late eighteenth-century Huaylas, and their replacement by appointed *mestizo* governors and tribute collectors,[41] the *alcaldes* emerge in the 1790s and subsequent decades to lead Indian community protests against the newly imposed and illegitimate neo-*caciques*. The separation of chiefly powers was part of the repression of hereditary *kurakas* that followed the Tupac Amaru II insurrection of 1780 and the establishment of the reformed intendency regime in 1783. In Huaylas, the prevalence of appointed *caciques* undermined chiefly authority and the viability of indirect rule via chiefs, and it frequently produced contentious litigation in the late colonial period.[42] The petition of the "alcaldes de indios" of Huaraz in 1790 to the subdelegate of Huaylas anticipated postcolonial petitions signed by *alcalde ordinario* authorities:

> Having suffered unspeakable prejudices as a result of not being able to possess the lands of their respective repartitions, which were assigned by royal census, because the *cacique* has appropriated them all without the least compassion [for his Indians]; and being so burdened . . . with the fulfillment of their tribute obligations, *mita* [corvée] service, and other duties to the republic; and since they are excluded even from their small plots because the said *cacique* has sold them; and now they have named a *mestizo* called Luís Maguiña as new *cacique,* and he maims and abuses the Indians to the extreme of breaking the staffs of the *alcaldes* at the door of the church; and for these reasons and because said new *mestizo cacique* is foreign to the propertied *cacique* lineage . . . the [Indians of Huaraz] beg that the legitimate Don Diego Gonzáles Rimay Cochachin be admitted as their *cacique.*[43]

The petition claims that the *cacique* (an illegitimate heir of Indian descent, who was subsequently replaced by the neo-*cacique mestizo* Maguiña) had appropriated community lands for himself or had sold them to meet tribute burdens (another frequent protest voiced by the *alcaldes* in late colonial Huaylas). The Indian peasants of the community, including the *alcaldes,* however, were saddled with tribute obligations, corvée service, and "other duties to the republic." The "republic" here, of course, was the "republic of Indians." The new *mestizo* tribute collector did not belong to that republic, and to top things off he abused the authority of the *alcaldes* by dashing their sacralized staffs of office, or *varas,* on the steps of the church.[44]

By 1817 *alcaldes* in Huaylas appear at the top of tribute lists, or *visitas,* where previously only chiefs were listed.[45] Many appointed *caciques* are dismissed from their positions, and the *alcaldes* take up the responsibility of tribute collection, in some cases as early as 1813.[46] Thus, when Bolívar arrives in the 1820s and abolishes the *caciques* in favor of petty non-Indian officials, many have already lost their power and have been displaced by the elected, rotating *alcaldes.*

The diminished stature and dependency of post-Independence *varayoc* on local officials and judges is suggested by the 1832 petition for official confirmation presented by the *alcaldes pedáneos* of the *parcialidad* of Allauca of the newly christened Pueblo Libre (formerly Huacra) between Caraz and Yungay. In this petition, the Indian *alcaldes* present themselves as meager local officials with precarious authority over "their" recalcitrant *indígenas.*

Their roles included purveying collective labor and aiding in contribution collection. In many ways, they look like a species of community police.

Nevertheless, this subordinate function, linked as it was to local Indian notions of *republicano* obligations, was probably critical for the collection of the contribution. Indeed, by 1850 the prefect of Ancash openly admitted the axial roles of the *alcalde* authorities, timidly suggesting to his superiors in Lima that they be granted official recognition as tax collectors in the Indian hamlets.[47] This request, like Prefect Saldías's in 1904, was firmly rejected by the Ministry of Government as unconstitutional and antiliberal: to admit the pivotal role of Indian authorities of colonial origin in the everyday apparatus of the republican state was heresy.[48]

But nineteenth-century *varas* (local shorthand for *alcaldes*) could be more than mere lackeys and tax collectors. Indian *vara* authorities in Huaylas, for example, continually appealed to the literacy clause of the Law of 1828 to defend Indian parcels from passing into non-Indian hands. In 1853, the *alcalde pedáneo* of Quillo (located in the Chawpi Yunga, or Vertientes, zone of the Cordillera Negra between Carhuaz and Casma) defended community lands when he charged that ten *originarios* of his community had sold their *topos* illegally to petty *mestizo* officials and to local landowners. The case illustrates both the use of the 1828 literacy clause in defense of threatened repartition lands and the webs of local clientage among corrupt officials that could undermine that defense.

The *alcalde* of Quillo argued that the ten who alienated their plots could not read or write; therefore, the sales (which he argued did harm to the community and to the individuals' own families) were illegal, clearly violating the literacy clause of the Law of 1828. The local justice of the peace conducted an oral hearing, or *juicio verbal.* The hearing revealed that some of the sellers could shakily sign their name, but nothing more. It was also stated that the plots had been sold for goods in kind, not cash, and that the sales had not been registered; cane liquor, oxen, mules, and a coastal orchard were among the goods ostensibly bartered for the plots. According to the *alcalde,* the swindlers, which included two *mestizo* ex-governors of the district, had gotten the Indians drunk and taken advantage of their ignorance to "relieve them of their possessions which the law and the nation hold in respect."[49]

Considering the evidence, the local justice of the peace decided in the *alcalde*'s favor, again citing the Law of 1828. Attempts to return possession to the Indians were resisted by the new owners, however, who appealed the decision to the higher *juez de primera instancia* (Primary Claims Court judge) in Huaraz. The higher judge reversed the lower justice of the peace's decision on technical grounds: the local judge, he said, had not notified all interested parties before repossessing the lands in question.

The justice of the peace's communications with the higher judge in Huaraz sound out the tensions unleashed by the 1828 law and reveal the difficulty of enforcing the literacy exemption at the local level. For the local judge, tribute revenue and the continued taxpayer status of *contribuyentes originarios* in the *matrículas de contribuyentes* were of great concern. But for the higher judicial authority in Huaraz, it appears that personal relations of petty clientage prompted him to declare a technical infraction and thus annul the community's defense.

Alcaldes also defended Indian *forastero* access to alpine commons, and when the preferred avenue of legal petition was foreclosed, they sometimes found themselves leading revolts against transgressive and, in their eyes, "unpatriotic" state authorities, as in the Atusparia insurgency of 1885. The petition presented in 1846 to the subprefect of Huaraz by Manuel Ysidro, the *alcalde de campo* of the Estancia of Marian, poignantly revealed the *vara-yoc* role in blocking the nineteenth-century drive by landlords to enclose, or "lock the gates," to high Andean common pastures in Huaylas. In question was the creeping enclosure of the *quebradas* (wooded alpine ravines) that led up from the valley towns to the high puna grasslands, or *jalka*, of the Cordillera Blanca to the east. The enclosure of the ravines violated a tense expectation between landless *forasteros*, or "contribuyentes sin tierras," as they were officially known, and departmental administration in Huaraz. This expectation revolved around previous state protection of public access to the native "quenua" or "quishuar" trees (*Polylepis* sp.), which grew only in the *quebradas* and which were freely cut and hauled by landless Indians, then sold and consumed as firewood in the valley towns.[50]

In 1842 the *apoderado fiscal*, or treasurer, of the Department of Ancash outlined the official justification of this resources-for-contribution compact between Indians and the state:

The contribution that the indigenes satisfy is not excessive and besides it is necessary. It is not excessive because they are granted certain prerogatives in the payment of parish fees, tithes, etc., and because they have free access to the *quebradas* or forests for the extraction of sticks of wood for the market; to this one must add that the contribution of the *originarios* is lightened because of the assistance they obtain with the repartition lands they possess. It is necessary because in the instances when they have stopped contributing by virtue of a pardon, we experience a scarcity of workhands, since the indigenes need only one piece of rough clothing per year; and their fields, although small, proportion them with their simple foods, being the only thing that they like [to eat], and they desire nothing else. They do not strive to abandon their idleness which is characteristic of them except at the time when the contribution is collected.[51]

In the departmental treasurer's view, the Indian head-tax was a necessary measure which ensured a cheap supply of seasonal labor at tax-collection time, given the Indian's "characteristic idleness" and his utter lack of interest in luxury consumption.[52] The reason for protecting Indian access to the natural woodstands of the alpine ravines was similarly self-interested. The Indians were the sole suppliers of fuelwood to the kitchens of townsmen, including those of petty officialdom. When landlords moved to fence or otherwise enclose and restrict Indian access to this resource, townsmen would object if the result was to cut off, or make more costly, their cheap supply of cooking fuel. The conflict over access to firewood, therefore, could pit the interests of landlords against those of local officials, townsmen, and Indians.

The Indian *forastero* view, as rendered in the language of a legal petition signed by the *alcalde* of Marian, was as follows:

[W]e find ourselves oppressed by the payment of tribute as unhappy *forastero* Indians without lands or recompense of any kind; that since the time of our ancestors all the Cordilleras were open for getting firewood and bringing it into town and with the money earned thereby we paid our tribute, tithes, and first fruits (*primicias*). But today the gates to the cordilleras are closed under lock and key, especially in [the *quebradas* of] Llacac and Cojup, which have belonged to us since time immemorial, and none of the former landlords had placed any obstacles before us. But now the señores Don Miguel Mosquera and Don Gregorio Cobo have ordered that they close the gates, and we find ourselves oppressed by an unjust sacrifice. In virtue of this we repair to the integrity of this court, so that taking pity on our sad orphancy, and finding ourselves reduced to extreme poverty, [you might] order by virtue of your recognized authority that they give us room to work and contribute religiously to the state.[53]

In his routine response to the *alcalde* of Marian's petition, the subprefect of Huaraz requested a report from the non-Indian governor of the District of La Independencia (formerly Waranka Ychoc Huaraz), who was then the *mestizo* Don Manuel Jurado, since the Estancia of Marian and its

Indian *alcalde* fell under his jurisdiction. Don Manuel's brief reports to the subprefect and the prefecture, respectively, confirmed the customary access granted by the colonial state and upheld by previous republican authorities in Huaylas. In his report to the subprefect, the district governor noted that

> one of the principal sources which the Indians make use of to pay their contributions is the firewood that they gather in the *quebradas,* and whose woodstands are recognized as common property. Proof of this is the fact that the first landlords were never able to impede woodgathering there, and when they tried, the authorities curbed such abuse. For example, the deceased ex-prefect Don Juan Mejía ordered [in the 1820s] that the *quebradas* be opened to public extraction of wood. In another [eighteenth-century] case on the same point, the deceased Don N. Carbajal, landlord of Aco and owner of the Rurec Quebrada, lost a decision in the Supreme Court against the miner Don N. García in virtue of the fact that landlords are considered owners of the topsoil (*casco*) and the pasture, but not of the natural woodstands that grow wildly and are not planted. Thus, if this abuse is not curbed, the first consequence will be that the Indians will be cut off from the only resource they have for paying their contributions; and second and most important, the town will be without one of the primary necessities of life.[54]

Furthermore, the governor pointed out that there were "indestructible bases" for common property rights in Law 14, title 17, book 4, of the *Recompilation of the Laws of the Indies.* In 1559, he noted, King Philip II had issued a royal decree stipulating that "the Indians may freely cut wood in the forests (*montes*) for their use, and that no impediments be placed on them except that they not cut [the trees] in such a manner that [they] cannot grow and increase."

As in many other such cases, Don Manuel cited colonial decrees to establish the time-tested legality of Indian access to the natural woodstands of the cordillera. In this and subsequent cases, the contention that the Laws of the Indies were still in force was reviewed and debated by departmental and ministerial authorities alike. The authorities would conclude that the Laws of the Indies were indeed still in force so long as specific articles were not derogated by the Constitution or by subsequent republican legislation. Departmental notary archives demonstrated that in the colonial Land Recomposition of 1712, which was based on the initial Composition of 1594, all the vacant lands above those assigned to the dual *warankas* of Huaraz and *el común del pueblo,* and reaching up to the Cordillera Blanca, were declared *ejidos* (commons). Yet the petition of the *encomendero* (Spanish overlord) Garci Barba in 1621 and the *visita pastoral* of Archbishop Mogrovejo in 1593 also showed that vast *encomendero* herds of sheep, numbering in the tens of thousands, were driven and pastured in these same common lands. The Recomposition of 1712, however, also recognized the individual claims of Spaniards and Creoles who had "purchased" Indian lands from financially strapped Indian chiefs or who had otherwise been granted lands in the area for having "served His Majesty."[55] The result was considerable tenure confusion. Notwithstanding, the colonial recomposition titles were not "blank check" private property under royal Spanish law. Property was always subject to "the will of the king," and the "natural fruits" of the land could not be owned as such. What was "natural" was the wealth of the king; thus, access to property was within the powers of his grace.

By the 1840s and 1850s, however, more exclusive notions of private property had entered Peruvian legislation and (especially) landlord consciousness. Bounded dominions were increasingly claimed by landlords in their efforts to extend and consolidate their vaguely defined estates. Such efforts to fully privatize estate dominions occurred in the late eighteenth century but, as Karen Spalding correctly argued, the designs of late colonial *hacendados* were more readily deflected by protective colonial legislation.[56] As the *alcaldes* of Huaraz would put it in their petition of 1887, colonial landlords had abstained "out of fear that the councils, justices, and ministers would apply the fines stipulated in the Law [of the Indies]."

But now colonial composition titles were willfully misinterpreted to be equivalent to liberal private property—that is to say, an exclusive form of property which implied a sacrosanct right to restrict access. For, as Manuel Jurado noted,

> today no one is ignorant of the fact that when the Royal Patrimony sold a farm it excluded the forests, waters, etc., declaring these to be common property, as one can plainly see in the titles of acquisition and in other laws and treatises which expressly declare that you cannot alienate common property. Thus, not even the livestock breeders of the *quebradas* can call themselves owners of the trees that the earth produces for the general good of the people, and as the primary necessity of the villages; and not even you, Señor, can avoid taking care that the laws of the land be upheld, as it is declared in the Constitution of the state.[57]

With the liberal abolition of the "indigenous contribution" in 1854–55, fewer legal bottlenecks obstructed liberal property rights, and in any case the opulent, Lima-based "guano state" was generally uninterested in collecting petty fines in the provinces. The lack of concern of the liberal state in the post-1854 period would invite further enclosures. Indeed, for the evicted Indian José Mendosa, this renewed aggression on the part of landlords was, in his words, worse than what the Spanish "conquistadors of America could have done to the descendants of Manco Capac, aided as [this landlord is] by his intimate relations of friendship with the local judge."[58]

The "Liberal Revolution"

Castilla's "liberal revolution" of 1854 was initially trumpeted by adherents as Peru's "real independence." The foundational, Bolivarian ideals of the early 1820s had, in their view, been betrayed by conservatives and *caudillos*. Now they would make good on the promise of 1821 by manumitting slaves, abolishing the "castes," and "liberating" Indians from tribute. But leaving aside (or suspending) the rhetoric of liberals and of Creole nationalist historiography, Castilla's revolution may be read within the regional tradition of what might be called liberal caudillism (as opposed to "nationalist caudillism") or perhaps South American "bonapartism." This brand of enlightened caudillism was anticipated by Bolívar and San Martín in the 1820s, and by Andrés de Santa Cruz in the 1830s, and resurrected by Andrés Cáceres in the 1880s, and Nicolás de Piérola in the 1890s. The "enlightened liberal" discourse of Castilla's mid-century revolution was remarkably similar to San Martín's. Echoing many of the same keywords of the 1820s, Castilla (who also fought in the 1820s Independence campaigns) decreed in 1854 that

> starting in 1855 the indigenous contribution is suppressed, and thenceforth they will not contribute except in the same way that the rest of the inhabitants of Peru do. . . . Emancipated from the humiliating tribute imposed upon its head three and a half centuries ago, and elevated by the natural effect of civilization, Peru will gain a numerous and productive population in the indigenous race, which will undoubtedly offer her a richer contribution.[59]

Repeating San Martín's rhetorically useful error—for the "tribute" was long since renamed and reformed as "contribution"—Castilla would emancipate Peru's downtrodden "indigenous race" so that it may "be elevated by the natural effect of civilization." As in the abolition of tribute decreed by the Cortes of Cadiz in 1812, which entailed what for the Junta Tribunal of Lima was the impractical and unwise "elevation of the Indian Nation to the level of the Spanish," Castilla would sunder the awkward ethnic-fiscal categories of "indíjenas" and "castas" and replace them with a unitary citizen tax known simply as the *contribución personal* (poll-tax).

Castilla's proposed liberal poll-tax, which would displace the "humiliating tribute" (read: the postcolonial "indigenous contribution"), was to be paid by all adult male citizens of Peru, with exceptions for priests, soldiers, the elderly, and the disabled.[60] Unlike the coercive thuggery that had supposedly accompanied collection of the "tribute" or indigenous and *casta* contributions, the universal citizen poll-tax, it was promised, would be collected in an enlightened manner. But like the Bolivarian liberals of the 1820s who saw their decrees undone in the Constitutional Congress of 1828, Castilla never established his liberal poll-tax. It, along with several other liberal reforms proposed by the Mariscal, was blocked by an alliance of conservative and liberal representatives to the National Convention of 1856.[61] The universal citizen poll-tax, or *contribución personal,* would be implemented for the first time only in 1866 — predictably by decree of yet another dictator, Mariano Ignacio Prado. But his decree, which met with resistance in the highlands, was just as quickly rescinded by the Peruvian Congress in 1867. The poll-tax appeared again in 1879, but now under the guise of the "impuesto de guerra" or war tax declared by yet another liberal dictator, this time by the self-proclaimed "Protector of the Indigenous Race," Nicolás de Piérola. The 1879 poll-tax would finally come to its bloody conclusion in Huaylas-Ancash in the Atusparia insurgency of 1885, and would then have to be officially abolished by its own author in 1895.

Generally considered a watershed event in modern Peruvian history, Castilla's "liberal revolution" signaled Lima's midcentury sea change toward the free-trade liberalism which was then becoming dominant throughout Latin America, and which began to emerge in Peru during the 1840s (partly under Castilla's own modernizing guidance as customs minister). Still, Lima's midcentury liberalism, though triumphant over the eclectic protectionist nationalism practiced by early republican elites, was subsidized in an illiberal, statist fashion by the fantastic revenues derived from the monopoly that the Peruvian state held over the guano (nitrogen-rich bird dung) trade with Europe.[62] As the modernizing coastal elite prospered, and as "pharoanic" (and, Paul Gootenberg argues, not-so-pharoanic) development projects were hatched in its salons,[63] the opulent "Lima State" would drift away from the interior highland regions. For at the same time as the central state set out to appease provincial elites and (physically) conquer the Andean interior with "civilizing" and export-led railroad construction projects (which, in the Huaylas-Ancash case, went bust), it would also effectively vacate its previous, albeit precarious role as mediator of agrarian class and political relations.[64]

Manuel del Río, Peru's minister of finance, had warned that the fiscal autonomy afforded by guano revenues could produce "dislocation" between the country's taxpayers (primarily Indian contributors) and Lima.[65] If the renewable tax base were abolished for ideological or political reasons, the central state would come to depend increasingly on export revenues from the sale of non-renewable guano, while its domestic tax base would erode to the point of no return. The "customary" fiscal bond between taxpayers and the central state would come unglued. Del Rio's gloomy prediction proved true for Huaylas-Ancash, where by the 1870s "dislocation" was manifest—and by the 1880s, fatally so. The fiscal dislocation of Lima from the interior regions also disrupted state-peasantry political relations and made it easier for Chile to conquer Peru by occupying Lima in the War of the Pacific (1879–83).[66] Subsequent to the Chilean occupation, the region-alized and dislocated nature of political culture and the aggravated class relations of society in the Andean sierra would manifest itself in civil war and, eventually, social war.

Thus, contrary to the liberal, integrationist designs of Castilla, the un-replaced 1855 abolition of "tribute" would have the effect of dislocating provincial Andean society from the central state in Lima, and of allowing agrarian class conflict to fester unchecked in the interior. The liberal state's absence in the hinterlands made it easier for landlords to enclose com-mons, charge access fees, and procure debt-ridden, landless Indian workers for their estates. In Huaylas, enclosures of the Andean pastures and natu-ral woodstands of the *quebradas,* or alpine ravines of the Cordillera Blanca, would be critical for the thousands of landless Indians, or *forasteros,* who depended on access to public resources for their livelihoods. Landlords in Huaylas enclosed alpine pastures not so much because they wished to ex-pand production—market incentives for expansion were weak here—but rather because they could thereby capture indentured Indian labor, which allowed the undercapitalized *haciendas* to survive under conditions of eco-nomic stagnation. Landlords thus allowed Indian access upon condition of the payment of *gabelas,* or user fees. In effect, Indians increasingly paid "tribute" to landlords—and not to the state—for access to the formerly pro-tected commons. When, during the war years of 1879–85, *caudillos* would collect poll-taxes as war taxes, the effect was to charge a "double-tax" on peasants (both landed *originarios* and tenant *forasteros*) without offering any reliable state guarantees of access to formerly public or community lands.

In practice, then, the late nineteenth-century "personal contribution" or poll-tax was little more than a species of *caudillo* war-tax and emphatically not a tributary levy paid in exchange for access to the means of production.[67] The personal contribution was thus the antithesis of the colonial "reciprocal pact" of land for tribute noted by Platt for Bolivia.[68] The poll-tax was usually collectable only with coercive methods, or with an individual *caudillo*'s personal promise of immediate political advantage or protection, and it was mainly applied to financing the regional or national campaigns of competing warlords.

Huaylas-Ancash was not isolated from the national unrest that had swept Castilla into power (once again) in 1854–55. Ramón Castilla's movement was based to the south, in ever liberal Arequipa, but the military campaign made itself strongly felt in the central highlands, where the Mariscal himself fought[69] and where local revolts broke out against the incumbent regime of José Rufino Echenique. One such revolt took place in Huaraz in 1854. The Huaraz revolt was directed primarily against the unpopular and violent military conscription practiced by the Echenique government, which desperately needed men to combat Castilla's growing insurgency. Resistance to the draft, and to the counterinsurgency troops sent from Lima to put down the rebellion, was accentuated by the general panic caused by the *verruga peruana* epidemic then ravaging the Indian *estancias* of Huaylas.[70] According to local reports, "about 2,000 Indians" incited by pro-Castilla elements drove the incumbent prefect and his entourage from Huaraz, whence they were forced to take refuge in the nearby town of Carhuaz. Indians may have been attracted by the rhetoric of liberal reformers, some of whom had taken up the cause of the Indian and argued, in seemingly contradictory terms, that "they be put in possession of their ancient lands, *ejidos*, hills, pastures, and the rest, which they have been dispossessed of by the greediness of others."[71] The popular Huaraz revolt was put down in bloodshed, though, and hundreds of conscripts were marched off to the port of Casma, whence they were hastily dispatched on an overloaded steam barge for Lima. Embarking at night in stormy seas, the ship slammed into a reef off Casma and, in one of the great tragedies of the civil war, all but the captain perished. This black event magnified Huaraz's supreme displeasure with the Echenique regime. When Castilla captured Lima the streets of Huaraz came alive with festivities.[72]

Castilla's program of liberal reform, however, would subsequently raise serious doubts among the region's indigenous peasantry and the local authorities. The 1856 *testimonio* of the local municipal agent of Cochabamba,

Manuel Morales, betrays one of the possible readings of the abolition of the *contribución de indígenas,* which accompanied the manumission of slaves as the centerpiece of Castilla's liberal revolution:

> It is obvious that in the *pueblos de indios,* where the *mestizos* who call themselves whites have settled, most are mortal enemies of the Indians, full of arrogance and with the footsteps of conquistadors. . . . [T]he Indians, despite being the majority of the state, obtain nothing but . . . a hoax: As proof, Your Excellency, deign to cast your gaze over the 82 deputies to the present National Convention [of 1856] and you will see that there is not one Indian among them who can represent them and speak for them. . . . [I] make this observation only because in many *pueblos* . . . the whites have propagated the idea—with discredit to Your Excellency's paternal designs—that if the Indian tribute has been extinguished it is so that their lands may be taken away and sold, and that in effect Your Excellency is going to send land surveyors.[73]

In this and other cases, the abolition of the postcolonial indigenous contribution—re-created in 1826 after the late colonial "voluntary" or "unitary" contribution, which in turn had renominated and displaced, in enlightened liberal fashion, the *real tributo de indios*—raised critical questions concerning the tenure of Indian lands, particularly those colonial "repartition," now "Republic" lands, claimed by the state. Although almost discursively identical to the 1812 abolition declared by the Cortes de Cadiz, Castilla's liberal-nationalist abolition of the contribution would irreversibly alter the terms of state–peasantry relations in Peru.

After 1855, indigenous peasants in Huaylas-Ancash would no longer argue that their status as *originarios republicanos* or even as *forasteros* who "contributed religiously to the state" should, *in itself,* guarantee or constitute a powerful argument for contingent access to an inherited plot of land in the parceled, ex-colonial "lands of the Republic." As we have seen, prior to 1854 peasant contributors often deployed contribution-for-land arguments and *republicano* status in cases of contested possession, despite the Law of 1828 which granted them title or ownership rights (and, if they could demonstrate literacy in Spanish, the right to transfer those rights). In the 1830s and 1840s, landed peasants could submit contribution receipts as evidence in defense of claims to plots, and as proof of good standing as taxpaying village citizens or *republicanos.* On the surface, these arguments were contradictory, since if the peasant was by law the private titleholder of his plot, he should not have to back up that claim with tax receipts. In practice, however, most peasants did not legalize their usufruct possessions with titles until much later in the century, if then. (If they did legalize individual plots with titles during the first half of the nineteenth century, no record has survived.) Without such title (and perhaps even with it) the best claim to a contested plot in the parceled, community "lands of the Republic" was *contribuyente originario* fiscal status and/or the legal demonstration of inheritance of such status from colonial forebears. The postcolonial fiscal system was a modified version of the late colonial one, and in order to function it had to recognize the descendants of colonial *tributarios originarios* as rightful holders of their usufruct (as of 1828, semiprivate) parcels in the "lands of the Republic." The reciprocal land-for-contribution linkage, then, obtained only to the extent that the lands in question were considered state property or dominion—either the Peruvian Republic's or, under colonial rule, the king's.

Manuel Morales's case, however, did not concern such lands. Indeed, the point of his personal *testimonio* was to prove that the threatened lands in question had not been repartition lands, but rather *tierras sobrantes* or *tierras de composición* "purchased" or "composed" by his community and its chief by way of the colonial *recomposición y venta de tierras*. The Recomposition of 1712 was a species of royal auction where various parties submitted land claims and pledged generous "donations" to the Crown of so many hundred pesos in exchange for royal titles of "perpetual possession."[74]

Contrary to the flat notion of "community lands" common in the ethnographic literature on the Andes, the colonial *pueblos de indios* of post-Toledan Huaylas held diverse lands classified under several distinct categories, each with differing tenure rights and obligations. *Ejidos, tierras realengas, tierras sobrantes, tierras de guaranga, tierras del cacique,* and *tierras del común* all appear in notarized colonial land registers. The critical tenure distinction, however, was between *tierras de repartición* and *tierras de composición.*

Tierras de repartición, which I have translated literally as "repartition lands," could not under normal colonial circumstances be legally alienated. They were the material basis of chiefly mediated tributary relations between the "Indian republic" and "the king." These lands were considered Crown dominion by right of conquest and were assigned by special delegates of the Crown to Andean chiefs and their tributary communities—the *guarangas, pachacas,* and *ayllus*—as well as to the *común,* or "republic," of the congregated *pueblos de indios* that the communities shared. The lands were in turn redistributed to tribute-paying peasant households as usufruct plots and pastures. In return for access, peasant households paid the *tasa* (tribute) to the collection agents of the chiefs, the lesser *principales, camachicos,* and *alcaldes.* Tributes were deposited at intervals by the chiefs in the *cajas de comunidad,* or community chests, until full tribute payment to the magistrate or *corregidor* came due.

The *tierras de composición,* or "composition lands," on the other hand, were lands "composed" by chiefs for their *warankas* (communities). These "composed" lands were not directly subject to royal tribute obligations. As corporate property under Indian dominion, these lands could be (and were) alienated provided that license was granted by the colonial magistrate (and such permission frequently was granted in colonial Huaylas).

The two most significant dates in the colonial history of Indian land tenure in Huaylas were 1594 and 1712. The initial *composición de tierras* (1594) legally established previously unwritten Indian claims, whereas the *recomposición y venta de tierras* (1712) legalized the transfer of "vacant" or "extra" Indian lands to Spaniards and *mestizos* but also the legal acquisition of untitled lands by chiefs and communities. In nineteenth- and twentieth-century land disputes, these two textualized "documentary events" are unfailingly cited to legitimate or to challenge claims. In effect, the Composition of 1594 and the Recomposition of 1712 conform the textual historical horizons of Indian territoriality in Huaylas-Ancash.⁷⁵

In 1594 recognized Indian lands in Huaraz included those undocumented precolonial holdings of particular chiefs and *ayllus* ("from the time of the Inka") which could be legally validated with sufficient oral testimony. In 1594 each *ayllu* was assigned repartition lands, as were the *warankas* ("tierras de guaranga"), the *kurakas* or chiefs ("tierras del cacique"), and the community-at-large or republic ("común del pueblo"). The *común del pueblo* also included Indian *forasteros* under an appointed *cacique de forasteros,* who was sometimes also the hereditary *originario* or *waranka* chief. The *tierras del cacique* and *de guaranga* were mostly lands redistributed to peasants by the chiefs, and dedicated to peasant cultivation in exchange for tribute payment. *Común del pueblo* or *ejido* lands included Crown or public commons open to all members of the community for grazing and for the extraction of firewood, glacial ice, and other alpine natural resources. These lands were normally the high pastures and *quebradas* that began at elevations where the parceled and lower *ayllu, waranka,* and chief's lands left off. Thus, smaller plots redistributed for peasant cultivation gave way to open commons as one moved up the slopes of the Andean cordilleras to the east and west of the valley. The upland commons, however, were rarely demarcated in precise terms. They normally extended from this *ayllu*'s lands to that mountaintop, or from this chief's land to that alpine lake. The lower-elevation agricultural lands, however, were generally subdivided in rectangular units measured in *varas* (Spanish yards) and were cultivated as *topos* (i.e., as parceled *tierras de repartición*). These were assigned by the chiefs, *principales,* and *alcaldes* to peasant tributary households. Peasant households worked plots by mobilizing Andean forms of interhousehold reciprocal (*rantin*) and festive community labor (*minka* and/or *la república*). This colonial pattern of subdivided household plots under cultivation with complementary common pastures at higher elevations is recognized in the contemporary ethnographic literature as Andean agropastoral organization.[76]

In 1712 the repartition lands could not be alienated and were not for sale, but any "vacant" or "extra" lands were. As a result of the demographic decline of the indigenous population, which was severe in the seventeenth century,[77] there were now plenty of such lands in Huaylas, especially in the alpine pasture, or *jalka* uplands, situated above the repartition lands of the communities, and some were sold by financially strapped chiefs to non-Indians.[78] By the late eighteenth century, the majority of the now fragmented Indian lands in Huaraz were not repartition lands but, rather, composition lands "purchased" or "composed" by Indians themselves (mostly chiefs) from the Crown.[79]

These "composed" lands were not subject to the tributary obligations that accompanied the distribution of repartition lands. In effect, the composition lands were corporate property exempt from the land-for-tribute "reciprocal pact" between the state and landed Indian society described by Tristan Platt for colonial Bolivia.[80] One historical consequence of Indian purchases of composition lands was that when the postcolonial liberal state privatized the repartition lands and altered the land-for-tribute linkage by granting private ownership rights to usufruct-holding contributors, it could not eliminate all Indian community lands, for the "tierras compuestas con su Magestad" remained unaffected.[81] However, when the Indian population of Huaraz began to recover and then expand in the nineteenth century, the historical significance of the colonial sales of composition lands by financially strapped chiefs would become painfully evident. After the nineteenth-century privatization of the repartition lands, the composition lands remained; but these remaining lands would not be nearly enough to support the expanding Indian population of Huaraz. This is one powerful reason why the ill-defined *ejidos,* or alpine commons, became so crucial by the end of the nineteenth century in Huaylas-Ancash.

If a nineteenth-century community could prove that it had "purchased" composition lands from the Crown, as Manuel Morales did, it could claim perpetual ownership and thus be exempt from privatization and tribute-abolition laws affecting "Republic" or state lands. Indeed, Morales's nineteenth-century defense is what made possible the modern community's very survival. We have his 1850s defense precisely because it was filed with Peru's Bureau of Indian Affairs in the 1940s as proof that Cochabamba was indeed an "indigenous community" deserving of legal recognition as such.

In effect, most of the so-called community lands that survived into the twentieth century in Huaylas-Ancash were not lands subject to tributary obligations at all. Instead, most appear to have been colonial *tierras sobrantes* "composed" by chiefs on behalf of their communities either in 1594 or 1712. In contrast, the repartition lands, which were assigned to chiefs and redistributed to the *warankas, pachacas,* and *ayllus* in return for tributary payments, were subject to an uneven and incomplete process of privatization over the course of the nineteenth century. Being linked to the indigenous contribution until 1854, the "tierras de la República" would be eroded, piece by piece, by individual land transfers.

In 1855, liberal reformers struck the literacy clause of the 1828 Constitution which had "negated the citizenship of Indians and Mestizos who could not read or write."[82] In theory, any Indian could now transfer his title as he saw fit. But as Morales warned, some aggressive "*mestizos* who call themselves whites" took advantage of the reforms to buy Indian lands, and to foreclose debts on Indian properties. Yet individual household ownership of *topos* did not necessarily imply the death of Indian "republics" in Huaylas-Ancash. Many aspects of production and reproduction remained collective or corporate, and subject to obligatory, but festive participation in *la república* labor brigades and the associated politics of community prestige invested in the rotating *varayoc* posts. In addition, access to colonial composition lands, and to the diminished but ill-defined *ejidos* or commons, could still be claimed, and sometimes upheld, in republican courts.

After 1855 conflicts over land between Indians, *mestizos,* and so-called whites appear to increase in Huaylas-Ancash, although to what extent remains at present unquantified given the fragmentary nature of local notarial records for the period.[83] In the 1860s and 1870s, civil disputes over commons were especially frequent in the Vertientes zone of the Cordillera Negra region, adjacent to coastal sugar and cotton plantations. As in other parts of the Peruvian sierra, these disputes frequently involved *cofradía* (religious brotherhood) property, private landowners, Indian communities, municipalities, and petty officials.[84] The liberal state passed legislation urging municipalities to lease community lands, brotherhood properties were banned, and other Church properties passed into the hands of the new Public Assistance Agency, or Beneficencia Pública. These measures generally increased the enclosure pressures on peasant communities.

In 1871, in the Cordillera Negra region of Tapacocha west of Recuay, the

Indian community of Tapacocha initiated a civil case against the local justice of the peace, whom they accused of usurping and enclosing community
lands. According to community litigants, the justice had taken half of their
lands, introduced cattle in their communal potato fields, and constructed a
stone fence down the middle with help from field hands recruited in the
local *pueblos* of Cotaparaco and Tapacocha. In their defense of community,
"the interested *comuneros* opposed the construction of the dividing wall and
even demolished the part of it that the [perpetrators] had managed to construct."[85] The available documentation on this case is incomplete, and no
sentence was passed. Of greater significance here, however, is that such
nineteenth-century fencing would repeatedly elicit firm resistance.

The pitched social battles over enclosure would soon be overshadowed,
but not canceled, by the War of the Pacific. International conflict would de-
volve into civil and social war as the consequences of unresolved postcolonial
contradictions, enclosure, and dislocation became violently evident. Andean
peasants and their leaders would confront this violent conjuncture informed
by an ambivalent history of political engagement with the postcolonial state.

This ambivalent history of engagement (and disengagement) had generated new predicaments for peasant politics. Andean peasants now moved in
the postcolonial limbo between tributary subject and citizen taxpayer. This
limbo, which constituted the space of postcolonial state-peasantry relations
and provided the generative conditions for postcolonial Andean political
communities, was largely unimaginable (except as negation or transition)
within the teleological discursive frameworks of enlightened liberalism and
Creole republicanism. In the Spanish language juri-political sphere, the
identity of this limbo or predicament was named "indígena" from above and
"republicano" from below. The slippage between offical Creole discourse on
"indígenas" and the deployment of "peruanos" and "republicanos" among
Quechua peasants seeking to resolve the local contradictions generated by
the uneven fiscal and property policies of an instable and sometimes liberalizing postcolonial state meant that peasant political practice in postcolonial
Huaylas-Ancash was receptive to, hidden by, and subversive of, the emergent republican (dis)order.

CHAPTER 3

Republicans at War

I n the meeting of Indian alcaldes *that took place yesterday . . . several of them made it clear to me that, the draft having been put into practice as a means of organizing the army, a considerable portion of the Indians have abandoned their homes and moved their residences to the mountains, or they have hidden in caves to elude the recruitment agents. . . . The Indians are poor men who have nothing with which to meet their needs except the fruits of their daily labor. It would not be surprising if the coercive means employed to wrench the poll-tax from them had the effect of exasperating them, making it possible that here, as in some places in the central highlands, social war—more bloody and dismal in its results than the civil war—will break out.—Provincial Mayor Vidal to Prefect Vargas, Huaraz, 1883*[1]

The Indians have harassed us by heaving boulders down upon us, cutting off our water supply, and blocking the roads. Thousands of them have crowned the hills, uniting themselves and traversing the mountains as if by magic.—Colonel Callirgos Quiroga to the Peruvian Central Command, Yungay, 27 April 1885[2]

In the midst of the terrible storm in which the Republic is enveloped, the uprising of the indigenous race and its combat against the white race, which barely forms one-sixth of [the Republic], threatens to lend formidable proportions to the national problem. The movement in Ancash appears to obey most purely an indigenous agitation. Since its appearance we have been able to do little else but follow the story with uneasy interest, trying to discover its real character and tendencies. In it lies the fate of the Republic.—El País, 7 May 1885

It has not been the idea of communism or of racial hatred that moved the Indians to rise up in mass and combat the iglesista forces; no, they have had no other desire than to see the triumph of the Constitution and . . . to support General Cáceres, EL GRAN REPUBLICANO, as they call him.—El Comercio, *2 June 1886*[3]

In late February 1885 an official broadside was posted around Huaraz. It announced that all "contributors," most of whom were indigenous peasants, must pay two semesters (that is, two soles) of the *contribución personal,* or poll-tax, at once. To facilitate tax collection, it was the duty of the two non-Indian district governors to order the *alcaldes ordinarios* of each district to submit the *matrículas,* or tax lists, of the indigenous peasant hamlets under their respective jurisdictions. In 1885 the *alcalde* of Huaraz's "first" District of La Independencia was Pedro Pablo Atusparia of Marian, and his "second," or counterpart, in the District of La Restauración was Pedro Guillén. In turn, they requested the lists from each of their subordinate *alcaldes pedáneos* and *alcaldes de campo* at the subdistrict (parish) and *estancia* (hamlet) levels.[4] But the pending collection of the poll-tax was greeted with trepidation by the twenty-four or twenty-five subordinate peasant authorities of Atusparia's "first" district. When the lesser *varayoc,* after meeting with their peasant communities, reported that they were unable to comply with the order, Atusparia sought literate legal assistance to draft a petition to the prefecture.

In the petition of 1885,[5] Atusparia (and probably Guillén) requested that the tax be reduced by half and that additional time be granted to deliver the lists. The authorities and some unsympathetic observers, though, declared that the petition was couched in a threatening tone. Yet given the relentlessly formal tone of subsequent and previous petitions, which were composed with "all due respect" and decorum for the authorities, this claim, which appeared in letters printed in the Lima press, was probably an alarmist provocation.[6] In any case, the avenue of legal petition was abruptly cut off when Atusparia, who was obliged to sign the petition in his capacity as "first" *alcalde ordinario,*[7] was jailed for contempt of authority and then tortured.

The governor of La Independencia District, José Collazos, had ordered that the *alcalde* Atusparia be made to confess the name of the petition's "redactor." Among other things, Atusparia got the "barber treatment": his long braid, the mark of age rank among the *alcaldes* of some Andean peasant communities, was reportedly chopped off.[8] When the governor's frenzied, counterinsurgent search for authorial conspirators failed to turn up the desired ventriloquist, all twenty-four of the lesser *varayoc* authorities of La Independencia District were imprisoned,[9] and "those who still wore long hair" were reportedly subjected to the same humiliation.[10] As in other such cases, the non-event of failing to capture the desired non-Indian conspiratorial agent brought down repression on an *alcalde*'s head.

The next afternoon, a crowd of Indian peasants—probably following Pedro Guillén and the twelve or so *varayoc* authorities who represented the hamlets of La Restauración District—approached the plaza.[11] Troops guarding the plaza (where the jail and government offices stood) panicked, opening fire on "the Indian rabble" at close range. As the sun rose over Huaraz, townspeople peered up to see the surrounding hills crowned with the silhouettes of, depending on the source, from four to eight thousand peasants. Near complete mobilization of the hamlets surrounding Huaraz had been achieved overnight.[12] Aware of the dire meaning of such a display, Huaraz's "notables" and the officers of the Artisans Battalion (which consisted of young recruits from Lima), then stationed in the plaza, apparently released some of the *alcaldes*, offering what must have been seen as bad faith promises of reconciliation.[13] In any case, last-minute wavering on the part of trembling notables came to no avail. By three o'clock in the afternoon, the Artisans Battalion, charged with upholding the regime in Huaraz, was completely routed. Fleeing survivors were driven out of town, whence they scrambled up the slopes of the Cordillera Negra to the west and then hurried down toward the Pacific coast. The prefecture, along with the Archive of the Departmental Treasury, which held the tax registers, was set ablaze, and many homes and shops of local Blue, or *iglesista*, sympathizers of the regime, were sacked. The so-called *indiada* and its liberated *alcaldes* now controlled Huaraz.[14] But behind them, and ready to move into positions of political leadership, stood Red, or *cacerista*, conspirators. On 4 March 1885, local Red nationalists constituted a new prefecture. The Atusparia insurgency, however, was far from over.

Countdown to 1885: From International to Civil War

Notwithstanding Benedict Anderson's cultural emphasis on the internal construction of "nation" as a meaningful imagined political community, certain nationalisms are generated in conflict, upon the violent construction of contrast. From Napoleon to Bismarck, nineteenth-century autocrats sought to create and seal patriotic allegiance to an emerging nation-state through infantry wars against neighboring Others. The drums of war and the defense of fatherland or homeland (*patria*) might, in the conflict approach to nationbuilding, unite an emergent nation otherwise divided by ethnic and class differences. Such an external opportunity to unite the nation in the common defense of homeland had presented itself uninvited at Peru's front door when Chilean troops came knocking in 1879. Peru failed utterly at this test, but in its failure it revealed, albeit in terms that proved threatening to the Creole elite, that the much-abused Andean peasantry had national political potential.[15] Huaylas-Ancash was a tragically important case of that undervalued, and unimagined, political potential.

The War of the Pacific (1879–83) would not have taken on its critical political nature as a test of Peruvian nationbuilding had Chile not decided to seize the highly valued nitrate-mining territory of southern Peru (and Bolivia) and then to occupy Peru's central coast and highlands, including Lima, in early 1881. The Chilean national state, which enjoyed the ironic postcolonial advantages of having been on the poor colonial periphery (subject to viceregal Lima), emerged from the trials of civil wars and incipient industrialization in the middle decades of the nineteenth century.[16] Chile's nationbuilding process was further consolidated by southward expansion into the Araucanian Indian frontier, where the Chilean Army resolved its "Indian question" in a violent and decisive manner similar to the "final solution" adopted in Argentina and the United States. By the 1880s Chile was in a position to challenge the financially weakened, post-guano-boom Peru for dominance over the lucrative nitrate mines of the Atacama Desert. (The guano boom came to an end in the 1870s as unrenewable reserves declined and synthetic fertilizers were developed.) At the time, the Atacama region was the national territory of Peru and Bolivia, but many of the nitrate mines were owned and operated by Chilean, British, and Anglo-American capitalists, and many of the mine workers were also Chilean.

After a series of iron-clad naval battles off the Atacama coast in which Chile emerged victorious, Peru and Bolivia sent infantry and cavalry forces south to stem the tide of land invasion. Master of the seas, Chile quickly outflanked Peruvian and Bolivian forces, landing battalions along the central Peruvian coast. Bolivia soon retreated from the fray, and Peruvian forces, badly beaten in the south, pulled back to defend Lima. In late 1881, Chilean regulars landed near Lima and overwhelmed a largely unprofessional force of poorly armed Peruvian soldiers, citizens, and Indians hastily recruited in the adjacent countryside—and in the Andean highlands.

Lima fell quickly and chaotically into the hands of the Chilean expeditionary force. Nicolás de Piérola, who assumed dictatorial powers at the outbreak of hostilities in 1879, was nominally in command of the defense of Lima. He and his circle of officers slipped away from the chaos, taking refuge in the rugged central highlands and establishing Peru's government-in-exile in Ayacucho. Piérola was later joined by Colonel Andrés Avelino Cáceres, who was soon elevated to general and made commander-in-chief of the Central Army of the Peruvian National Resistance. However, the appointed, civilian president of Peru, Francisco García Calderón, who assumed his post in 1881, remained in Lima. His "Magdalena government," although officially constituted in an international "neutral zone" established in suburban Lima,[17] emerged as an unpopular surrogate government compromised by the Chilean command, which occupied the seat of government in downtown Lima. Besides being occupied, Peru was now clearly divided. Some Peruvians, especially elites in Lima and the adjacent coastal plantations, supported García Calderón and peace with Chile at any cost; others, mostly concentrated in the central highlands and supporting Piérola, called for a war of national liberation to erase the disgrace of foreign occupation and forestall the loss of national territory.

The War in Huaylas-Ancash

Peru's war with Chile did not hit home in Huaylas-Ancash until near the end of the international conflict in 1883, although Chilean expeditionary forces occupied some coastal plantations and port installations,[18] as well as the unfinished Chimbote railway to Huallanca, between 1880 and 1882.[19] In the latter instance, Chilean forces were attracted by the presence of the provisional government of Vice-Admiral Lizardo Montero, who represented the now exiled President Francisco García Calderón and whose entourage established its national headquarters in Huaraz between February and July of 1882.[20] In addition, native sons of Huaylas-Ancash had been recruited for the defense of Lima in early 1881, and recruits and resources had been mobilized for the war effort on the southern front since 1879.[21]

After the fall of Lima, Ancash Prefect Tadeo Terry organized small National Guard contingents for the anticipated defense of Huaraz, regrouping the dispersed recruits fleeing the occupied capital. Terry collected war quotas (*cupos*) to support troop formation and departmental government, for fiscal subsidies from the central government in Lima were severed.[22] Like other highland authorities adhering to the defiant Piérola, Prefect Terry acted "with the firm resolution to continue making war" on the foreign invader.[23]

But in May 1881 the surrogate "Magdalena government" of García Calderón sent an expeditionary force to remove Terry.[24] The force of 450 guardsmen was led by the distinguished Colonel Isaac Recavarren, then prefect of Lima, and was part of the regime's effort to reconsolidate itself as the constitutional government of Peru.[25] Recavarren would remove Terry and install Nicanor Gonzáles, a "landlord from the Ancash coast linked to the coastal oligarchy," as prefect.[26]

The García Calderón regime initially represented the interests of the coastal plantation elite, then suffering the depredations of Chilean occupation. Among this elite group, including landlords from the Huaylas-Ancash coast, most were eager for peace. Highland nationalists, however, including some industrialists and many *hacendados,* saw the García Calderón regime as supported by traitors who put their private interests before the national interest of "peace with dignity."[27] Although Recavarren and the would-be prefect Gonzáles received an enthusiastic welcome when they arrived in the traditionally conservative town of Yungay,[28] they were met quietly in Huaraz. In a sly tactical move, Terry had disbanded his forces as Recavarren approached; he then regrouped and laid siege to Recavarren once the colonel had settled in Huaraz. During Terry's siege of Huaraz, more than half of Recavarren's guardsmen defected to the "national forces," and only about a hundred remained to retreat to Lima with Recavarren in late June.[29] As the defeated Recavarren pulled out, the prominent priest and provincial intellectual Fidel Olívas Escudero[30] blasted the expedition: "The war and hostilities brought by the Chileans could not have been more ruinous and tenacious than those wrought by our constitutional brothers. . . . Ancash denies recognition of and energetically rejects the [Magdalena] government, which it considers spurious and illegitimate, and [Ancash] is prepared to spill its last drop of blood before accepting [such a nefarious regime]."[31]

The residue of Recavarren's first expedition to Huaraz was popular resentment and hostility toward a Peruvian regime that seemed to bring more grief to its citizens than the still-distant Chileans. When Recavarren returned to Huaraz in 1883 — albeit this time under orders of the nationalist hero Andrés Avelino Cáceres — he could not enter the region with a clean slate. Recavarren would later overcome much, but not all, of the wary resentment. He did, however, learn some important lessons from the 1881 fiasco. In 1883 Recavarren, now commander-in-chief of the Northern Army of the National Resistance, appointed Olívas Escudero to the post of chief medical officer.[32] He also allowed the formation of popular fighting units, called *montoneras* and *guerrillas.*[33]

Late in 1881 the national political scene had shifted. Cáceres broke with Piérola, who went abroad; the general now recognized his former enemy. When Cáceres turned against Piérola and recognized the "Magdalena government" of García Calderón and (Vice-President) Lizardo Montero,[34] Recavarren was ready to come to his aid in the fight for "an honorable peace" with Chile.[35] Cáceres and Recavarren now agreed that an honorable peace for Peru (i.e., one without territorial concessions) could only be negotiated from a position of strength. In short, a credible nationalist military effort would be brought to bear on the Chilean occupation forces; spirited resistance and costly casualties inflicted on the enemy, they reasoned, would force the Chilean Congress to withdraw its forces and seek a negotiated settlement with the legitimate government of Peru.

When García Calderón was forced into exile in Chile, Montero assumed duties as acting head of state. Leaving his northern post in Cajamarca, Montero set up a provisional government in Huaraz, in effect making it the capital of the Peruvian Republic from February to June 1882.[36] In a fateful decision, Montero named General Miguel Iglesias to replace himself as "Political Chief of the North."[37] After unsuccessful negotiations in Huaraz with the U.S. emissary Prescott, Montero moved his government from Huaraz to Arequipa in late June.

Meanwhile, Chilean forces had occupied northern ports and now threatened to invade the highlands. As Chilean forces approached highland Cajamarca, Iglesias dispersed his troops without offering significant resistance. By late August, Iglesias broke with the Montero government. He then issued the infamous "Cry of Montán," which called for peace on Chilean terms and for "national regeneration" under his leadership. Far from presenting a united nationalist front against Chile, Peru was now preparing for civil war. The opposing camps, which would persist until 1886, came to be known as the *iglesistas,* or Blues, who favored peace with Chile, and the nationalist *caceristas* or *monteristas,* the Reds, who continued the armed struggle both against Chile and the *iglesistas,* whom they saw as collaborators with the enemy.

Most of highland Peru, including Huaylas-Ancash, rejected the Cry of Montán as treachery, although significant numbers of prominent landowners, on the coast more than in the highlands, supported Iglesias. Iglesias then called for national elections to his "Congress of the North," the counterpart of Montero's "National Congress" scheduled to convene in southerly Arequipa. When Iglesias sent a notice of congressional elections to Prefect Bruno Bueno in Huaraz, Bueno's response was one of intense indignation. Bueno slandered Iglesias as a traitor and a national disgrace, and he vowed to resist him with whatever means possible. Dissident proclamations against Iglesias were issued in Huaraz and elsewhere.[38]

The Northern La Breña Campaign of Colonel Recavarren, 1883

In March 1883 General Cáceres named Recavarren commander-in-chief of the "Expeditionary Forces of the Central Army to the Departments of the North." His orders were to return to Huaraz and raise an army with which

to march on Cajamarca and smash Iglesias.[39] Recavarren's task was critical
to the national military strategy envisioned by Cáceres. By forming an army
in Huaylas-Ancash and marching north on Iglesias, Recavarren would unite
the northern and central highlands, forming a united nationalist front that
could then turn on the Chilean occupation forces in coastal Lima. Yet, for
such a critical task, Cáceres could spare only a small and poorly equipped
battalion from his threadbare Central Army,[40] itself under constant danger
of attack by superior Chilean forces sent from Lima.[41] Recavarren was to
raise his army nearly from scratch, in a matter of two months (or less) and
without the added incentive of Chilean repression that proved so critical to
Cáceres's own recruitment successes in Junín, the central highland department to the south of Huaylas-Ancash. It must be noted that in contrast to
Junín, which was the main theater of resistance in highland Peru during the
war, Chilean incursion and repressive actions were only hearsay in most of
Huaylas-Ancash when Recavarren returned in 1883. Indeed, the only serious episode of repression prior to 1883 was at the hands of Recavarren's own
"pacification" expedition in 1881.

Once in Huaraz, Recavarren immediately began the formation of the
Ejército del Norte. Each of the seven provinces of the Department of
Ancash[42] was ordered to submit from a hundred to two hundred able-
bodied men: that is, "all persons suited for military service without regard
to class or condition, consulting only physical aptitudes required in the use
of firearms." The civilian population was also called upon to render arms,
cattle, mules, horses, hides, cloth, food, cash, and other war levies (gunpowder, dynamite, and tools from miners) "in proportion with the fortune
of each."[43] Recavarren's policy was to use persuasive, patriotic methods for
garnering support. His staff kept a balance sheet of exactions and donations, and the income and expenditures of his army were made public.[44] He
was also quick to reprimand subordinate officers for not carrying out his
orders to the letter. Yet the gentleman officer from Arequipa was not above
taking drastic measures when persuasion did not produce the desired results. In the crunch, Recavarren ordered his subordinates to exact whatever
they could and by whatever means necessary.[45] Collection of the poll-tax,
revived as an *impuesto de guerra* by Piérola in 1879, was enforced, and recruits were also drafted by force. The consequences of these war exactions
were considerable. As in the Independence and Restoration campaigns of
1821–24 and 1838–39, the region's peasantry would pay heavily in lives, livestock, pasture, crops, cloth, and cash.

Despite the rushed and coercive elements of the 1883 campaign, some
relatively independent, patriotic peasant *guerrillas* and *montoneras* were

formed to support the *fuerza de linea,* or regular army. As in the better-known case of Junín (albeit, for the moment, on a smaller scale), the *guer-rillas* were composed mainly of Indian peasants and miners, often with local militiamen or ex-gendarmes at their head. It is significant to note that the most important locale of *guerrilla* formation in Ancash prior to the invasion of Chilean forces (in late June 1883) was not on Atusparia's turf around Huaraz, nor in the densely populated Huaylas Valley through which Cáceres's Central Army would march, but along the northern periphery of the Department of Ancash—from the strategic passes of the Cordillera Negra region to the northwest of Huaraz, particularly around Moro and Jimbe, north through Macate and Atun Huaylas, and on to the peripheral towns of Pallasca and Mollepata in the northeast.[46] *Guerrillas* were organized here, rather than in the Huaylas Valley or heartland where the peasantry was concentrated, because it was along the mountainous northwestern front that Recavarren correctly anticipated brief Chilean incursions, and it was here that he would most need *guerrilla* tactical support for the planned march on Iglesias in Cajamarca.

The *guerrilla* and *montonera* bands of the northwestern rim of Huaylas-Ancash engaged in hit-and-run tactics against small Chilean platoons venturing on shore from naval vessels anchored at the ports of Chimbote, Samanco, or Casma. In 1880, 1882, and 1883 Chilean forces made punitive incursions, collecting war levies and destroying property. The Agustín Castro Montonera operated here in 1882–83, harassing Chilean units stationed in Samanco and Chimbote; this band also carried out reprisals against collaborationist landlords, including the Anglo-American leaselord of Jimbe, Alonso Cartland, whose interesting case is discussed below. In Moro, the Castro Montonera ambushed a Chilean punitive mission on 5 July 1883, but the Chileans quickly countered, killing forty of Castro's men and wounding Castro himself, although he managed to escape.[47] Castro's *montonera* would be followed later by the feared Cochachin Guerrilla, which dominated the region for much of 1885.

But the main, if unanticipated, military action of 1883 in Huaylas-Ancash —which would lead to, and follow from, the decisive Battle of Huamachuco—would take place near Huaraz, and in the Callejón de Huaylas, in late June and early July. Superior Chilean forces had closed in on Cáceres in Junín, whence he was obliged to retreat with his entire Central Army north toward Huanaco, and from there across the southern Cordillera Blanca to Huaraz, where he would join forces with Recavarren's Northern Army. Huaraz's current Indian *alcaldes,* however, had not been "properly informed by the authorities" of the meaning of these events.[48] Instead, Recavarren had moved his army northward to Atun Huaylas, where he was preparing to march on Cajamarca. Without Recavarren and his command present, Huaraz's elite let Cáceres's Central Army pass with all due respect, but then turned to openly embrace the superior Chilean force chasing him.[49] Huaraz's elite had seen the writing on the wall: Chilean troops far out-gunned Cáceres, and Recavarren's Northern Army was too distant to act.

Recavarren's Northern Army finally met the Central Army in Yungay, and from there both armies escaped the enclosing Chilean forces by traversing the high Llanganuco Pass eastward toward Conchucos, whence they proceeded northwest to the decisive Battle of Huamachuco. After boldly taking the initial advantage at Huamachuco, the Peruvians, who had gambled everything on the battle, ran out of munitions and men in the heat of battle, after which the Chilean forces proceeded to cut apart Recavarren's and Cáceres's armies. The disaster was the turning point of the resistance. The Chilean command would declare the Peruvian resistance over. Subsequently Chile withdrew from Peru after Cáceres recognized the Treaty of Ancón, which ceded the Atacama nitrate territories and forced Peru to pay war reparations.

The frenetic pace of the northern La Breña campaign was decisive in shaping possible peasant responses. In contrast to Cáceres's defensive predicament in Junín, Recavarren's military goals, which were offensive (to march north on Iglesias), did not require many *guerrilla* or *montonera* bands. Neither Huaraz nor any other town or village in the Callejón de Huaylas was sacked or burned by the Chilean occupation forces (except Pallasca and Mollepata in early July 1883, where Chilean forces desperately retreated from the attacking armies of Recavarren and Cáceres). This was in sharp contrast to the devastation wrought on the villages of Junín. As Nelson Manrique noted, in Junín "the depredations and abuses committed by the army of occupation served as efficient recruiters of new combatants."[50] The catalyst of repression was still absent in most of Huaylas-Ancash. When the Chilean enemy did finally arrive in force, it was too sudden and insufficiently repressive to elicit, in a timely fashion, a unified peasant front of resistance. With the Peruvian armies desperately marching up and down, forcefully extracting mules, livestock, crops, and men, leaving a trail of blood and desertion in their wake, the wary position of the peasantry was the best suited to the occasion. That wary distance would not always and everywhere be appropriate, however. In the last weeks before the decisive Battle of Huamachuco, peasants were rapidly mobilized in Huaraz, and possibly in Yungay and elsewhere in the Callejón de Huaylas as well.

After Huamachuco: From Civil War to Social War

After the disaster at Huamachuco, General Cáceres, Colonel Francisco de Paula Secada, and what was left of his battered cavalry escort limped into Atusparia's Huaraz (Recavarren, who could not limp, lay with a gangrenous leg on an isolated *hacienda* near Sihuas). But in Huaraz the defeated general was unexpectedly greeted "by the *indiada*, which had formed *guerrilla* bands to harass the enemy." The excited peasant crowd was estimated at two thousand lancemen (*rejoneros*) and rock-hurlers (*honderos*), ready for battle with the Chileans.[51] Atusparia's kinsmen, it would appear, had mobilized en masse after all. Although some errant Chilean troops, outmaneuvered by the Llanganuco traverse, were ambushed by Indian peasants as they plied the Quebrada Honda pass above Huaraz, most of the Chilean forces had quickly abandoned the region before Cáceres returned. The come-lately Indian mobilization of Huaraz thus welcomed the Peruvian general at a moment when he could not use them. They would not, at least for now, come to know their enemy in battle. We do not know where Atusparia was at the time, nor how he acted in the face of these events. But of one thing there is little doubt: the poorly timed misencounter of 1883 would hail the violent encounter of 1885. In 1885, the enemy *did* present himself. Only now, as history would have it, he was wearing a Peruvian uniform.

With the defeat of the La Breña command at Huamachuco, and the scattering of its forces, Iglesias began to consolidate his fragile "government of national regeneration" with the decisive assistance and protection of the Chileans. The consolidation of *iglesista* rule was not uncontested, however, for the *cacerista* Reds would regroup and carry on the resistance. In Huaraz, the invading Arriagada Division had quickly moved on, leaving behind a pro-Iglesias prefecture organized by collaborators accompanying the Chilean force.[52] Almost as soon as the Chileans left Huaraz, the Reds, now led by the *puguista* prefect Pedro Tovar, seized the Prefecture of Ancash.[53] The mobilization of the Indians of Huaraz must have immediately ensued, or possibly precipitated, this action.

Although Tovar took over the prefecture as soon as the Chilean forces left, his reign appears to have been extremely short. In a private letter to the convalescent Recavarren, Augusto Cisneros wrote that "small departmental politics are an outrage: there is no legal government, *iglesista* or *monterista*." In "big national politics," Cisneros continued, things fared worse for the sullen patriots of the resistance: the strongman Piérola, returning from Europe, had officially adhered to the Iglesias regime.[54] For another observer, though, the *iglesista* bent of "small politics," as represented by the new prefect of Ancash, Señor Angeles, was becoming apparent. A confidant of Cisneros described the new prefect's move to censure Huaraz's most important newspaper, *La Autonomía*.[55] The most recent victim of censorship was the "young writer" Luis Felipe Montestruque, who would later be named "secretary" in the revolutionary *cacerista* prefecture that was swept to power in March 1885 by the Atusparia insurgency. Montestruque's editorials had been cause for Prefect Angeles to shut down the press.

In one editorial, entitled "El porvenir se aclara" [The Future Is Becoming Clear], Montestruque asserted that the Chilean Congress preferred to make peace with the legitimate Montero-Calderón government, not with the "imposter" Iglesias. The Chileans, wrote the author, considered Iglesias to be an illegitimate dictator. Iglesias was simply "an ambitious pygmy" sustained only "by the bayonets" of the unscrupulous Chilean commander in Lima, the hated Admiral Patricio Lynch. Montestruque added that the Chilean Congress and people were "not at all in agreement" with Lynch's policies in Peru. The author exhorted Peruvians to reject the farce of Iglesias—which even their enemies rejected—and to anticipate a ready solution to the war under the legitimate government of Montero, which was represented militarily by Cáceres and politically by the National Congress convened in Arequipa. This legitimate body, he added, was disposed to signing an honorable and just peace, without territorial concessions, with the Chilean Congress.

By October 1883 an unambiguously pro-Iglesias prefect was installed in Huaraz. Prefect Juan Vargas was sent from Lima to form a National Guard contingent in Huaraz to protect private property, collect taxes one year in advance, enforce military conscription, and suppress dissident municipal government.[56] As the *iglesista* "pacification" and "regeneration" policy of military conscription and poll-tax collection was implemented in Huaraz,[57] an unheeded warning was issued by the provincial mayor of Huaraz, Juan del C. Vidal: "In the meeting of Indian *alcaldes* that took place yesterday . . . several of them made it clear to me that, the draft having been put into practice as a means of organizing the army, a considerable portion of the Indians have abandoned their homes and moved their residences to the mountains, or they have hidden in caves to elude the recruitment agents."

Vidal asked Prefect Vargas to limit the general conscription to "vagabonds and derelicts," noting that the conscription worked against the government's expressed desire to hold free elections, since all those subject to conscription were likely to stay away from the ballot box. Moreover, according to Vidal, many of the nonvoting "indígenas" had ceased participating in municipal public-works projects (*la república* labor) out of fear of being drafted. Another consequence of Indian evasion was that private employers were short of hands, and the poll-tax was uncollectable.[58] On this last point, Vidal warned: "The Indians are poor men who have nothing with which to meet their needs except the fruits of their daily labor. It would not be surprising if the coercive means employed to wrench the poll-tax from them had the effect of exasperating them, making it possible that here, as in some places in the central highlands, social war—more bloody and dismal in its results than the civil war—will break out."[59]

The governor of La Independencia District, however, denied the accusations of the provincial mayor, claiming that the Indian *alcaldes* had been duly informed, both in Quechua and Spanish, "that the order was not to recruit, but rather to separate out the dangerous elements that injure society, and that the *alcaldes* should designate such individuals [for the draft]." Prefect Vargas dismissed Vidal's notice. Municipal government (*alcaldía provincial*), he declared, had no right to represent the Indians, noting that the Indian *alcaldes* could freely represent themselves directly to the constituted state authorities of the prefecture and its dependencies (the district governors) if they had any complaints.

Significant was Prefect Vargas's insistence that the Indian *alcaldes* had a direct channel to the prefecture (the provincial arm of the central state), and that municipalities had no legal right to represent their grievances to the state. Such a policy of direct relations between Indian communities and the prefecture was consistent with the *iglesista* policy to repress municipal government. However, in Huaylas-Ancash the Indian *alcaldes* had consistently voiced their grievances directly to state authorities, from the local to the national level. In the coming years, *alcaldes* would address petitions to district governors, provincial subprefects, the departmental prefect and, beyond them, to the President of the Republic. In general, municipal mediation of Indian politics appears to have been relatively less significant in postcolonial Huaylas-Ancash than it was, for example, in Junín.[60] This relatively direct line between local Indian communities and the state would turn out to be a powerful weapon in the hands of the *alcaldes*.

But Prefect Vargas's unpopular reign in Huaraz would be cut short. Not six months later, one of Puga's roaming captains attacked Corongo, and the Nicolás Porturas Montonera (which operated out of Hacienda Angasmarca) occupied Sihuas and Pomabamba, to the northeast of Huaraz.[61] By mid-June 1884 Porturas, proclaiming himself prefect of Ancash, prepared to invade the Callejón de Huaylas.[62] Prefect Vargas marched with a small cavalry force to combat Porturas at Atun Huaylas, where he took up defensive positions in the very trenches dug by Recavarren a year before to fend off the Chilean attack. Meanwhile, Puga approached with his *montonera* force of, according to Vargas, 670 men. The "Political and Military Chief of the North" chased Vargas out of the department.[63]

José Mercedes Puga seized Huaraz. Retreating from momentary setbacks in Cajamarca in his ongoing war with Iglesias, Puga had sent urban Chinese members of his *montonera* as emissaries to the coastal plantations, where, in conjunction with Porturas, they caused the massive flight of bonded Chinese laborers to Puga's ranks.[64] Puga installed Porturas as prefect of Ancash. In nearby Huari, Puga appointed Federico Cáceres subprefect. Cáceres lost no time carrying out punitive strikes against the property and persons of "traitors," recruiting "200 indígenas" to do the job. Shortly after taking Huaraz, though, Puga moved on to the more strategic prize of Trujillo, leaving Huaylas-Ancash to the appointed authorities. Prefect Porturas lasted only about three months, however, as local *iglesistas,* led by the imprisoned subprefect and governor, José Collazos, staged yet another coup in Huaraz on 9 October.[65] Porturas fled to Sihuas in November when a powerful "pacification force" commanded by War Minister Juan Echenique marched on Huaraz and installed the now infamous *iglesista* prefect, Francisco Noriega.[66]

Like most nineteenth-century prefects who came to Huaraz with high expectations, Noriega found the departmental treasury "in a lamentable state, exhausted of funds."[67] After suspending "the quotas and other extortions that the revolutionary *caudillos* had imposed,"[68] Noriega began a single-minded campaign to identify state-owned lands and to collect unpaid rents. At the admonition of certain "notables" of Huaraz, who decried the breakdown of the justice system, Noriega also intended to reopen the temporarily suspended Superior Court of Ancash. Given Lima's unwillingness to fund the court, however, Noriega, like his successors, would be obliged to raise funds locally to pay for its operation.[69] The desire to reopen the court, applauded by the local elite, generated additional fiscal pressure on the peasantry.

Realizing that the Municipality of Huaraz was occupied by authorities sympathetic to Puga,[70] and following instructions from Lima, Noriega suspended municipal functions and assumed direction of municipal works, which were reassigned to the Subprefecture of Huaraz, then occupied by José Collazos.[71] Noriega sold the rights to collect municipal duties (*mojonazgos*) to his local allies, and he ordered several untimely municipal works projects (roads, bridge repair, church reconstruction, cemetery construction, house whitewashing, house numbering with placards, etc.) with the aim of raising funds through fines or obliging residents to pay fees.[72] Just before Noriega's arrival, the *iglesista* Provincial Mayor Vidal, who was restored to his post by the Collazos coup, ordered that the gates of the "old cemetery" of Huaraz be locked so that the ritual offerings and festivities associated with the popular Day of the Dead (All Souls Day—All Saints Day) could not be held. Vidal noted that "the custom of allowing the public access to the cemetery on the first and subsequent days [of November,] to commit irreverent acts scarcely consonant with civilization, subsists. . . . As this municipality has an interest that this practice become extinct . . . I give the necessary orders so that the gates of said cemetery not be opened."[73] Henceforth, the dead were to be buried in the new cemetery, even though it was unfinished. The governors of the twin districts of Huaraz, including Collazos, ordered that the construction of the new cemetery commence immediately, with drafted Indian labor from the hamlets and barrios. Indian "republicanos," or brigade workers, faced a stiff fine if they did not show up for work.[74]

These renewed drives to raise needed funds caused consternation in Huaraz among nearly all sectors of the population, still suffering from the devastating effects of the military exactions of 1883–84. In addition, 1884 was a year of drought, and the harvest was negligible. Livestock herds had also been depleted by the campaigning armies of Recavarren, Cáceres, Arriagada, and Puga. These last two factors put additional economic pressure on the peasantry as well as on the less fortunate *hacendados*. With the consequent wartime and drought-related shortages, prices of basic goods danced to astounding heights.

The Ministry of Government in Lima had realized that stiff exactions in the postwar period would likely produce discontent. Prefect Noriega, for example, received an official notice on 15 November, warning him to "abstain from imposing any exactions or taxes not established by law."[75] Noriega subsequently met with the "notables" of Huaraz to decide a course of action for raising funds. The "junta de notables" decided to implement the poll-tax which, contrary to postrebellion accounts published in Lima's newspapers, was perfectly legal at the time and, indeed, was the preferred option for funding the Superior Court of Ancash until 1895.[76] The poll-tax had been reestablished as a war-tax by Piérola in 1879, and the Iglesias regime had generally upheld its collection. In December, Noriega requested from the Ministry of Government a copy of the Census of 1876, with which to establish the necessary registers for tax collection.[77] On 2 January, Noriega reported that the tax register would be completed by the end of the month and that collection would commence in February. He requested funds from the central government to print 200,000 tax receipts, and on 15 January his request was approved. The Ministry of Commerce ordered that the receipts be printed and that "sufficient quantity to collect the tax" be sent to Huaraz. By early February a commission was installed in Huaraz with the purpose of forming the tax register.[78] By 21 February, however, the tax receipts promised by Lima had not yet arrived. Faced with the rising costs of provisioning a growing army of recruits, Noriega ordered the provisional printing of 12,000 tax receipts which could later be exchanged for those being sent from Lima.[79]

As early as middle to late November, however, Noriega had betrayed a vague sense of his own vulnerability and isolation. With the departure of Echenique's battalions, the prefect could depend only upon his cavalry escort of fifty men to uphold his rule. Concerned with the real or imagined threat of the Porturas Montonera to the northeast, Noriega requested that Lima send a force of a hundred men with which to begin the formation of the Ancash Battalion.[80] Noriega also requested equipment to restore the telegraph line to the port of Casma, cut by the Chileans in 1883, as it was the only direct line of rapid communication between Huaraz and Lima. Lima turned down the request for lack of funds, as it had when the previous *iglesista* prefect, Juan Vargas, made the same request.[81] In late November the War Ministry informed Noriega that the Artisans Battalion, an inexperienced guard unit of 120 young recruits, would be assigned to Huaraz.[82]

By January 1885 the "Artesanos de Lima" Battalion was in Huaraz. Without funds to support the new troops, Noriega was obliged by February to request a monthly subsidy from Lima to avert open mutiny in the barracks: "The extreme scarcity of funds for attending to services in the department . . . obliges me to request the remission of a monthly contingency [fund] to sustain part of the 'Artesanos de Lima' Battalion which is under my orders for only the time it takes to impose the poll-tax, since once this job is realized the surplus funds [collected] from my [department] will even be able to assist the Lima treasury."[83]

Noriega's assertion that he would soon have enough cash from the poll-tax bonanza to meet the needs both of the Artisans Battalion and the prefecture, with extra to send to Lima's treasury, was an inaccurate assessment of his situation. Perhaps wishing to impress his superiors in Lima, to the very end Noriega insisted that the lucrative poll-tax could be collected. He reported on 21 February that, despite the fiscal crisis of the treasury, his department "enjoyed complete tranquillity."[84] By 27 February, Noriega had added some 130 recruits to the Artisans Battalion, although they lacked sufficient funds, arms, uniforms, and other essential equipment.[85] One week later Noriega would report that the Artisans Battalion had been completely routed, and that he himself had narrowly escaped with his life.

The Day After

On 3 March 1885 the deposed Prefect Noriega, together with what remained of the bloodied Artisans Battalion, huddled somewhere in the mountain passes between Huaraz and Huarmey. Noriega's desperate pleas for reinforcements were answered when the National Guard force of Colonel Lorenzo Gonzáles landed at the tiny port of Huarmey. Gonzáles, however, was soon ambushed in Yautan by Indian *guerrillas* led by the *cacerista* captains, José and Justo Solís. Gonzáles and Noriega were forced to retreat. At this point, there was little hope that the *iglesista* forces would be able to retake Huaraz. Sergeant Manuel de la F. Mazuelo surveyed the unpromising conditions:

> On the day we left Lima on this important mission, my force was content and enthusiastic about having the chance to do combat with the enemy . . . but today both the officers and the troops find themselves very dispirited. . . . [T]hey shout . . . for their back pay and immediate return to Lima, making a show of how maltreated and unclothed they are as a result of the long forced marches they had made since they disembarked at Huarmey, and then the retreat from Yautan [where they were badly beaten]—without having gained any advantage thereby. As a result many have fallen ill and are no longer fit for combat . . . and they are not at all animated with the idea of a countermarch on Huaraz.

But more than these sorry conditions, an imminent sense of dread had disabled the troops, and had begun to alarm the officers as well. Sergeant Mazuelo:

> On the other hand, I should also report that the troops get continuous news from Huaraz, and it instills much fear in them, that the enemy is innumerable and that only one town [e.g., Caraz] has not risen up, and that the rebellion has become general throughout the entire department, and they calculate about 20,000 to 25,000 Indians occupying impregnable positions [and] armed with all manner of weapons, and they fear that they will suffer the same fate as Artisans Battalion in the first uprising. And as the ferocity of the Indian rebellion has increased, they have instilled terror in our diminished troops, and it now appears to them impossible that they will be able to pacify and combat them. . . . My troops prefer to return to Lima . . . rather than be sacrificed by the Indians. . . . For these reasons I implore you, Sir, to . . .

advise the government of our situation since it may not be fully aware of the great danger which threatens the department.[86]

The news reaching the sergeant's camp was not inaccurate. Once the tremors made by the dance of thousands of Indian feet had begun in the hills around Huaraz, its movement rushed—as one observer put it—"like an avalanche" down the well-worn social channels of the densely populated Callejón de Huaylas. In a matter of days, more peasant combatants were fielded than General Cáceres or Colonel Recavarren combined could have dreamed of in 1883. Peasants now besieged all the major towns of the valley. Just downriver from Huaraz, the town of Carhuaz was rapidly seized by the local peasantry, who responded to the persecution, and leadership, of their own local *alcaldes*. A small-time Indian miner, Pedro "Uchcu" Cochachin, appears to have led a band of *guerrilleros* from Carhuaz. Cochachin was not the *alcalde pedáneo* of Ecash[87] in 1885 but, in popular memory at least, he had previously held the *vara*, or staff of office.[88] It is unclear whether Cochachin held any appointed position, political or military, in March 1885.[89] The hamlets of Rupas, or the northeastern "half" of Carhuaz, were apparently mobilized by the *alcalde pedáneo*, Juan Cebrino.[90]

Farther downriver the main locus of rebellion was (Uma) Mancos, a small village (and *hacienda*) just to the south of Yungay. Yungay was then the second-largest town (after Huaraz) in the fertile Callejón de Huaylas and was home to the cream of the provincial landed "oligarchy." Still farther down the valley, related revolts were staged in (Atun) Huaylas and Macate.[91] By late March the concentration of peasants in Mancos, initially led by Simón Bambarén, prepared to attack Yungay and its Urban Guard. The level of anguish in "white" Yungay ran high as Bambarén massed peasant legions on the heights to the south of town. As in Huaraz, the hills around Yungay were decorated with thousands of haranguing peasants from the surrounding hamlets. This massive mobilization in Mancos caused the first alarms of an ominous "race war" to be sounded by reactionary Blue elites in Yungay. Fearing for their lives and possessions, many of Yungay's "white families" fled downriver to the nearby town of Caraz.[92]

On Palm Sunday the assault on Yungay began. The first attack faltered, and Bambarén was killed. At this point the "revolutionary" *cacerista* prefect, Manuel Mosquera,[93] appeared with Atusparia, Guillén, and their peasant legions to take command of the siege.[94] Prefect Mosquera, like everyone else present, knew that Yungay's "notables" had publicly declared allegiance to the government of Miguel Iglesias.[95] Mosquera's legions stormed Yungay on Holy Saturday. The by now poorly munitioned Urban Guard of Yungay was driven from its positions. As they scrambled in the direction of Caraz many were cut down, including the despised guard commander, Manuel Rosas Villón. As in Huaraz, the victors proceeded to burn and plunder the property of guard members and of the more prominent, *iglesista* notables of Yungay.[96]

Before taking Yungay "a sangre y fuego," Prefect Mosquera addressed this political ultimatum to Commander Villón and "the notables of Yungay":

> I know that you have more than two hundred rifles collected in that town, with which to resist the government of His Excellency General Cáceres and with which to decisively protect the wicked government of Iglesias; [I also know] that Yungay and Caraz are serving as a vehicle for the arrival of the ex-prefect Noriega to the capital of the department. On another point, about a hundred widows of those killed in Yungay have presented themselves before me asking for assistance, and therefore I remit to you the following conclusions. *1st:* The moment you receive this note you will remit to this prefecture an act signed by all the notables of Yungay recognizing the government of General Cáceres. *2nd:* You will remit to this camp the forty rifles that have been offered and a hundred more, equipped with the respective ammunition packed in crates and in good condition. *3rd:* [You will remit] 5,000 soles in coin for the mentioned widows and for the army which should return to Huaraz. The realization of this last condition should be facilitated with the cooperation of the titular prefect Don Ignacio Figueroa.[97] *4th and last:* You have three hours to meet the remissions requested. If by twelve o'clock the commission that you should name, and whose safety I will guarantee, has not handed over the request I shall find myself in the painful necessity of having to take that plaza unconditionally.
>
> > May God protect you.
> > Manuel Mosquera[98]

After taking Yungay, the peasant legions led by Prefect Mosquera set their eyes on Caraz, the last stronghold of the pro-Iglesias faction in the region. The notables and clergy of Caraz persuaded the rebels to spare the "families" that had taken refuge in Caraz; the triumphant rebels would march into Caraz in peaceful procession. All Huaylas was now in Red hands.

In control of the entire Callejón de Huaylas, but fearful of an attack on Huaraz by Noriega and *iglesista* reinforcements from Lima, Mosquera, Atusparia, Cochachin, and the *ejército republicano* (as Reyna called it) returned to Carhuaz and Huaraz. The scene was described in alarming terms in a letter printed in Lima's *El País* on 11 April:

Until April 2, Yungay was the refuge of persons fleeing Huaraz and Carhuaz, and one can imagine the confusion of the families huddled in Yungay, without mules and peons to retreat with. All the families had to retreat to Caraz on foot, and it too began to be attacked on the 8th with a considerable reinforcement of Indians from Huaraz and Recuay. In Caraz they made considerable efforts to defend themselves with the assistance of [the colony of] foreigners and the Urban Guard. In spite of [those] efforts, the Indians by now would have taken the town, since its defenders also had the Indian rabble of Atun Huaylas and Macate to deal with. The priests García and Fidel Olívas Escudero went out of Yungay on 31 March draped in the sacred vestments with the aim of calming the Indians in Mancos, but this appears to have been useless and they had to return to town because of threats. After taking Yautan by force [from Colonel Gonzáles] the Indians have removed Prefect Mosquera and have handed leadership of the insurrection over to the Indian [Pedro] Manuel Granados, and military command to Pedro Atusparia and Pedro Guillén, both *alcaldes ordinarios* of Huaraz. . . . The instigators from Carhuaz and Huaraz are dedicated to reinforcing the defense of the mountain passes and destroying the roads. For the defense [of the passes] they can count on the Indians, with the great numbers of their race, on a few rifles, and principally on the fact that the [government's] troops are bound to run out of bullets. . . . The Indians of Carhuaz [led by Pedro Cochachin] have sacked the warehouses of the Austrian Mining Company in Uchco where they have found food, tools, dynamite . . . and . . . gunpowder. If energetic and at the same time prudent measures are not taken quickly now to contain the avalanche of the Indian rabble from the provinces of Huaraz, Huaylas, and Huari, the movement will soon spread to the rest of the provinces and the loss of life will be greater and it will cost that much more to achieve the pacification of the department.[99]

With such alarming rumors of the "avalanche of the Indian rabble" spreading rapidly in Lima, Iglesias named Colonel José Iraola to be prefect of Ancash, with orders to march swiftly on Huaraz and crush the rebellion.[100] The *iglesista* "Northern Pacification Force" disembarked at Casma on 12 April. The next day, Iraola informed the minister of war in Lima of an unanticipated turn of events: "The news I have received from the interior is favorable, and I believe that there will be very few obstacles to overcome to obtain the pacification of the department."[101]

Iraola had received news of a secret plan to welcome his forces in Yungay. But it is also likely that he learned of the cowardly assassination of José Mercedes Puga in Huamachuco,[102] which conveniently removed the most serious military threat to Iraola's expedition.[103] Still, the narrow passage up the mountains to Yungay was heavily defended by Pedro Cochachin's *guerrilla* (and possibly by the Solís Montonera as well). The scene was remarkably reminiscent of the famed (because nationalist) peasant defense of Quebrada Huarochiri in Junín against the Chilean invaders of 1883. Iraola reported:

> During our march . . . we have sustained unnerving combat with the Indian rabble that had crowned the heights and harassed us with boulders and firearms. In the five tenacious and sustained battles that we have seen in this march against thousands of Indians, the valor and enthusiasm of the troops and officers has surpassed my hopes. . . . [M]uch intrepidness and abnegation has been required to crown the [nearly] inaccessible heights and then fight hand to hand to drive the savage hordes from . . . impregnable positions.[104]

Iraola's counterinsurgent "pacification" force arrived in Yungay to a warm reception secretly organized by the *gente decente* of the town. However, he would soon be dismayed by a massive peasant assault unleashed from Mancos:

> The troops, which had just arrived fatigued and bootless, had little time to rest, however, since at dawn . . . we were surprised by a rude attack from the indigenous forces commanded by Dr. M. Mosquera. I calculate that they were about 5,000, and of these about 200 were perfectly armed [i.e., with firearms]. After about four hours of tenacious fighting, we had them on the run. We had thought we had severely punished them with this defeat, but despite this they returned about 9 A.M. in equal numbers, although with less valor, to attack us. But they were equally beaten back and were inflicted, as in the previous battle, with a considerable number of casualties. On the 27th they left us alone, at which time I received a parley from Dr. Mosquera, in which he offered to send his delegates to enter into an agreement. But in place of them I received a new note in which he informed me *that no longer being able to contain the hordes that surrounded him, he would*

regrettably have to destroy Yungay with his 50,000 warriors [emphasis in original]. The bearer of this strange note had only just left when we began to note that from all the hills surrounding Yungay, as well as at the bridge leading into town, there descended infinite masses of Indians, which I calculate at more or less 12,000 hailing from all the provinces of this department. The attack was tremendous. I ordered my troops to convenient positions and a few moments later the enemy opened fire on us, and we responded with the total calm of the serene and valiant soldier. Six hours of incessant combat during which our forces were the rival of any in valor and serenity, and we were able to push them into a complete retreat. Indian casualties on this day were numerous, but on our side we lost only two officers and thirty soldiers. On this day, as on previous ones, we took a few prisoners; and they declared that the *alcaldes* Atusparia and Granados had, according to some, been killed, and according to others, wounded.[105]

Mosquera's first demand of Yungay had been that its inhabitants pledge allegiance to the government of Andrés Cáceres. There was no mistaking the political intentions of the siege. Mosquera had also appealed to Iraola's patriotic conscience: "[A]s a Peruvian first, and before your allegiance to Señor Iglesias . . . you should look after the *pueblo* [of Yungay] that has received you with such hospitality. . . . I am only responding to the blind tenacity of a group of bad Peruvians who perpetuate the rule of [Chilean Admiral] Lynch in this disgraced land."[106]

In the next day or two, however, what became clear was that Mosquera exercised rather tenuous command over "his" peasant legions. Informing Iraola that he was forced to suspend talks because the *guerrilleros* obliged him to take Yungay "by blood and fire," Mosquera absolved himself from personal responsibility by adding that "the valiant warriors who commit themselves to such a favorable cause will be responsible for its consequences before the country and before history. You and I will safeguard the principles of humanity and Civilization, even if it is over our dead bodies."[107]

But when the peasant legions suffered heavy losses in several unsuccessful assaults on Iraola's well-munitioned positions in Yungay, Mosquera quickly sought an "honorable" resolution that might save himself, Iraola, and Yungay from the ignominy that might befall them if they were held responsible for "spill[ing] sterile torrents of blood in a dishonorable manner before the country." Mosquera now suddenly confessed that, like Iraola, he too wished to avoid the "demolition of property that has always served as a source of vitality and progress." But Prefect Iraola, now firmly in command of the military situation, arrogantly replied that he would inflict a terrible lesson on the "savage horde."

Iraola's guns and artillery mowed down wave after wave of charging peasants: the "lesson" was a bloody massacre of great proportions. The killed and maimed included Atusparia, Granados, Bambarén, and the local *cacerista* journalist and ideologue Felipe Montestruque—Mosquera's secretary and the probable author of at least some of the communiqués sent to Prefect Iraola. In his last communiqué to Mosquera, Prefect Iraola noted that "after three attacks by your forces on this city all you have achieved is to blanket the fields with cadavers and spill torrents of blood, whereas I have not a single fatality to lament. I understand that your patriotism must suffer. . . . I accept your proposal for talks, which will take place in Huaraz, and so I advise you to retire your forces to those places you judge convenient."[108]

On 3 May—the *día central* of the patron saint festival of Huaraz— Iraola's troops and officers were pleasantly surprised when they met only brief resistance from the Solís Montonera at the Calicanto Bridge leading into the rebel stronghold.[109] Solís was pounded and quickly dispersed with artillery fire, and Iraola entered Huaraz.[110] Once in town, Iraola dispersed those Indians congregated in celebration of the patron saint, "El Señor de la Soledad." Negotiations began with the *alcaldes,* including the wounded Atusparia and the lesser *varayoc* from La Independencia District, as well as with *cacerista* leaders. Solís suddenly reversed his defiant stance, abandoning Cochachin as the latter prepared to assault Iraola. Iraola met with Solís and several *alcaldes* on 10 May, promising to meet their conditions if they ceased hostilities immediately.[111] He then publicized the proclamation which suspended collection of the poll-tax—which had been declared in Lima by President Iglesias, upon Prefect Noriega's dismissal—and the hated and abusive military conscription.[112]

But on 11 May, Iraola's forces were assaulted by yet more thousands of hostile Indian *guerrilleros,* now led by Pedro "Uchcu" Cochachin of Carhuaz. Iraola reported that

> The *indígenas,* tenacious in their purpose to persecute and annihilate
> my forces, . . . began to gather from all the *pueblos* of the provinces
> of Huaraz, Huaylas, Huari, and Huarmey since the 5th [of May], and
> commanded by Pedro Cochachin (called Uchcu) and other bad guys
> they surrounded and laid siege to the population, crowning the hills
> immediately dominating the town, and especially the heights above
> the Calicanto Bridge, where the bulk of his *montoneros* were concentrated. They commenced their first assault on the 9th, measuring their

shots against ours, and on the 11th at 5 P.M., after unnerving and bloody battle, they were completely routed. A few hours earlier, Sergeant Major Don Justo Solís had surrendered with the Montoneros of the North under his command. With this last clash of arms, whose details can be found in the *parte* [field report] . . . that I remit . . . in original, order has been restored in the department[;] the *indígenas*, who for more than two months have been given over to robbery and devastation, will return to their ordinary occupations, and I am now adopting measures to see that this end is realized.[113]

An excerpt from the field report, dictated by Sergeant Isidro Salazar, reported the frontline military details of "restoring order." It was another massacre:

> We engaged in renewed hand-to-hand combat of unequaled butchery . . . but we did not long hesitate, for all it took was to see the enemy to throw ourselves upon him and vanquish him with a heroism worthy of every eulogy, leaving the fields sown with cadavers, and taking their impregnable trenches. This was the assignment of the division that you so decisively commanded, which is to reestablish order wherever it is altered. In this situation and the heights having been crowned by our forces . . . the Indians left in our sight at least fifty dead, and an incalculable number of dead and wounded lay scattered about in the brambles. In this manner they paid very dearly for their temerity.[114]

Phantom *Caudillos*, Counterinsurgent Prose

The counterinsurgent prose[115] of the *iglesista* military commanders engaged in the repression of the Atusparia insurgency may be read against, but also within, the grain. As William Stein noted, the Cochachin assault of 11 May, like the earlier siege of Yungay by Granados, Bambarén, Atusparia, Mosquera et al., was not the "barbarian" or "savage" attack of an Indian "horde" bent on exterminating "white families" ensconced in barricaded towns. And Cochachin was not the maniacal and ferocious *chancador de huesos*, or "bone cruncher," of folklore, bent on exterminating "whites." Indeed, fragmentary evidence suggests that Cochachin probably thought he was fighting a tactical, prolonged resistance until Red reinforcements could arrive. Reinforcements, however, did not arrive; the nationalist *caudillos*, for the most part, remained phantoms. And when supposed allies did arrive, as in the case of Colonel Manuel Armando Zamudio, they carried an inhospitable "restore order" agenda.

At his summary execution in late September 1885, Pedro Cochachin reportedly confessed that he was a *guerrilla* commander recognized by the *cacerista* command.[116] Jorge Basadre wrote that "Cochachin was appointed general commander of *guerrillas* in Ancash," although without providing his source.[117] Stein, too, suggests that Cochachin hoped for support from *cacerista* forces operating outside the region.[118] Although Cochachin may have been self-appointed, hope for outside help on his part would not have been idle in May 1885.

For nationalist forces in the north were on the move in early May, just as they had been in early March. Following the *iglesista* assassination of Puga on 16 March, the new "Jefe Superior del Norte" would be Tomás Romero y Flores. Romero y Flores pledged to carry on Puga's fight, and later proclaimed himself prefect of Ancash as well. Romero operated with his *montonera* in the Province of Pataz as well as in Pallasca and Otuzco along the southern edge of Puga's former territory. He was preparing an assault on Trujillo on the very day (10 May) that Cochachin—before Solís's unanticipated peace—intended to take Huaraz back from Iraola.[119] Like Cochachin, Romero y Flores carried on a defiant resistance; the Northern Chief even refused to recognize Cáceres's peace with Iglesias, just as Cochachin had not accepted Atusparia's peace with Iraola. But Cochachin, as far as we know, never met Romero y Flores.

Another, more significant misencounter between militant peasant leaders and phantom nationalist *caudillos* marked the course of the Atusparia insurgency. The *ejército republicano* at the March 1885 siege of Yungay could also have reasonably expected reinforcements from the north, an expectation which possibly abated fears of reprisal. For the powerful *montonera* of José Mercedes Puga was on the move in early March. Puga, the sworn enemy of Iglesias in Cajamarca, had just captured the strategic town of Huamachuco from *iglesista* forces. But on 16 March, when the *caudillo* descended into the center of town to survey the spoils of his victory, he was ambushed by snipers. Puga's victorious forces swiftly executed the perpetrators in grisly fashion, then turned around and marched north, solemnly escorting their beloved *caudillo* to rest on his vast *hacienda* near Cajabamba.[120] A more bitter fruit of victory is hardly imaginable. At this point the historiography of Puga and his *montonera* ends, albeit without noting why he had taken Huamachuco in the first place or where he was heading.

It is now clear that Puga and his *montonera* were, as the critical communiqué put it, "abriendo paso a Huaraz."[121] Had Puga not been struck down by the sniper's bullet, his forces would in all probability have marched unimpeded into Huaylas-Ancash, much as they had in June 1884. They would have taken the northern town of Caraz unopposed and would have then met with Mosquera's and Atusparia's forces gathered in Mancos. In short, the Reds would have taken the northern towns of the Callejón handily and rather earlier, and Puga's forces would (perhaps) have then backed the Cochachin Guerrilla in the defense of the Quillo Pass, where the "pacification" expedition led by Prefect Iraola and Commander Callirgos would have found their passage obstructed not only by the "magic" of Andean peasants armed with spears, slings, and boulders, but by a considerable force of seasoned *montoneros* armed with rifles and canon and mounted on horseback.

In military terms, it is reasonable to assume that the upward march of Iraola's pacification expedition, which arrived in Yungay on 24 April, would have been rather more arduous.[122] Indeed, the peasant legions led by Atusparia and others—if, and this is a big if, they could strike an alliance with Puga—might have controlled the department for many months, possibly even until December, when Cáceres reached a compromise agreement with Iglesias and rode triumphantly into Lima. A Red nationalist stronghold backed by thousands of Indian peasants in Huaylas-Ancash might have tipped the balance of forces, nudging Cáceres toward an early military victory over Iglesias, thereby averting the necessity of compromise.

But perhaps it is only distracting and utopian to extend this counterfactual exercise (to absurd conclusions). The fact is that an encounter between Puga and Atusparia did *not* happen. Moreover, complicating factors on the national scene limit any simple projection of events from Huaylas-Ancash. Perhaps the reasonable point to which the counterfactual argument can be extended is this: had Puga not been assassinated in such an untimely fashion, he would in all probability have become a major player in the so-called Atusparia uprising. (Would it now be known as the "Puga insurgency," had the *caudillo* dominated the scene?) This is not an impossible reading, especially given the fact that Puga had done exactly the same thing not one year before. Huaylas-Ancash once again offered him a worthy prize: the chance to reclaim the strategic zone, free his southern flank, and *encaudillar* the region's masses for subsequent offensive actions.

But the matter also has, and had, more ambiguous and probable implications. Who in Huaylas-Ancash was betting on Puga's help? Even if we assume that Puga's march went unannounced, the question remains one of reception. Would peasant rebels hail Puga, the "Jefe Superior del Norte," as the recognized leader of their cause? Or would they give Puga a cool reception, maintaining an autonomous distance from him? Having subdued Iraola's pacification force from Lima, would Puga have turned to repressing the "savage horde" and its Indian leaders, as Cáceres himself had the year before in Junín, when Tomás Laime and his patriotic band of peasant *guerrilleros* were executed in Huancayo?[123] Or would the independent and unpredictable Puga have seconded radical Indian demands to eradicate the Blue presence in the region? In short, could a strategic nationalist alliance be sufficiently durable in Huaylas-Ancash in 1885 to withstand the diverse agendas that, in Junín at least, had driven a wedge of repression between peasant patriots and *cacerista* "constitutionalists"?

We cannot know what would have happened with Puga at the helm in 1885, but in the case of Prefect Mosquera and subsequent *cacerista* military officers (like Colonel Zamudio) the answer is clear. As in Junín, the *cacerista* elite distanced itself from "the savage hordes" by suddenly closing ranks with *iglesista* alarmists.[124] The preserved correspondence at the siege of Yungay between the rival prefects, Mosquera and Iraola, betrayed elite fears (then rampant among *iglesistas*) that the "civil war" was escalating beyond the control of either political faction.

One *cacerista caudillo* did arrive in 1885, albeit several months too late. It was another misencounter of sorts. Colonel Zamudio, ostensibly sent by Cáceres "to give guarantees to these towns" (code words for pacification) and claiming to be the new "Jefe Superior del Norte" (also claimed by the defiant Romero y Flores), was not much of a threat to Iraola in late July 1885. Zamudio, who was privy to the hushed conspiracy that would soon carry Cáceres to power in Lima, wrote to Iraola explaining that "perhaps at this very moment all the military officials of Lima have deposed Iglesias, proclaiming a change of government." Zamudio invited the *iglesista* Iraola to join him "in the great work of pacifying the Republic . . . to prevent further bloodletting among brothers." Standing his ground, Iraola replied firmly to Zamudio's invitation: "It has been four months since I came to this department with the important mission of reestablishing order where it is altered, to put a stop to the extermination and devastation with which the savage hordes consumed the towns, invoking the name of the *caudillo* who you obey."[125]

Zamudio tried to stir up support in Recuay, but to little effect. As far as we know, he did not make contact with Cochachin, who carried out his defiant peasant resistance in the mountains to the northwest. Instead, Zamudio and his small force were easily captured by Iraola when they attempted to hold up an arms shipment from Lima.[126] Meanwhile, Cochachin was hounded by racist posses, who torched peasant hamlets as they chased the elusive "outlaw" up the Cordillera Negra. Fearing that Cochachin would be reinforced by Romero y Flores, Iraola sent a punitive military expedition to Mato in late August. In Mato, Iraola's troops confronted, according to one report, sixteen hundred *guerrilleros*. Government troops joined the posses, or "urban guard units," from Caraz and Yungay in dispersing the Cocha-chin Guerrilla and razing the village of Mato.[127] A month later, Cochachin was betrayed by his *compadre*, who, under orders from the subprefect of Santa, had invited Pedro to his home in Quillo, where an ambush awaited. Cochachin was summarily tried and executed in Casma.[128]

The Anti-fiscal Hypothesis

Judging by their actions, the mobilized peasant *republicanos* who initially seized Huaraz in early March had clear strategic objectives: (a) free the *alcaldes;* (b) remove the abusive authorities particularly the district gover-nors; (c) if the Artisans Battalion did not submit, destroy it; (d) punish "notables" and other collaborationist *argollas*,[129] and sack their properties; (e) burn the prefecture, which housed the departmental treasury archive of tax registers and receipts which Prefect Noriega had begun to collect in January; and (f) pillage the stores of Chinese merchants, who sold goods at exorbitant prices and who may have been seen as collaborators with the regime.[130]

The torching of the archive of the departmental treasury, or Caja Fis-cal, revealed in no uncertain terms the political and strategic objectives or, as one informed observer put it, the "cierto sistema"[131] of the insurrection. But the loss of this archive also gave birth to wild rumors, among them the notion that the *indiada* had burned Huaraz's notary archives (*escribanías públicas*) as well, thereby destroying all public records of private property.[132] This rumor was part of the alarmist, counterinsurgent campaign which depicted the events of March in highly polarized and racist terms. Such rumors notwithstanding, it appears that only the archive of the treasury and the prefecture was lost.[133]

The burning of the fiscal archive was cited as evidence supporting the hypothesis, first advanced by Wilfredo Kapsoli, that the Atusparia uprising should be seen as an "anti-fiscal movement."[134] This label has, with modi-fications, been accepted by subsequent scholars including, in part, Stein.[135] As these authors employ it, the anti-fiscal notion partakes of both liberal and vulgar marxist postulates that assume (a) that all fiscal exactions by the state are necessarily exploitative because they intrude upon the peasant's individual freedom or resources; and (b) that the state is always merely the blunt instrument of the dominant class. The first notion was commonly es-poused by *limeño* liberals in 1885, and the second is still heard today. What these arguments ignore is that if all fiscal exactions were necessarily exploit-ative, then the problem of explaining rebellion is reduced to explaining its opposite, namely, why peasant rebellion is so rare — a historical question they fail to address, or even raise. When this problem of the historical paucity of rebellion in peasant politics is interrogated, as James C. Scott has, then the anti-fiscal label quickly loses its luster, and is revealed for the reductionist and after-the-fact construct that it is. It does not address the critical, historical question of timing: Why now and not then?[136]

In this case, the question of timing is clarified when we compare the events of 1885 with the non-events or near-revolts of 1888 and 1904, for example, or when we consider the rebellion within the long history of state-peasantry fiscal relations. In the near-revolts of 1888 and 1904, which are discussed in chapter 4 below, the escalation of conflict was curbed. But in 1885, the non-event of failing to capture the prefect's desired, non-Indian authorial agent elicited repression of the *alcaldes;* the legal avenue of protest via petition removed, repression of Indian leaders was answered by measured protest in the streets, the violent, further repression of which elicited massive mobilization. This chain of events was not inevitable, as analysis of the non-events of 1888 and 1904 makes clear. Long-term historical analysis of nineteenth-century state peasantry fiscal relations reveals that the double poll-tax of 1885 may be seen as abusive for conjunctural and social historical reasons, not for structural or sociological ones (i.e., not because of an a priori, or innate anti-fiscal predisposition of the peasantry). The emergency, wartime poll-tax, initiated by dictatorial decree of Nicolás de Piérola in 1879, carried no tributary legitimacy since it was not accompanied by state protection of Indian access rights to commons. The poll-tax could now only be legitimate for political or "national" reasons, that is, for the defense of *patria.* In 1885 (as in 1883, when it was also resisted), the tax was hastily imposed at a moment of acute economic crisis by an illegitimate, collaborationist regime installed by the Chileans and opposed by most of the highland Peruvian population. Thus, the political or nationalist rationale (*patria*) for the tax was also lost. Nevertheless, it was the violent rejection of *alcalde* mediation and negotiation that apparently provoked mass rebellion in 1885, a point to which I will return in chapter 4.

Variations on the Anti-fiscal Theme

Most newspaper accounts, and some of the historiography based on them,[137] blamed Prefect Noriega's personal "excesses" for "inciting" the Indians of Huaraz to revolt in 1885. But Noriega's vilified actions were not substantially different from those of nearly all other prefects of the period. Like those colleagues who came before and after, Prefect Noriega arrived in Huaraz only to find the department's coffers (predictably) empty. He would vigorously apply the poll-tax to raise desperately needed revenue; he would work to raise a military force, primarily to collect the tax, and would otherwise try to "maintain order"; he would strive to reopen the Superior Court, so as to settle festering disputes (including those involving state properties), and this, too, would be funded with anticipated poll-tax revenues. The new prefect would also investigate and reclaim squandered state properties, and order that they be leased at a profit; and to carry this out, he would replace local Red officials with compliant Blue functionaries. Noriega's routine measures, countlessly repeated in nineteenth-century Ancash, did not in themselves cause the revolt of 1885. Indeed, the accusations hurled at Prefect Noriega were equally predictable, and countlessly repeated, during the politically factious postcolonial history of the region.

Such accusations inevitably elicited the necessary contestations. Prefect Noriega countered that it was not he—after all, he was only following orders from Lima—but rather the wicked landlords of Huaraz who were behind the revolt. Noriega claimed that certain landlords, possibly of *cacerista* persuasion, had appropriated state lands without paying due rents. These same delinquent landlords fomented the revolt, he argued, because they did not wish to pay the rents, and because they did not wish to pay the poll-tax for their peons. But the collection of the poll-tax was normally in harmony with the economic interests of the landed elite. As with the colonial tribute and the postcolonial contribution, the liberal poll-tax tended to attract reluctant Indian labor to the *haciendas* in search of the necessary cash for its payment. Nelson Manrique argues that the poll-tax was an adjunct to debt peonage in the late nineteenth century; by paying the tax for his peons, landlords ensured their continued indebtedness and thus their labor.[138] Indeed, Colonel Francisco de Paula Secada's published letter, which defended the accused landlord Aloys Schreiber from Noriega's attacks, would emphasize the prolandlord nature of the poll-tax.

Noriega had accused Schreiber of mobilizing, even arming, his peons and, in the case of his son Germán, actually leading them in rebellion. Schreiber, an Austrian immigrant who married and settled in Huaraz in the 1850s, started out as a merchant and later accumulated two or three *haciendas;* he leased others, including Hacienda Vicos, which was the property of the Beneficencia Pública, or Public Assistance Agency, of Lima. He appears to have been associated with the Constitutionalist Party,[139] which General Cáceres formed in 1884 to shore up landlord support for his campaign to unseat Iglesias. Germán later became congressman for Ancash. Another son, Oscar, became the treasurer (*apoderado fiscal*) of Huaraz in 1887, charged with compiling new poll-tax registers under the postwar *cacerista* regime.[140]

The Schreibers, in fact, were far from being "anti-fiscal." After the civil war and the legalization of the new Cáceres regime, they eagerly sought the re-establishment of the poll-tax.

All such causal explanations of the insurgency, and the echoing "tertiary discourse" of historians who uncritically relied upon them as sources, reproduce the elitist bias of what Ranajit Guha has called "the prose of counterinsurgency." This paranoid prose denies the subjectivity and collective agency of subalterns by searching for the causes of revolt in the "redactors" of petitions, in corrupt provincial officials, in wicked landlords, and in other conspiratorial elites or "subversive" (in this case, anti-fiscal) agents who may be identified and apprehended by the police. This "primary" counterinsurgent prose is then transposed in "secondary" accounts, such as those appearing in Lima's newspapers,[141] which in turn are read by historians who, in their "tertiary" accounts, argue that peasants are sociologically incapable of leading their own revolts.[142]

The War of Words and Blood in Hacienda Jimbe

The ex-prefect, Francisco Noriega, had also implicated several other lease-lords in the supposed "anti-fiscal" conspiracy of the *gamonales* (wicked landlords) which in his view was behind the Atusparia insurgency. Noriega wrote that

> in keeping with the obligations of my post, I endeavored to investigate and identify all the properties possessed by the state in the department by reviewing denunciations and searching through the archives. I re-possessed . . . two valuable *haciendas* that belong to the state treasury and that were possessed without proper titles. As my investigations advanced and since innumerable farms exist which are in the same condition as those aforementioned, they tried to instigate an uprising and, in effect, they exploited the Indian's natural repugnance for the poll-tax to that end. . . . [T]hey took advantage of the certified simplicity of the Indians and were successful in setting off the rebellion.

The two unnamed "valuable *haciendas*" mentioned by Noriega were probably Jimbe and Utcuyacu, although it is not impossible (but unlikely, since the rents of Vicos did not correspond to the departmental treasury but, rather, to the Public Assistance Agency of Lima) that he also included part of Hacienda Vicos (Collón), then leased by Schreiber. However, Noriega did not "discover" the first two, except in the sense that they were new to him. The rents of these two large, state-owned *haciendas* had preoccupied past prefects, and they would continue to concern the future prefects of Ancash as sources of departmental revenue.

The vast Hacienda Jimbe was leased to the Anglo American Alonso Cartland, an affinal relative of Miguel Iglesias who, not surprisingly, had readily collaborated with the Chileans during the war. Prefect Noriega had sent a contingent of the Artisans Battalion to repress and evict Cartland's so-called tenants and to forcibly collect unpaid rents from them. These "tenants," legitimate members of the community or *pueblo* of Jimbe, were accused by Cartland of invading *hacienda* lands. On 25 January Prefect Noriega ordered that Cartland's possession be restored, and it was made so on 10 February.[143] The "smoking gun" turned up on 4 March, when "an employee of the revolutionary prefect, Doctor Mosquera, found . . . in the [abandoned] bag of the ex-prefect Colonel Noriega . . . seven certificates . . . for [41,440] silver pesos that the operator of Hacienda Jimbe, Don Alonso Cartland, owes to the treasury in rents."[144] Noriega's treasurer had been apprehended by the Atusparia insurgents on his way back from Jimbe, where he had been sent by the prefect to collect rents—not from Cartland but from his so-called tenants, the *comuneros* of Jimbe.[145] In short, Cartland, one of those leaselords in serious arrears with the departmental treasury, was the last person to mastermind a peasant rebellion against Noriega. Indeed, much more likely was a revolt by the peasants of the *pueblo* of Jimbe who, in Prefect Noriega's pre-insurrection eyes, were the real "usurpers" of state property in Jimbe, not Cartland.

The Jimbe episode, like the dramatic cases of *hacienda*-community conflict that enveloped Junín during and after the War of the Pacific,[146] suggests that peasant social struggles could become entangled with the political contingencies of the war. Hacienda Jimbe became state property as a result of the midcentury liberal reforms which disinherited ecclesiastical estates. The state took possession of the *hacienda* in 1871, when the last heir of the Matos family, which had secured usufruct rights from Lima's Augustinian Convent of St. Thomas in the 1850s, passed away. From 1871 to 1876 the *hacienda*'s products were sold, and the proceeds were deposited in Ancash's departmental treasury. In late 1876 the estate was leased for a period of ten years to a Señor Rodríguez. Rodríguez was under contract to maintain 500 to 1,000 breeding mares and stallions "for the service of the state"; in turn, the state had agreed to supply the stock. But in 1879—as war with Chile became imminent—the contract was modified. The Peruvian state was no longer in a position to supply breeding stock; instead, it settled for an annual fee of 4,000 soles to be paid by the tenant.[147] Rodríguez left Peru soon thereafter, never to return. He designated the family friend Alonso P. Cartland to assume the remaining eight years of the Jimbe lease. Cartland, who also administered the vast, formerly Jesuit sugar plantation of San José in the Nepeña Valley, took possession of Hacienda Jimbe in 1879.[148] At the time, Hacienda Jimbe was one of the most extensive estates in the Cordillera Negra region. It covered the entire western slope from around four thousand meters above sea level near Rayan (southwest of Atun Huaylas) down to below a thousand meters near the outskirts of Moro, on the coast, thus extending over the entire upper watershed of the Jimbe River, which fed the Nepeña River below Moro, making it a strategic source of irrigation water for the rich bottomlands of the coastal valley.[149] The coastal valley of the Nepeña River was devoted to sugarcane plantations (among them San José, San Jacinto, and Motocachi) which were worked by African slaves until 1854 and then by Chinese coolies or bonded laborers.

In 1887 Cartland explained to the *cacerista* authorities how he had taken possession in 1879, and he recounted the series of misfortunes that, in his version of events, had plagued all efforts to farm the estate. Cartland's account was intended to justify his demand that the authorities compensate him or, if that were impossible, extend the original lease. The state as landlord, he argued, had not fulfilled its contract as guarantor of his possession. Cartland explained that

> upon taking possession I could see for myself the state of complete ruin that the *hacienda* was in. . . . I found myself with a farm that although abundant in lands, and with rights to the necessary [irrigation] water for cultivation, had in fact been dismantled. . . . Despite such difficulties . . . and the fact that the war with Chile posed further obstacles to my plans . . . I began . . . to clear the land and repair the [irrigation] canals, and to construct new canals and fencing and even a house. . . . But on Monday the 21st of January 1883, the legal representative of the inhabitants of the community of Jimbe, Don Vicente Gutiérrez, presented himself to me. Together with eight of them he advised me that the judge of the Primary Claims Court had awarded possession of these lands to the community. . . . Even though I presented . . . the documents that confirm my possession, I was forced to leave the *hacienda* immediately. . . . They confiscated my crops and left some of their people in my house to impede my going in.

Cartland explained that he later recuperated that section of the *hacienda* called "Salitre," albeit at "great expense, and by endangering my life." But he was still "deprived of the rest of the farm and of the water which the Indians had appropriated for themselves." He was also hurt by "the [Chilean] occupation, whose soldiers cannibalized national property like Hacienda Jimbe, causing me more damage, which in my status as foreigner I was unable to avoid, including the destruction of my house, machinery, and crops." After this misfortune, Cartland rebuilt the farm and entertained renewed hopes of bringing in a good harvest. It was then that "these parts were invaded by the demoralized and cruel hordes of the so-called *montoneras.*"

Agustín Castro, "who called himself military commander of Santa and chief of *guerrillas,*" had led "these ragged and lawless bandits without regular organization," in an assault on Hacienda Jimbe, "pillaging and burning, and even taking me prisoner." Yet this was not, according to Cartland, the last eviction he would suffer. During the civil war, the "indígenas" of the community of Jimbe blocked his attempts to repossess the farm, and in 1885 he was again removed and punished, this time by the "indiada," led by Pedro "Uchcu" Cochachin.

The substantial aspects of Cartland's declaration can be clarified with a closer look at events on the ground. In 1881 the *pueblo* of Jimbe solicited a *juicio de deslinde* with the *hacienda* to determine the legal boundaries of community and *hacienda* lands. The community charged that the *hacienda* had usurped a large section of their lands and pastures, located in the upper elevations of the estate. Under Peruvian law, in order to execute the *deslinde,* or boundary demarcation, it was necessary first to notify all interested parties. The law specifically required placing legal summons in a newspaper "published in the capital of the Republic." The Prefecture of Ancash at the time, headed by the patriot Tadeo Terry, did not recognize the "Magdalena government" of García Calderón, since in its view "Lima was occupied by the enemy." Instead, it recognized Ayacucho as the capital of the Republic, for that was where Nicolás de Piérola had established his government-in-exile. In short, the unusual circumstances of the war meant that legal summons for the boundary demarcation should be publicized in the pages of an Ayacucho newspaper.

Of course, none of the interested landlords of the adjacent coastal plantations bordering on Jimbe could have responded to a notification made in isolated, and censored, Ayacucho. Most resided in Lima, and they were favorably disposed toward the "Magdalena government." This presented a legal snag for the community of Jimbe, which could not carry out the *deslinde* without proper public notification of all interested property owners sharing common boundaries with the community, nor without the proper authorization of the Ministry of Public Finance.

But when the Montero government made Huaraz the capital of the Republic in 1882, this snag was suddenly unhung. The community of Jimbe could now publish an official summons in a Huaraz newspaper and have it properly authorized by Montero's ministry. Unfortunately for the community, Montero's government in Huaraz had ordered that Hacienda Jimbe be auctioned because, according to the records, Cartland had not paid the rent, and Montero's cause was in dire need of funds. The state auction would include the lands claimed by the community, although it appears that the Montero government was then unaware of the community's claim.

After the auction, the community notified the Montero government of its claim and requested that the auction be annulled. The community then published legal notices in the Huaraz newspaper, *La Autonomía*, summoning interested parties to the act of *deslinde*. The demarcation, which was favorable to the community, was carried out on 26 September 1882, several months after Montero's government had moved south to Arequipa. Among the signatories of the legal act of *deslinde* was Agustín Castro.

Possession was officially granted to the "Comunidad de Jimbe" on 15 January 1883. On 4 April, the community notified the judge in the case that Cartland still occupied community lands. Exercising their right of possession, community representatives requested that Cartland be removed, if necessary by force. On 9 April, Cartland was notified via the Huaraz newspapers that if he did not vacate the premises in three days, he would be "lanzada por la fuerza pública." The local justice of the peace was commissioned by the higher court, and on 12 April 1883 he constituted himself in Jimbe to hand Cartland the eviction notice personally. When he arrived, however, the justice found the *hacienda* "voluntarily unoccupied without there being anyone present to evict."[150] This documented inspection by the justice of the peace in April scarcely agrees with Cartland's version of "the forced eviction that was inflicted on me in March of 1883."

The community's lawful possession of the lands was nevertheless reversed two years later, when Cartland was repossessed by order of Prefect Noriega. Noriega was simply following orders from Lima.[151] But on 19 July 1885 the *hacienda* was attacked, this time by the Cochachin Guerrilla.[152]

After the *caceristas* assumed power in 1886, the "Pueblo de Jimbe" quickly incorporated itself as a new district. With no small measure of ingratiation with the new chief, the *pueblo* joyfully christened their new district "Cáceres del Perú." In 1887 José Vicente Gutiérrez, appointed legal representative of the *pueblo* of Jimbe, presented his version of the land conflict, and it was totally contrary to Cartland's. Writing to the subprefect of Huaylas, he explained:

I must permit myself to speak frankly; said Señor Catlan [*sic*] fails to tell the truth. On the date that he claims [that I evicted him,] yes, it is true that I did come before him in response to his invitations, and with a group of those with interests in the case; and after a friendly conversation I persuaded him not to be afraid because no individual who belongs to the community is going to hurt him in the least, be it in his person or his crops, by virtue of the fact that they are men of order, fathers of families, and holders of regular interests. But he [Cartland] has presented these things in a very distinct color. In reality Señor Catlan [*sic*], taking advantage of the affinal relations that exist between himself and the President of the Republic, Don Miguel Iglesias, has harassed and harmed my clients and put them in a desperate situation, obtaining by entreaty . . . that the prefect of this department [Noriega] send a platoon of soldiers to make effective an unjustified collection of rents on the lands that had been restored to the community. And if Catlan [*sic*] suffered anything prejudicial, it was by the [hand of the] *montoneros* that happened to be stationed in the *pueblo*. But according to what I've been told, the aforementioned Cartland was the origin of the prejudices he suffered. . . . Catlan [*sic*] led a part of the Chilean force to Jimbe whence the Chileans, with the pretext of persecuting the *montoneros*, converted Jimbe into a pile of ashes, taking from the community all the livestock which they have been unable to recover, and as a result they are now living in extreme mendicancy.[153]

But it was the report of the new governor of Cáceres del Perú that was the most damning to Cartland's version. Manuel Alegre was a sly architect of words, and in this case he was keen to point out that Cartland's particular choice of words disguised his actions:

Señor Cartland plays with the word *indígenas*, first associating it with a force formed by some of those individuals thus called, and then attaching it to "tenants" with the intention of defaming the good name of the citizens of this *pueblo*. [This has been done] with wicked and slanderous purpose, because the only force of *indígenas* that presented itself in these parts was that led by Flavio and Apolinario Cochachin [i.e., the sons of Pedro]. That force and its leaders, which came out of the mountains of the Province of Huaraz, did not know Señor Cartland, and for this reason, and because he was a foreigner, they could not have had an adverse disposition toward him. And not one individual of this *pueblo* could be counted among the ranks of Cochachin.

All these fundamentals make absurd and impossible the robbery that with studied subtlety is imputed onto these mindful citizens.

Alegre then confirmed what everyone knew: Cartland was a confirmed collaborator with the enemy:

Finally, the enemy's forces . . . did not damage the interests of [Señor Cartland]. This is confirmed by the fact that he has made no reclamation to the government of Chile; and this is decried by public voice, which presents him as an ally of the soldiers of that government, [a]s the guide whose counsel and direction saved those soldiers from the mines that Agustín Castro had set for them in certain passages, [and who was] responsible for the razing of this *pueblo*. . . . It was, without doubt, in attention to the public outcry that Castro, who fought for the honor and independence of his *patria*, and who knew well that if the Chileans ever caught him they would kill him, divorced himself from Cartland's friendship, and counted him among the enemies of the country and ceased seeing him as a neutral.

The *cacerista* prefect José María B. Sevilla's view of the land conflict in Jimbe in 1887 was radically different from either Cartland's or those of the community's representatives, reflecting as it did the desire of Ancash's departmental treasury to reduce its ballooning fiscal deficit. For the paranoid Prefect Sevilla, the Jimbe conflict was a conspiracy designed to parcel and privatize the *hacienda* and thereby rob the state of its patrimony. (Had Prefect Noriega not argued the same?) Sevilla argued that Cartland and his friends and relatives—namely, Eugenio Gonzáles and Juan Luna, each of whom occupied "a high social position" in *iglesista* circles—were fully cognizant of the carelessness of administrators in charging rent, and that they tried to exploit the situation by instilling in their peons and tenants the idea that "the *hacienda* was theirs and not the state's" and by obliging them to revolt against Cartland. The point of this "feigned uprising" was to fragment the *hacienda* and let the Indian community have the least important lands, while the authors of the conspiracy got away with the most valuable bottomland, thus swindling the state out of its rightful possession. As evidence, the prefect cited the fact that Cartland still maintained the best lands, and that the representative of the community had made the revolt "palatable" by soliciting and obtaining in the recent session of Congress that Jimbe be constituted as a new district in the Province of Santa, thus breaking off from the Province of Huaylas. Most notable, he said, was the "Machiavellianism" with which the peasants of Jimbe took "a glorious name in the history of the country" and "gave it to their *pueblo* [in order to] satisfy and flatter the [president] of the nation."

The war of words in the Jimbe case was striking. The *pueblo*'s political metamorphosis into the District of Cáceres del Perú was purely self-interested. But Sevilla, like his paranoid predecessor Noriega, would see conspiracy where none existed. Indeed, antagonism and retribution characterized relations between the collaborationist Cartland and the community that had been sacked and burned after Cartland led the Chileans to their door. Nor is it likely that Agustín Castro, not to mention Cochachin, would conspire with the likes of Cartland, whose dubious reputation was *voz pública*. District Governor Alegre detected the weighted use of the term "indígenas," employed indiscriminately by Cartland to associate the villagers of Jimbe with both the Castro Montonera and Cochachin's "indiada." The verbiage betrayed the political motives of all three parties (Cartland, the Prefecture, the *pueblo*), engaged in what for the moment would be a conflict without resolution.[154]

Noriega's case, which blamed wicked leaselords for causing the rebellion, was ultimately based on misrepresentations like that of the Jimbe affair, combined with the popular but unfounded notions of the Indian's "natural repugnance" for the poll-tax, and his "certified simplicity" or political gullibility. Schreiber's self-defense[155] emphasized his disassociation with the rebellion, which in his view was a spontaneous uprising of the Indian hamlets of Huaraz, led by the persecuted *alcaldes*. Schreiber added that Noriega's claim that the rebels had burned the notary archives was also false. The rebels, Schreiber noted, had burned only the archive of the Caja Fiscal, "because they believed that with its destruction the tax registers would also disappear"—a belief that turned out to be well founded. Finally, he added that his peons from Collón and Vicos had not taken part in the rebellion. Indeed, most sources indicate that the *alcaldes* led the resistance against the inflated poll-tax in 1885, just as they would in subsequent years. There is no sound reason to think that their patrons made them do it or, more seriously, that they were ever capable of such a thing.

In the late nineteenth century the majority of Indians in Huaylas-Ancash were not *hacienda* peons or *colonos*, although most were not fully independent smallholders either. Many were semi-independent smallholders and sharecroppers who worked at a variety of tasks. Some were pastoralists. Most were landless woodcutters, charcoal makers, and artisans who sold their labor and products in town to make ends meet.[156] Almost all were members of land-hungry *estancias* (hemmed-in hamlets) with elected *alcalde* authorities. Although the land base of these hamlets was acutely deficient in the late nineteenth century, this did not mean that all were captives of the *haciendas*. In short, the economic dependency of Indians on landlords was great, but it did not translate into total political dependency or a one-way clientism.

The Rhythm of Resistance and Insurgency, 1883–85

Two conjunctures of causation were fundamental in the transition from avoidance protest to legal petition to open rebellion in Huaraz. The first concerned the volatile contradiction of a tributelike (though in reality liberal) poll-tax that carried no state guarantee of Indian access to usufruct plots or to alpine commons, but instead was a "double tax" imposed in addition to (illegal) landlord access fees. This contradiction, combined with the increased demands of *la república* corvée labor and with the constant threat of military conscription—at a moment when peasant households were experiencing economic distress—placed Indians and their local leaders in a volatile predicament. The second, more decisive contradiction that determined the timing of rebellion was the explosive combination of a violent rejection of the petitions submitted by the *alcaldes* and then the humiliation of the persons and authority of the *alcaldes* themselves. From here, political objectives (both peasant and *cacerista*) and the defense of the initial gains made determined the expansion of the insurgency.

In 1883, under the *iglesista* prefect Vargas, peasant tactics had been largely confined to "voting with one's feet." To avoid the crunch of poll-tax, public works labor, and military conscription, peasants simply moved to the hills.[157] During the Recavarren campaign of 1883, peasants with a choice preferred to fight as independently organized *guerrillas,* rather than be recruited as footsoldiers and be forced to sacrifice their freedom to come and go, a freedom that their domestic economies and cultural inclinations demanded.[158]

Under the relentless fiscal pressure of 1884–85, peasants sought the proven road of petition via the *alcaldes,* who in turn routinely sought out the skills of literate legal experts. Only after these legal means were violently rejected by state authorities was a limited, tactical show of force considered in Huaraz. When this tactical show of force was brutally repressed—several hundred peasants were fired upon in the plaza—full-scale mobilization was at hand. Still, had state authorities then released all the *alcaldes* and met their modest demands, the rebellion might have been averted, as occurred, for example, under similar circumstances in 1904 (see chapter 4). In 1885, though, the *alcaldes* were humiliated. In defense of their leaders and themselves, the hamlets mobilized, descending in irresistible numbers on the prefecture and the barracks.

Having taken the decisive step to punish and banish the authorities from Huaraz, the peasantry and its leaders faced a number of political imperatives. Given the sudden, escalating nature of the rebellion, Atusparia's first move was to restore order in Huaraz. With the prompting of *cacerista* conspirators, the rebels named sympathetic *mistis*, or non-Indians, to the posts of prefect, subprefect, and secretary of the prefecture. The ready appointment of *caceristas* as political leaders of the new regime would, it was mistakenly deemed, assuage any reasonable fears by whites of "race war" in Huaraz, thus affirming the political nature of the revolt.[159]

Moreover, it is clear that no other option was imaginable in the midst of civil war. *Caceristas* were ready to take over, and they proclaimed that General Cáceres would meet all the Indians' social and fiscal demands. *Caceristas* in Huaraz were pleased to see Noriega and his forces routed, and some were undoubtedly involved in the early stages of the revolt. Spokespersons like Manuel Mosquera, Luis Huídobro, and Justo Solís announced that General Cáceres, who represented "the legitimate government of Peru," had already abolished the poll-tax (although this claim was not entirely true) and annulled other oppressive measures enacted by the Iglesias regime.[160] These spokespersons probably claimed, as Colonel Zamudio did later, that Cáceres was about to destroy the treacherous Iglesias and that, therefore, the risks of repression were minimal. With *caceristas* in positions of political authority, the Indian rebellion would suddenly become the torchbearer of a nationalist movement tragically indifferent to its existence. General Cáceres, like Puga, was the *alternativa ausente* of the moment.

Despite the presence of *caceristas* at the top, the *alcaldes* led by Atusparia were responsible for the grass-roots mobilization of the hundreds of Indian hamlets in the Callejón de Huaylas and even, apparently, beyond the Callejón to points south and east in Chiquian (Bolognesi Province), Huari (Conchucos Province), and Dos de Mayo (Department of Huanuco). Rebel leaders with some military experience from Recavarren's Northern La Breña Campaign, or other training, emerged from the Indian ranks: Simón Bambarén in Yungay, Pedro Granados and, later, Pedro "Uchcu" Cochachin, among others. Some of these Indian or *cholo* militiamen, including Cochachin, may have been invested with the accumulated prestige of having held *alcalde* posts in the past.

Cacerista allies were thus kept at arm's length, their control being contingent. In the heat of rebellion, the peasantry gained greater relative autonomy of action — the essential difference of April and May 1885 and the factor that most contributed to white fears of a "race war" unleashed by an uncontrollable "savage horde." But the "savage horde" was actually no horde at all; rather, these rebels were an organized peasantry composed of "natural" units, which most probably resembled the *republicano* work brigades of each community, led by its respective *alcalde* authority.

The "Magic" of Peasant Mobilization

During the embattled march to Yungay through Cochachin's mountainous territory, Colonel Callirgos Quiroga, Prefect Iraola's field commander, reported to his commanding officer that "the Indians have harassed us by heaving boulders down upon us, cutting off our water supply, and blocking the roads. Thousands of them have crowned the hills, uniting themselves and traversing the mountains as if by magic."[161]

What was this "magic" by which thousands of Indian peasants united themselves in battle against the *iglesista* troops? What was the mechanism of what one observer called the "avalanche" of "Indian rabble" that descended upon Iraola at Yungay? How does one read this "prose of counterinsurgency" inscribed in the military reports of the *iglesista* "pacification campaign"? Merely to assume an "enthusiasm" for revolt, as Ranajit Guha suggested in another context, would be an analytically poor guess in this case.[162] Instead, the fragmentary documentary evidence on peasant social and political organization suggests something more grounded in the postcolonial history of local political culture. Indian peasants throughout Huaylas-Ancash were likely mobilized for combat along the same organizational lines as they were for such mundane and festive tasks as work brigades, tax collection, or patron saint celebrations and, not surprisingly, by the same local authorities who did that organizing: the various *alcaldes* or "staff-holding" *varayoc*. The overlapping dimensions of peasant "republicano" political practice are one reason why Ernesto Reyna could write that the "military expedition [of Atusparia and Mosquera from Huaraz to Manco] resembled a procession of dancers going to celebrate Easter Week in Yungay," and that this Indian army was given the name of *ejército republicano*.[163] The mundane "magic" of the staffs was augmented by insurrectionary codes, including smoke signals, emotive dances, drink and coca, and possibly red flags—all of which signaled war. Rumor also contributed to mobilization, and *cacerista* elements probably played a role in its propagation, albeit not in its reception or transmission.

William Stein has cited the absence of Indian resistance to Iraola in Huaraz on 3 May, arguing that the religious cult of the local patron saint (El Señor de la Soledad) "interfered with the social struggle."[164] But key details of the events of 3–11 May call this reading into question. There is little doubt that the Indians celebrating their revered patron saint in the quarter now known as "La Soledad" were surprised by Iraola's appearance at the gates of Huaraz. They probably expected Iraola and his troops to wait for reinforcements in Yungay. As it turns out, this was not an uninformed or unreasonable assumption. Indeed, Iraola's own officers voted *not* to march on Huaraz in the *junta de guerra* of 1 May, electing instead to wait for a cavalry reinforcement (which, however, was then pinned down by *guerrillas*)[165] and for an ammunition and arms shipment Iraola had requested from Lima.[166] Stein's interpretation also relies on the assumption that the "cult" was a one-day affair. However, the patron saint festival of El Señor de la Soledad is not, and was not, a day-long celebration. Izaguirre's folkloric sketch of the "Fiesta del Señor"—published circa 1885 but surely not a description of that year's critical events—suggests that the fiesta normally lasted longer than a week.[167] In recent decades (more so before the devastating earthquake of 1970), the "octava" of the fiesta, which is celebrated on 10 May, attracts far more Indian peasants than the "día central," or 3 May festivities, which are characterized by neighborhood processions of town dwellers, led by town officials, notables, and priests. It is also noteworthy that Cochachin had "measured his forces" against town militias on 9 May before initiating the assault against Huaraz on 10 May (only to postpone it one day because of the unanticipated defection of Justo Solís). Did Cochachin wait until 10 May so that he might first swell his ranks with the peasant fiesta-goers who were streaming into Huaraz for the celebration of the "octava"? Did the self-assured orders issued on 10 May, which commanded Solís to make ready for the attack, indicate that Cochachin was amassing strength? Did the presence of Iraola's troops in Huaraz discourage peasants from descending to the plaza of La Soledad, as one keen observer noted, obliging them instead to gather on the hills around town, in effect augmenting the threat posed by Cochachin? These cultural probabilities, although unproven, cannot be dismissed out of hand.

The patron saint festival in Huaraz, like the carnival celebration, has served historically as a magnet for peasants, who stream in from the outlying hamlets into the plaza and chapel of Huaraz's eastern quarter, La Soledad. The procession participants carry hewn and pictorial images of the crucified Christ (El Señor) to the city's Chapel of La Soledad for the parish priest's benediction.[168] Most common (particularly at carnival) is a simple cross, adorned with wreaths. The Pastoral Inspection of 1848 demonstrates that most of the rural chapels in the *estancias* of Huaraz also observed the "Holy Cross" as their patron saint.[169] In effect, then, the processions would likely have channeled thousands of peasants into Cochachin's camps atop the hills which encircled Huaraz.[170] That Cochachin's peasant *guerrilla* force did swell to more than five thousand Indians on the hills of Huaraz during the festival days of early May suggests that the festivities did not impede the struggle but, quite possibly, bolstered it. The same can be said for the Easter Week processions which attracted thousands of "dancing" peasants to the siege of Yungay.

Indeed, an anonymous description of Iraola's occupation of Huaraz suggested that Indian leaders were inclined to see the celebration of the patron saint as an opportunity to revive the resistance, perhaps to launch a new offensive. Undoubtedly this resistance would have included moral and religious elements, including the common ritual offerings to the patron saint of Huaraz, in expectation of the reciprocal protection that the saint might afford his benefactors in battle. The anonymous account, which appeared in the 22 June edition of *El Comercio*, depicted the scene in alarmist and racist, but in other ways revealing, terms:

> On the 3rd [of May] the [government] forces occupied this plaza [of Huaraz], surprising the Indians who were celebrating a festival in La Soledad; they fled terrified, leaving their dead behind. They had proposed to decapitate and rob the whites after the festival, but happily [for us] they were surprised at [the] height [of the festival], and so their malevolent intentions were derailed. . . . One Pedro Cochachin, a miner from Uchcu called "Uchcu Pedro" by the Indians, had come from Yungay with a band of armed men and, not admitting defeat, he promised victory to the Indians and made himself supreme chief of all the Indians. . . . Two days after this plaza was occupied [by the troops] "Uchcu Pedro" began to threaten the population daily, and occasionally sustained serious combat, since he now had under his orders perhaps more than five thousand Indians.[171]

In Stein's instrumentalist view, which was also common among liberal elites of the period, Andean ritual practice and the entire *varayoc* tradition itself are seen as tools of domination,[172] forms of "false consciousness" instilled and controlled by *gamonales* and the local clergy.[173] To be sure, priests did attempt (and sometimes succeed) at wielding the power of Catholic ritual, and of Indian *vara* authority, in the interests of pacification and domination; but such attempts did not always work, nor did they preclude peasant agency in shaping local religious and political life. The *alcaldes* could make their own political alliances in consultation with their respective hamlets, and ritual practice, including the solemn duty of patron saint propitiation, was an integral part of the *varayoc* authority that made such *republicano* action possible.

One could argue that these modes and signs of mobilization confirm the view, espoused by Heraclio Bonilla, that "primitive" or ethnic "tribalism" characterized the motivations of Andean insurgents,[174] but closer scrutiny of the colonial and postcolonial history of the hybrid, Spanish-Andean institution of the *alcaldes* suggests otherwise. In Huaylas-Ancash the subaltern network of *alcalde* authorities, although segmented and subordinate to provincial officialdom since Bolívar's decree, was capable of transcending (if necessary, in short order) the localist, or "closed-corporate" nature of postcolonial Indian communities. Indeed, a ranked, pan-communal hierarchy of sorts existed, and it made its veiled but still powerful presence felt at several critical junctures in Ancash's postcolonial history—most notably in 1885, 1887, 1888, and 1904. Also, this subaltern political network was not necessarily "traditional" but, rather, marked the postcolonial resurgence of local Indian *republicano* authorities, which advanced unchecked during the period of the guano state's liberal retreat from direct tributary relations with the peasantry (ca. 1855–79). In subsequent petitions, the *alcaldes* would represent themselves as "true citizens" of the nation and legitimate servants of the Peruvian Republic. Their followers apparently saw them as such, and even some of Ancash's prefects, who counted heavily upon them, would have agreed. Of course, allegiances were primarily local, but local allegiances had been inextricably tied to tributary state structures, now withering away. It was the withering of those structures, exacerbated by the lawless and multiple exactions of campaigning *caudillos,* that precipitated the erosion of state–peasantry relations.

Were the *alcaldes* and the peasants they represented, then, nationalists, or perhaps "protonationalists," as Florencia Mallon has argued for the Junín case?[175] They clearly did, at least momentarily, ally themselves with the nationalist, *cacerista* cause. They served local officials by mediating relations between the Andean peasantry and the departmental authorities. But they were not "nationalist" in the finalist, bourgeois sense of the term. As Platt argued for the Bolivian case, the political practice of the postcolonial Andean authorities was informed by a historical sense of "tributary citizenship" in the *patria,* which sought state protection of certain "Indian rights" of colonial origin.[176] As I argued in chapter 2, in Huaylas-Ancash this notion was wrapped up in the hybrid identity of "republicano." Indians (both landed and landless) would render tribute or contribution, provide brigade labor, and perform soldierly service to maintain their "rights"—*if* the state kept up *its* end of the bargain, which was specified in the colonial Laws of the Indies.

Were the *alcaldes,* then, "constitutionalists" fighting for the "Gran Republicano"? That claim—heard from the pro-Cáceres newspaper, *El Comercio*—may have contained more meanings than its author intended. The imputed phrases of "Gran Republicano" and the "Constitution" permitted several possible readings, among which one was fit for consumption among *cacerista* elites of the newly formed Constitutionalist Party; another, however, could resonate among the peasant *republicano* combatants and their leaders, the *varayoc*. For defense of "republican order" for Andean peasants could also mean defending the livelihood of the local republics and "the community of Peruvians" via the observance of the "indigenous rights" inscribed in the colonial Laws of the Indies. Would the "Gran Republicano" defend those rights? This was all expressed rather convincingly in several petitions addressed to President Cáceres in 1887 and signed by the *alcaldes* of Huaraz, in the actions of the *alcaldes* after 1885, and by the haunting specter of the Atusparia insurgency, whose presence was felt in Huaylas-Ancash into the early twentieth century.

CHAPTER 4

Atusparia's Specter

We are aware of our sacred duty as true citizens to contribute to the sustenance of the nation. But today the circumstances of extreme poverty in which we find ourselves, as a consequence of the recent political convulsions . . . puts us in the irrepressible and absolute necessity of begging the attention of Your Excellency. [We] beseech . . . that you deign to decree that [the] Laws . . . of the Indies . . . be strictly adhered to, inasmuch as they be compatible with . . . the current Constitution and laws. The reasons upon which we base this solicitation are the following. . . . Under colonial rule we Indians enjoyed, as Your Excellency is very well aware, unrestricted access to the community of pastures, woodlands, and waters, as established by [the Laws of the Indies]. Thus, although we were subject to the tribute, we easily paid it by cutting firewood in the mountains and selling it in town, and by raising our little flocks of sheep in the high pastures, without paying anyone anything, not even to those who claimed ownership of the woodlands and pastures. Then came Independence and, no less than as if she [i.e., Independence] had been obtained only to benefit the mestizos and Spaniards [e.g., Creoles], we watched with pain as they began to place obstacles in the way of the exercise of our rights, pretending that the community of pastures, wooded ravines, and waters had disappeared. . . . That is how things remained until the year 1855 when tribute was abolished and they made us understand that those rights or, to put it better, the community which we had enjoyed for several centuries—in an absolute way under colonial rule and with only certain small restrictions afterward—had been correlative to the tribute and that it being abolished, so also was [our community] abolished. . . . How much our circumstances have changed, Your Excellency!—Nicolás Granados and Apolinario de Paz, alcaldes ordinarios of Huaraz, to President Cáceres, 1887[1]

[W]e have done everything in our power to regularize collection [of the polltax]. . . . [I]n this department . . . the great majority of inhabitants are indígenas *who do not comprehend the obligation they have to pay. They procure by a variety of means to evade it, even to the point of armed resistance, as in 1885, when they committed such savage and horrible acts that even today panic in the civilized part of the population has not disappeared.* — *Prefect Rodríguez to the Finance Ministry, 1893*[2]

[T]he titular alcaldes ordinarios *and* pedáneos . . . *dominate the communities and exercise all faculties in them, in effect making, if you will, an independent state of the* indígenas *in this department.* — *Prefect Huapaya to the Ministry of Government, 1904*[3]

The Indian *alcalde* Pedro Pablo Atusparia met the Creole *general* Andrés Avelino Cáceres for the first and last time on a misty June morning in Lima in 1886. Two of Lima's influential dailies saw fit to report the scene in these terms:[4]

> The *indígena* Don Pedro Atusparia, *alcalde ordinario* and chief of numerous Indians who, after defeating the *iglesista* forces commanded by Colonel Noriega, implanted constitutional order in the Department of Ancash, paid a visit to General Cáceres today. . . . [Atusparia] said that when the general passed on his way to Huamachuco [in the Northern La Breña Campaign of 1883] the authorities had not taken care to make [the Indians] comprehend what the international war [with Chile] was about, and that if they had known they would have mobilized thousands of lancemen in a single day. He also spoke of the poll-tax and asked that it be reduced. And lastly [Atusparia] lamented the shootings and assassinations committed against his race. . . . Atusparia offered to leave his youngest son, a nine-year-old, in the general's custody as a pledge of his perpetual fidelity, and so that "he might grow in your shadow, imitating your virtues." During the whole conversation they spoke only in Quechua, both the general and Atusparia.

The second newsprint version of the meeting included these passages:

> A very significant conversation took place today between Señor General Cáceres and the Indian Pedro Atusparia, chief of the Indian communities of Huaraz. . . . Atusparia . . . answered that he was sent by all the citizens of the indigenous race that conform the communities of Huaraz, to personally convince himself that General Cáceres, EL GRAN REPUBLICANO, as they call him, would finally assume supreme power. [He had heard] that [Cáceres] had been forced to consent to

a betrayal by a part of the current government that would have put power in the hands of *iglesistas*, against whom they had fought very hard, and . . . had never submitted to. . . . General Cáceres offered to busy himself with all those matters that at this moment preoccupy the Indians, and with those things about which Atusparia had spoken. He told Atusparia that he would send a commission to Huaraz to demarcate all the properties of the Indians and that, guaranteed by the government, they would henceforth be religiously respected. The general also said that one of his first projects would be to establish schools in those regions so that the Indians could enjoy the benefits of enlightenment, and advance themselves through their knowledge to the level of all the rest of the free and independent citizenry. On the theme of taxes, General Cáceres promised to Atusparia that he would reduce them until they had gotten on their feet well enough to make payments, so that the Indians would not consider them a heavy burden. . . . It would be difficult to describe the joy of the representative of Manco Capac's race when he heard the trustworthy and serious word of the future president. Atusparia left convinced that henceforth the Indians—until now the slaves of authoritarian abuse and violence—will be [treated as] Peruvian citizens, like everyone else, and that they will occupy a preferential place in the considerations of rulers.

To judge from newspaper accounts, the meeting of Atusparia and Cáceres might suggest that the wished-for moment of national reconciliation had finally arrived. When had patriotic Indians and revolutionary generals conferred—in Quechua no less—within reach of the walls of "Pizarro's palace" and in the name of national renovation and the liberation of the Indian? Although Atusparia was no Emiliano Zapata, and Cáceres no Pancho Villa (nor, indeed, even a Venustiano Carranza), and no photograph of the event has come down to us (although a photographer may have been present), this largely forgotten and tardy meeting of triumphant chieftains was perhaps equally forlorn for the missed and, in retrospect, subverted opportunity that it may be seen to represent.[5] Although wishfully (and demogogically) portrayed by the newspapers as a conciliatory parley of "the races," the content and the timing of the uneven exchange between Atusparia and Cáceres actually portended the widening postwar crevasse that would soon swallow the bridge of shared struggle which had briefly united them.

As a misread encounter that augured tension, the meeting of Atusparia and Cáceres can be read as an analogue for the ambivalent relations between Creole *caudillos* and Andean peasants which marked the period's turbulent political history. The misread encounters, or misencounters, between mobilized Indian peasants and phantom nationalist *caudillos* (Cáceres himself in 1883, Puga in 1885) marked the course of the Atusparia insurgency and would *not* be overcome in the postwar decades. Together with other forces, this history of misencounter would disallow the emergence of an inclusive or "normative" national state-formation process, and would instead widen cleavages between segments of Peru's diverse population.

It was not, after all, surprising that the medium of exchange between the wily *breñero* of Ayacucho and the inquiring *varayoc* of Huaraz should be some lingua franca manner of mediated Quechua speech, despite the marked differences in regional dialects. Cáceres had always appealed to his Indian compatriots in the highland tongue. Atusparia's shifting political predicament back in Huaraz may have urged him to witness the transfer of power in Lima (from Iglesias to Cáceres). Perhaps he needed the rhetorical ammunition afforded by the Quechua language's witness-validation suffix (*-mi*), in order to persuade his doubting, Quechua-speaking compatriots in Huaraz that "El Gran Republicano" had indeed come to power and, more important, that he was on their side.[6]

In Huaraz, Quechua-speaking peasants had reason to be suspicious. The once uncompromising nationalist hero of the Andean-based "Resistencia de La Breña" was now surrounded by his former *iglesista* and *civilista* enemies, some of whom colluded in the shady negotiations that lifted the general to the compromised presidency of the defeated and bankrupt Republic. Back in Huaraz, provincial officials were still prone to act as if the indigenous peasantry were the sworn enemy of the nation. Had they not heard that Cáceres, in whose patriotic cause the Indians had so fiercely fought, was about to become President of the Republic? And now that "El Gran Republicano" had finally taken Lima, did he not owe the Andean peasant "republicanos" of Ancash something for their support?

Such peasant expectations were not simply beggarly or passing fantasies in 1886. If anything, the post-guano, postwar *cacerista* state would now be the beggar (obliged, for example, to sign the infamous Grace contract, which handed Peru's assets over to foreign bondholders; obliged, for example, to reinstitute the troublesome poll-tax to finance the departments), and Andean peasants would, once again, be called upon to fulfill their role as the nation's bottomless pocket, the forever-plundered "reserva andina."[7] The postwar state's weakened position is one reason why the seemingly genuine pledges that General Cáceres made at the June 1886 encounter with Atusparia—which were not unlike those made by earlier generations of postcolonial *caudillos*—elicited the characteristic "we'll watch and see" response of the peasantry. After all, despite the counterinsurgent repression of April and May 1885, recalcitrant peasants now had the upper hand in depressed Ancash—if only by virtue of state default. Far from being business as usual, the violent conflict of 1885 and the preceding international and civil wars yielded a new correlation of forces in Huaylas-Ancash (as elsewhere in the central highlands) which was somewhat less unfavorable to the Andean peasantry.[8] The postwar *cacerista* state was weak, without funds, and unable to sustain repressive military expeditions against an "unpacified" peasantry. Landlords were suffering from the destruction wrought by war and a depressed economy; the postwar consolidation of landed estates noted elsewhere does not, at least immediately, seem to have occurred here.[9] The peasantry was also suffering and under assault; but now, in an irony of history, it was somewhat better positioned to survive collectively and thus resist unpopular state demands.

The Atusparia insurgency left an indelible mark of dread on elite consciousness. But it also had very concrete consequences for departmental administration, since it set rigid constraints on the fiscal viability of the provincial state apparatus in Huaraz, in effect curtailing the fiscal designs of the national state now led by Cáceres. In the postwar decades, elite fears of "race war" and of Indian rebellion against the poll-tax (and other exactions) were perennial in Huaylas-Ancash. Prefects were also increasingly concerned with the vaguely perceived threat that rising Indian population numbers signified. Indeed, a remarkable but imperfectly understood "Indianization" or indigenization process was under way in the Callejón de Huaylas of Ancash.

In this postwar context, peasant semiautonomy would be asserted. And the ready-but-wary stance would reveal itself the wiser. The general's pledge to survey and guarantee community lands would soon unveil itself as a liberalizing project—intended, in part, to abolish collective holdings.[10] The handful of phantom Indian schools would, it seems, enlighten no one. Even the general's welcome promise to temporarily reduce the poll-tax until the Indians "had gotten on their feet" was flimsy. The promised reduction materialized only after Atusparia's successors firmly resisted repeated attempts by provincial officials, acting under orders from Lima's Ministry of Finance, to collect the poll-tax. Indeed, it was only after Huaraz's Indian *alcaldes* addressed several remarkable petitions to President Cáceres himself in 1887, and then waited steadfastly for his reply—in the meantime raising the bloody specter of 1885 over the heads of provincial officials and the paranoid local elite—that President Cáceres finally kept his word (in 1889).

But Atusparia was also not what he appeared to be in the imaginative pages of the *limeño* press. No "cacique" or "chief of the indigenous race" at all, Atusparia was no more, and no less, than an illiterate peasant of some means from the tiny hamlet of Marian, albeit one with notable yet waning prestige in Huaraz. His prestige was earned by virtue of having filled the important annual post of *alcalde ordinario* of Huaraz's La Independencia District in 1885. That memorable year he found himself, nominally at least, at the helm of Peru's most impressive peasant mobilization since the great Tupac Amaru II insurrection of 1780. In June 1886, though, Atusparia was already an *ex-alcalde* and, unlike the general, his political future was uncertain. Following well-worn political custom, Atusparia and his *segundo*, or second-ranked counterpart, Pedro Guillén, had "passed on their staffs" of office, with the blessing of priests, to the next elected pair of *varayoc*, or staff-holders, at (or possibly even before) the calendric Feast of the Magi ("Fiesta de los Reyes") in early January.

Indeed, Atusparia would soon die under suspicious circumstances. Owing to the same atmosphere of national reconciliation and compromise that brought Cáceres to power, no judicial investigation, either of the many crimes perpetrated in rebellion or of Atusparia's death—to the lament of historians—would be held. Folklore has it that upon his return to Huaraz Atusparia was poisoned by his more militant followers, but no firm documentary evidence confirms this or any other version of his death. In any case, and in contrast to Cáceres, Atusparia himself appears to have left no immediate personal legacy other than his "hijo encomendado a Cáceres," who in turn appears to have led an insignificant and assimilated life in Callao—the port of Lima.[11] Only four decades later—under the auspices of Lima's left-leaning indigenism and, particularly, the passionate pen of the novelist Ernesto Reyna—would the name and figure of Atusparia be launched on its contemporary trajectory as floating (orbiting) signifier of sagacious leadership (*amauta*) and justified rebellion.[12] Although the personal figure of Atusparia was momentarily eclipsed by the forgetting Creole positivism of the "aristocratic republic" (ca. 1895–1919) the specter of the Atusparia insurgency would haunt the hills and valleys of Huaylas-Ancash in the decades immediately following 1885.

The Phantom *Contribución Personal*

Contrary to what the *cacerista* conspirators had promised in March 1885, the Peruvian state's enthusiasm for the *contribución personal*, or poll-tax, did not come to an end with the ouster of the *iglesista* authorities. Nor would the drive to resurrect the defunct Corte Superior de Ancash with local poll-tax revenues expire with Prefect Noriega's fiscal fiasco. In 1885, Noriega's miscalculations meant that the "contribution" for that year would be paid in blood, not in silver pesos or paper bills. And although the *caceristas,* now in power, doggedly supported the poll-tax and did everything they could to make it effective, after 1885 the tax was rarely collected in any form in Huaylas-Ancash. Indeed, between 1886 and 1895 (when the poll-tax was officially abolished by Piérola and Congress) on average less than 15 percent of the annual poll-tax due was actually deposited in the departmental treasury.[13] In Huaylas-Ancash, as in other parts of highland Peru, the *cacerista* program of national fiscal decentralization would fail because it was predicated upon paper budgets that relied upon an illusory poll-tax. Ironically, Piérola, who had decreed the tax in 1879, now abolished an unpopular mirage.

Contrary to some influential historical accounts, the Huaylas-Ancash case illustrates Peru's critical postwar budget gap more clearly, perhaps, than any other. In his study of the Atusparia uprising, William Stein concluded that the rebellion of 1885 actually did little to change the situation of Indians since, he claimed, they continued to pay the poll-tax just as they had before.[14] But this was surely not the case. Others, including the great Peruvian historian Jorge Basadre, assumed that Indians were meeting poll-tax obligations until Piérola and Congress "liberated" them in 1895. Citing a congressional commission report, Basadre asserted that the Department of Ancash "had as income in 1893 133,500 soles, of which 96,486 soles corresponded to the poll-tax," leaving the impression that this is what was actually collected.[15] It was not. Unfortunately, Lima's budget projections are unreliable indicators of the actual fiscal situation of the departments. To begin with, the projected figures cited by Basadre are not those of 1893, but of 1891.[16] Yet how much of the poll-tax was actually made effective in 1891? As of 31 December 1891 a total of 881 soles had been collected. In other words, 95,605 soles were still *pendiente!*[17]

If Piérola did not abolish an effective departmental revenue base, then what was he up to in 1895? Piérola's abolition had more to do with restructuring and modernizing an ineffectual revenue-collection system than with "liberating the indigenous race" from the fictitious yoke of "neocolonial tribute." These trumped-up declarations were, however, consistent with the populist demagoguery of the self-proclaimed "Protector of the indigenous Race." Departmental accounts after 1895 generally do not reveal a drastic decline in actual revenue, and where decline occurred it was not of the order of magnitude many historians have assumed. If the projected total of the departmental budget approached 140,000 soles in 1895, then the decline in 1896 to 10,975.85 soles (projected costs were then 14,511.33 soles) would indeed be draconian. In fact, the actual amount of poll-tax revenues collected and recorded for 1895 was a mere 3,533 soles.[18] Total revenues for 1895 probably did not far exceed 10,000 soles, although a reformist push to collect the unpaid taxes of previous years did nudge revenues up somewhat. Thus, the post-1895 departmental budgets were simply more realistic and in line with actual revenue. Also significant is the fact that in 1897 the budget nearly doubled to 22,302.90 soles, thus reaching higher levels of income than in 1895. It appears that Piérola's structural reforms of the tax-collection system were working in Ancash.

The political meanings of these figures are better understood through the words and actions of local actors. Basadre's congressional budget figures wither next to Prefect José María Rodríguez's words, written in October of 1893:

> About the letter . . . from the secretariat of Congress that accuses this [departmental] junta of negligence in collecting the poll-tax. . . . You will see that we have done everything in our power to regularize the collection [of the poll-tax] despite all the difficulties that confront us . . . in this department, where the great majority of inhabitants are *indígenas* who do not comprehend the obligation they have to pay. They procure by a variety of means to evade it, even to the point of armed resistance, as in 1885, when they committed such savage and horrible acts that even today panic in the civilized part of the population has not disappeared.[19]

The year 1891 was not much different. In May of that year, Prefect Nicolás Portal warned Lima that local revolts could lead to a general insurrection and that it was impossible to collect the poll-tax without resorting to coercive methods. He requested more troops and armaments, which Lima denied him because it had none to send.[20] In September the new prefect, Antonio Alarco, informed Lima that "having manifested the motivating causes of why the poll-tax has not been collected as it should, it has been noted that in the present year and in previous ones only a very small percentage of this rent has been deposited in the treasury; this is owing to the resistance of contributors and to the lack of a [military] force."[21]

But the fiscal and political problems of the 1890s were preceded by the even more illusory departmental budgets of the late 1880s. As military commander of the *iglesista* pacification force and prefect of Ancash, José Iraola had suspended the poll-tax as part of an accord with Justo Solís and the *alcaldes* of Huaraz, who agreed to cease hostilities in May 1885. In 1886 the poll-tax was reestablished by the still popular Cáceres regime under the new Law of Fiscal Decentralization, but in Huaylas-Ancash the tax was essentially uncollectable. The chief reason for this was that the Atusparia rebels had taken care to burn all the tax registers held in the archive of the Caja Fiscal (departmental treasury), which was housed in the gutted prefecture. Without the tax registers, or *matriculas*, there could be no legal collection of the poll-tax. And so the primary problem soon became how to "matriculate," or enlist, a wary and hostile Indian majority. This would turn out to be a sticky problem indeed.

In 1887, departmental records indicate that only 1,098.88 soles were collected in all of Ancash, 903 of these from the Province of Huaylas and zero from the Province of Cercado or Huaraz itself.[22] The total value of the 1887 poll-tax in Ancash was projected at 98,040 soles. Thus, as of 12 September 1888, 96,941 soles were still pending collection.[23] The total 1888 projected budget was in excess of 140,000 silver soles. After eight months of collection efforts, the *junta departamental* lamented that "the collected sum for the year 1888 has reached only . . . 15,127.45 soles; that is, less than 11 percent of the amount budgeted for the entire year. This is a disconsolate fact."[24]

The budget figures in themselves are undeniable evidence for noncompliance after 1885. Even more compelling, though, is the evidence found in Ancash's prefectural correspondence and Lima's ministerial dispatches. Still, the strongest evidence stems not from these, but from the petitions and actions of the Indian *alcaldes* themselves.

In March of 1887 the *alcaldes* of Huaraz petitioned President Cáceres, requesting that their people be exonerated from the poll-tax. The response of the Ministry of Government, however, was categorically negative. Instead, the ministry recommended that the (non-Indian) municipal authorities in Huaraz appeal to the Indian's patriotism which, they argued, could be relied upon to supply the poll-tax.[25] The petition, which was signed by the *alcaldes ordinarios* of the twin districts of Huaraz, plus the fifty lesser *alcaldes pedáneos* and *campos* of the surrounding hamlets, or *estancias*, made a personal pitch to Cáceres by reminding him of his Andean experience during the "La Breña" campaign of national resistance:

> Your Excellency, who has suffered hunger and thirst in our home because of the indigence that oppresses us; Your Excellency, who has touched the miserable condition in which we are sepulchered, [and] understands, even better than the undersigned, the impossibility of what they want to obligate us with; Your Excellency, who has contemplated, during the time that you soldiered with us, the reestablishment of republican liberties and institutions, our mode of social and individual being; Your Excellency, who has intimately observed the

pauperism to which we are subject from immemorial times. . . . Your Excellency, who does not ignore that with our own strength, blood, and lives we emancipated Peru from foreign domination,[26] and with the same contingent we repaired to the battlefield in the last international conflict, and without any other motive than love of *patria*. Your Excellency, who knows all this, and much more, you are our protective father who knows justice . . . and who will grant the present solicitation its corresponding passage.

The petition signed by the *alcaldes* of Huaraz presents the outlines of what "republican" state–society relations should be. In exchange for the peasant's tax contribution, they reasoned, the republican state was obligated to protect "their individual and social rights." Thus:

> Every contribution, Your Excellency, is a part of the income with which particular individuals contribute to the sustenance of the state, and with which the [state] indemnifies and makes retribution to them by protecting individual and social rights. The poll-tax, Your Excellency, does not and cannot have a reason for existence in the absence of either one of these [two] conditions: namely, income for the contributor and protection from the state. . . . For our race, and particularly in the Department of Ancash, both of these conditions are absent. . . . We have no income because we are not landowners . . . and even the small inheritance that belongs to us is now part of the *hacienda* of some landlord, and we take it from him for a limited time in exchange for our personal labor. . . . For us [since Independence] there has never been, nor is there now, any state protection.

The petition went on to explain that "since Independence" state protection of "indigenous rights" had degenerated into the rapacious exploits of rival *caudillos* and flaccid republican regimes, forcing Indians "to buy their liberty" or be "kidnapped" for "some criminal project." "Indigenous liberty" and "indigenous property" were the casualties of this *caudillo*-ridden, postcolonial disorder:

> Every regime that has fought to sustain itself in power, and every *caudillo* [faction] that has worked to overthrow it, has availed itself by decree or by force to draft free men by yanking them from their homes . . . to incorporate them by force under pain of death . . . to serve . . . what are almost always criminal projects[.] [N]ot having any other means of avoiding this noxious kidnapping than the money or goods with which we have bought our liberty. . . . This is the history of indigenous liberty

in its relations with the military politics of the country, and this is the protection that the state and the regimes and the rebel [*caudillos*] have dispensed. . . . Has this ill been remedied in Peru, Your Excellency? We are not yet sure. . . . In respect to indigenous property rights what shall we say, Your Excellency? Since Independence the exiguous goods of our fortune, fruit of the sweat of our brow, the few animals we have raised for our subsistence and for plowing, all have been inhumanely stripped from us by the disturbers of order and by its pseudodefenders, without there being one single *caudillo* or one single president who has taken pity on our fate. Such is the history, traced in broad strokes, of indigenous property in its relations with regimes and the enemies of those regimes. . . . [A]nd such has been the protection that one or the other has dispensed. . . . For all these express reasons and for others that we omit, we implore Your Excellency to deign to accede with justice to our petition, suspending the collection of the poll-tax in this province.[27]

Having taken the legal route of a direct petition to President Cáceres, Huaraz's Indians were not inclined to pay the poll-tax demanded by the departmental authorities until they heard from "El Gran Republicano" himself. The relationship of the *alcaldes* of Huaraz with President Cáceres had a powerful precedent: Atusparia's personal interview with Cáceres in 1886, when the general had promised to reduce the burden of the poll-tax on Atusparia's people. One year later, the *alcaldes* of Huaraz still awaited the fulfillment of that promise.

In April, Prefect P. J. Carrión informed Lima of widespread Indian resistance to the formation of the new tax registers, which were to be used to collect the poll-tax. He also warned Lima of an impending revolt.[28] The central government responded in a way consistent with its impoverished position. It could not send troops, and it could not waive the poll-tax because the bankrupt federal treasury was in no position to subsidize the departments. On 19 April the Ministry of Government made its recommendation.

[C]onsidering: (1) that rather than decree the suspension of the Law [of Fiscal Decentralization] which created the poll-tax, the government wishes to justify that measure; (2) that the sagacity and diligence of state and municipal authorities may contribute to the dissipation of the resistance of the *indígenas* against the payment of this tax. It is resolved: Inform [Prefect Carrión] that, making use of the natural influence that is invested in his authority and exciting the zeal of the subprefects and the municipalities, he [should] personally procure interpreters and through them convince the *indígenas* of the necessity that exists that they pay the poll-tax, which is destined to sustain the authorities and justices who are charged with protecting their lives and interests, and of upholding justice for them.[29]

One can imagine how unconvincing this resolution might have sounded to the ears of the *alcaldes* of Huaraz and the peasant population they represented. Now they were to pay the poll-tax to support the local authorities they most often detested, many of whom were held responsible for coerced exactions and for the very absence of justice. These local authorities were not to be trusted to defend "indigenous rights."

The ministry would argue that the only reason Indians resisted the poll-tax was that local officials and landlords collected "illegal kickbacks" (*gabelas ilegales*), in the form of eggs, firewood, and pasture. With the elimination of these extraofficial taxes, the state argued, Indians would comply with the legitimate poll-tax. There was an element of truth in this argument, but the weak postwar state was in no position to abolish the *gabelas,* or to protect Indian lands, even if it had wanted to—and it appears that it did not.

Resisting Enclosure: The Case of Marian

The historical significance of the 1846 petition presented by Manuel Ysidro, *alcalde de campo* of Marian, which protested the enclosure of the *quebradas* or alpine commons used by Indians to extract firewood (discussed in chapter 2 above), was magnified by the petition of 1 June 1887, directed to President Cáceres by the *alcaldes ordinarios* of Huaraz. The June 1887 petition underlines the dislocation in peasantry–state relations that kindled the Atusparia insurgency of 1885, when it was no coincidence that Atusparia, the leading *alcalde ordinario* in that fateful year, also hailed from the Estancia of Marian. Huaraz's notarial archives confirm that the conflict-ridden history of enclosure in the alpine commons above Marian remained unresolved.

In 1828, the landlord Miguel Mosquera had purchased Quebrada Llacac, "situated above Marian . . . with all its pastures, ravines, and corrals, with all its entrances, exits, uses, customs, servitudes, and everything else that belongs to it," from Paulino Gonzáles.[30] Pedro Nivín, however, "indio principal del Pueblo de Huaraz," had also claimed, and was granted, most of the same lands in 1811. In 1823 Pedro's widow, María Nivín, had unsuccessfully challenged Don Paulino's claim to Quebrada Llacac. But in 1890, "María Fernanda Yauli, widow of Atusparia," along with Juan Torres,

Manuel Rosario, Manuel Shuan, Julián Morales Collas, Cayetano Colonia, Manuel Emiliano, Cecilio Osorio, Sebastián Fabian, Julián López, Manuel Concepción, Vito Rosario, Julián Guillén, and Manuel Lorenzo Heredia, who identified themselves all as "peasants and *indígenas* from the Estancia of Marian," demanded a *deslinde,* or legal demarcation, of the "Recuay-huanca" lands at the mouth of Quebrada Llacac just above Marian.

As proof of their claim, the indigenous peasants of Marian presented a composition title from 1712 under the name of Chrisóstomo Nivín, "indio originario del Aillo Atun Guaraz." However, the colonial boundary markers were vague and easily contested.[31] Nor could the peasant litigants of Marian demonstrate descent from Nivín. The documents on the other side were also incomplete. The titles to a section of the lands, then held by Don Miguel Mosquera's widow, María Sánchez de Mejía, had apparently been "stolen" with other papers "en la época de la revolución de los indígenas" (i.e., in 1885) from Mejía's house in Huaraz.[32] But witnesses declared that Miguel Mosquera had constructed a stone fence sometime between 1834 and 1861 to demarcate his lands from other claims. Given the *alcalde* of Marian's petition of 1846, in which Mosquera is named as one of the guilty landlords who had enclosed the *quebrada* (see chapter 2 above) it is likely that this fence-building began before the date of the petition, which would mean that the "enclosure" of Quebrada Llacac had begun sometime between 1834 and 1846.[33]

Another clue to the Quebrada Llacac case was revealed when the witness Manuel Alzamora declared that Juan Torres had been his *leñatero,* or firewood purveyor.[34] Manuel Alzamora had initially been named subprefect of Huaraz by the Atusparia rebels in 1885, but he was soon replaced by the *cacerista* Luis Huídobro. Indeed, several reports suggested (among them, one that appeared in the 8 May 1885 edition of *El Nacional*) that Atusparia himself had worked for Alzamora. We do not know if Juan Torres was Alzamora's *leñatero* in 1885. However, Alzamora would have had an interest in Juan's free access to the *quebrada,* since it meant a cheap and steady supply of firewood for him. In 1890, though, most of Alzamora's testimony confirmed the claims of the adversaries, and the Indians of Marian lost the case.

The legal dispute over Quebrada Llacac is not quite a "smoking gun," but it strongly suggests that contested claims in the *quebradas* above Marian dated from at least the Nivín vs. Gonzáles case of 1823 (i.e., from the Independence period). Mosquera's stone fences and the link between Alzamora and his client, the firewood purveyor Juan Torres (and possibly Atusparia himself) also raises the question of linkage between the enclosure problem in the *quebradas* and the scarcity of firewood in Huaraz (which was further exacerbated by the insurrection, when firewood prices soared).[35] The direct involvement of Atusparia's widow as claimant in the dispute also suggests that Pedro Atusparia himself had a personal stake in the struggle to reclaim access to Quebrada Llacac.

Although the Marian case is highly suggestive, it was the petition of the *alcaldes ordinarios* of Huaraz in June 1887 that would confirm the linkage between the enclosure problem and resistance to the poll-tax. The petition was presented and signed by the *alcaldes ordinarios* who had rotated into office that year. Nicolás Granados and Apolinario de Paz spoke for "all the Indians of this locality." The petition's remarkable preamble declared that

> we are aware of our sacred duty as true citizens to contribute to the sustenance of the nation. But today the circumstances of extreme poverty in which we find ourselves, as a consequence of the recent political convulsions that the country and especially this department has suffered, puts us in the irrepressible and absolute necessity of begging the attention of Your Excellency. [We] beseech . . . that you deign to decree that Laws 5 and subsequent of the 17th title of the 4th book of the *Recompilation of the [Laws of the] Indies,* and also those relative to the personal service contained in the 12th title of the 6th book of the same *Recompilation* be strictly adhered to, inasmuch as they be compatible with rights established by the current Constitution and laws. The reasons upon which we base this solicitation are the following.

The 1887 "solicitation" of the *alcaldes* of Huaraz, although undoubtedly penned by a skilled "ventriloquist" or lettered legal advisor, amounts to a historical critique of the postcolonial state from the perspective of the erosion of colonial "indigenous rights." It is an invaluable and rare historical document of subalternist slant, and for this reason it is reproduced here at some length:

> Under colonial rule we Indians enjoyed, as Your Excellency is very well aware, unrestricted access to the community of pastures, woodlands, and waters, as established by [the Laws of the Indies]. Thus, although we were subject to the tribute, we easily paid it by cutting firewood in the mountains and selling it in town, and by raising our little flocks of sheep in the high pastures, without paying anyone anything, not even to those who claimed ownership of the woodlands and pastures. Then came Independence and, no less than as if she [i.e., Independence] had been obtained only to benefit the *mestizos* and Spaniards [e.g., Creoles], we watched with pain as they began to place obstacles

in the way of the exercise of our rights, pretending that the community of pastures, wooded ravines, and waters had disappeared, or that at a minimum, to access these, we now had to pay so much for every dozen bundles of firewood, or another so much each year for the pasture that our [animals] would eat. This we were supposed·to pay to those same exclusive landowners who before had never risked trying to charge us any fees at all for fear that the councillors, justices, and magistrates would charge them the fine specified in the cited Law 5 [of the Indies]. . . . That is how things remained until the year 1855, when tribute was abolished and they made us understand that those rights or, to put it better, the community which we had enjoyed for several centuries—in an absolute way under colonial rule and with only certain small restrictions afterward—*had been correlative to the tribute* [emphasis in original] and that it being abolished, so also was [our community] abolished. We . . . were gradually losing the exercise of the aforementioned rights; noting, in addition, that as we were losing them, the titular exclusive landowners of the ravines and pastures raised their access fees to the point that today they charge us one silver real for the extraction of one load of firewood; an arbitrary fee for each post that we extract for our workshops; seventeen silver reales for the pasture consumed each year for each cow; and five select lambs each year for the pasture consumed by every hundred sheep etc. And woeful are we if we do not pay the corresponding fee for firewood, because they will take the very shirts off our backs. And woe to us even more if we do not pay the fees corresponding to the pasture, because they take our livestock and keep whatever portion that they deem convenient. It will be argued, perhaps, that we have our expedient right to repair to the justices: true enough. But between certified paper, scribe, defense lawyer, clerk, etc., we spend ten times more than what we pay in fees, and without any guarantee that we will achieve justice. Because most of the time personal influence, bribes, or something else of the kind counts for more, especially when the Superior Court is located in a distant place, where we cannot easily take our grievances for lack of funds, as is currently the case. It was for nought that in 1862 [Prefect] Colonel Don Ignacio Dulant issued a broadside reminding [everyone of] the cited Laws of the Indies, because even if he had sufficient fortitude to make people obey his dispositions, subsequent prefects made it impossible for things ever to return to their former state. It was similarly futile that Doctor Don Bruno Bueno [prefect], with the subprefect being Don Justo C. Solís in the year 1882, issued another broadside, although less sweeping than that of the cited Colonel [Dulant], since they could not defeat the resistance of the titular exclusive landowners of the woodlands and ravines, on the one hand because [Bueno] was prefect for only a very short time, and on the other hand because more pressing duties of another nature did not permit him to see his good intentions through on this matter. It is noteworthy that since these broadsides [were issued] they have imposed a new access fee on us, which is one silver real for each load of [glacial] ice, as if the Cordillera Blanca herself were private property! On the issue of personal [labor] service, Your Excellency will see that according to the Laws of the Indies this was very circumscribed, and we were only obliged to work without pay in the opening and maintenance of important roadways, and in the construction and repair of bridges, but that if we were employed in some other work we were to be paid the respective wage in remuneration for the service. How much our circumstances have changed, Your Excellency! Today they make us work in all manner of public works for free. . . . Your Excellency, if all our rights are trampled upon; if the little that we have is not of our free disposition except in unusual cases; if we are constantly employed in unremunerated work—where are we going to get the necessary funds to pay the poll-tax? . . . And if we complain they call us insolent, and if our justified anger is translated into action, then they call us rebels and savages, and they go to the extreme of razing our homes with all our possessions inside, as indeed occurred in a not-very-distant epoch. Your Excellency, we do not want those sad scenes to be reproduced; rather [we prefer] to exercise the right of petition that the law grants us.

   This petition, which in two or three pages said more than most contemporary historiography, made it clear that what the "true citizens" of Huaraz desired was the peasants' "republican" engagement with the state, where access to the "community of resources," or commons, and protection from abuse were guarded by that state. How? By strictly adhering to the relevant articles of the colonial Laws of the Indies. But these laws had been undermined by "recent political convulsions" and gradually eroded by liberal reforms, including the abolition of "tribute" (the *contribución indígena*) in 1854–55, and thereafter by the abusive access fees charged by landlords. When they rose up in justified anger, as in 1885, their cottages were torched and they were labeled "rebels and savages."

   Whether in the hands of the *mestizo* district governor, Manuel Jurado, who defended Indian access to commons (see chapter 2 above), or in the hands of the protesting *varayoc* of Huaraz, the *Recompilation of the Laws of the Indies,* volumes of which were deposited in *escribanías* all across Spanish America, turned out to be a subversive document. The *Recompilation* was ordered done in the 1620s but was published only in 1681. It was intended not only as an index of the laws of the land but, as David Brading has pointed out, as a legitimation of Spanish or, more precisely, Habsburg-style colonialism.[36] In the more liberal Bourbon (late colonial) and postcolonial periods, this earlier legitimation would be the text most frequently cited by Indian communities and local authorities in defense of their lands and "rights" as Indians.

In the postcolonial history sketched in the petition, the political events of Independence, and of Castilla's liberal abolition of the contribution in 1854, are watersheds. "Indigenous rights" had been steadily eroded during the early Republican period, but the abolition of the contribution made things worse by tempting the appetites of formerly timid landlords. With the abolition of tribute, Indians were made to understand that their community rights had been "correlative" to it. If tribute was abolished, then too was "our community."

The seemingly marginal historical reference to the posting of a broadside in defense of indigenous rights in 1882, when the *caceristas* Bruno Bueno and Justo Solís were in office, was now an important element of political strategy. These men had led the resistance against Chilean and *iglesista* forces. But now they were again in positions of power, and the Indians of Huaraz expected patronage from them. Besides his role as *montonera* commander in the Atusparia insurgency, Justo Solís was also the landlord of Quebrada Shallap, situated above the hamlet of Unchus in La Independencia District. In 1885, Solís had used his local influence to garner Indian support in the district. In response to the *junta departamental*'s summons of all landowner titles to the *quebradas,* Solís readily agreed in 1887 that "from this point forward I concede to the Indians the right to freely extract the firewood they need from Quebrada [Shallap], pruning the trees of their branches in accordance with the restrictions and prohibitions prescribed by the *Recompilation of the Laws of the Indies* invoked by them."[37]

The 1887 petition of the *alcaldes* of Huaraz generated considerable debate in the Departmental Junta of Ancash, the governing body headed by the prefect.[38] A commission was established to study the matter raised by the *alcaldes'* petition, but its members submitted dissonant reports to the junta. The extraordinary session of 12 August is illustrative of the proceedings. After reading the petition of the *alcaldes* and the reports, the floor was opened to debate. Don Manuel Dextre Romero argued that rather than consider the petition of the Indians, it was first necessary to know whether or not the Laws of the Indies cited in the petition were still in effect. As a member of the commission, Don José de la Rosa Sánchez responded that he had taken the precaution of studying the law codes in minute detail, and he had not found that the Laws of the Indies had been anywhere specifically derogated. He noted that all previous laws remain in force in those cases which are not explicitly determined otherwise and that, therefore, in his opinion, the Laws of the Indies were still in force. Dextre Romero later retook the floor and argued at some length that, in the past, the Indians had enjoyed great advantages with the free extraction of firewood from the ravines and that this practice signified considerable losses for landowners. He also complained that the Indians' manufacture of charcoal made use of young trees, a practice, he said, which did permanent damage to the woodstands. The landowners, he argued, were the only ones responsible enough to ensure wise use of the resources. Don César A. E. del Río contradicted Dextre Romero and the others, arguing that if the point under discussion was in fact the competency of the Justice Department, then the central government would request a legal brief from the Supreme Court or from whomever else exercised jurisdiction. As a result, he agreed with Rosa Sánchez that the free and open extraction of firewood from the ravines must, in the meantime, be declared legal. Thereupon the debate heated up to the point that the session had to be briefly adjourned by order of the prefect. Reconvening for a vote, the junta heard the report of Rosa Sánchez and Señor del Río, which argued that the Laws of the Indies were still in force and which was passed by the majority.

The junta then passed a resolution concerning the *alcaldes'* petition. The petition was, in its opinion, "attendable" insofar as the free extraction of firewood and ice went, since the titles presented by the landowners of the *quebradas* of Rurec, Raju-Colta, Quilcayhuanca, Cojup, Collón, and Pariacaca made no mention of the woods and glacial snows contained in the ravines, a fact "which inclined them [the junta] to believe that those resources were reserved for the good of the community." The junta agreed with the petitioners that this right was confirmed by the Indians' customary use of these resources "before and after Independence until the year 1854 when, according to data we have procured, the Indians began to suffer perturbations of their rights of access, which gave rise to several promulgations from the prefecture."

But the same reasoning did not apply to the alpine pastures, the junta argued. These had been acquired by purchase from the colonial state and, thus, were "private property." The pastures, therefore, could not be destined for "common use" without infringing on Article 26 of the Constitution, which guaranteed absolute property rights. Thus, the junta opined that the composition lands which had been "composed with His Majesty" were to be considered private property under the liberal constitution. This was a blow to Indians, for under colonial law "composition lands" in fact had not precluded community rights of access. The legal redefinition of composition lands as private property would now undermine Indian arguments for access to common pastures in the mountains.

In Lima, the Cáceres administration responded positively to the petition of the *alcaldes* of Huaraz. The administration confirmed that the Laws of the Indies were still in force and were therefore to be respected. On 15 October, departmental officials in Huaraz were ordered to accede to the *alcaldes'* demands, since "the Laws [of the Indies] that favor the most numerous part of the population of the Republic, which requires their protection given the exceptional circumstances, are still in force." Moreover, Indians were not to be obliged to work for free in any tasks except those specifically mentioned in the Laws of the Indies. Provincial fiscal agents of the state were to see to it that Indians retained unimpeded access to "pasture, firewood, and ice on lands that are national property, or on those where some legal form of access has been established, with the exception of those duly accredited cases of private ownership of ravines or forested mountains." [39]

For the moment, the Cáceres administration's approach was conciliatory and supportive of "indigenous rights." This gave Huaraz's *alcaldes* reason for hope. As we have seen, the *alcaldes* had sent an earlier petition to Cáceres in March wherein they requested exemption from the poll-tax. Cáceres had not yet responded to that petition, but rumor had it that at least a reduction of the poll-tax (as Cáceres had pledged to Atusparia in 1886) would soon be granted.

Confronting the Poll-Tax

Although no revolt broke out in Huaraz in 1887—thanks largely to the political work of the new prefect, Leonardo Cavero, and to the wait-and-see stance of Huaraz's politically astute *alcaldes*—a revolt against the collection of the poll-tax did take place one year later in Chacas. Chacas was a mining center situated on the eastern side of the Cordillera Blanca, connected with Huaraz and Carhuaz via the rugged mountain pass known as Quebrada Honda, as well as by the Olleros Road, the old east fork of the Inka Way. Prefect Cavero summarized local reports of this revolt in his urgent communication of 30 June 1888 to the Ministry of Government in Lima:

> Whether the Chacas movement may be the first spark in a general conflagration, or simply an essay carried out by the Indians to measure our forces, it is necessary to augment [our forces] in the department immediately if we are to keep this isolated incident from becoming the start of a terrible conflagration. As Your Excellency should know, in Ancash in 1885 there was an indigenous uprising for reasons that are very long to explicate but that can nevertheless be condensed to these two: [1] abuses that the *iglesista* forces committed against them, and [2] the poll-tax. The revolt extended itself . . . from Huaraz, where it originated, to [the provinces of] Huaylas and Huari and could not be contained except with profuse bloodletting, after causing an immense injury and disturbance [of order]. In the present case the cause is not, and cannot, be the same, given that everything is in order and there are no abuses which are not quickly corrected. Nevertheless, the poll-tax . . . is not the most appealing or easily fulfilled obligation among those that the law imposes upon them.[40]

The Cáceres administration had reestablished the poll-tax, with the support of the legislative branch, as part of an experimental "fiscal decentralization" bill. Cáceres had learned from his experience in the resistance that the interior provinces longed for independence from Lima. He also knew that ceding some power to the interior provinces after the war could work to his political advantage. The mechanism for this decentralization of the state would be the separation of departmental budgets from the national treasury. This was an expedient move, since the national treasury was at the moment broke. In the absence of national subsidies from the federal government in Lima (subsidies which the departments had grown accustomed to in the "guano age" before the war) and given the widespread destruction of property, the burden of war reparations, and the subsequent national recession, the only means for satisfying departmental budgets was a poll-tax. The fiscal decentralization plan meant that the poll-tax would provide for the great bulk of the departmental budgets—in the Huaylas case, about 75–80 percent of *projected* revenues. In local terms, this meant that the indigenous majority would pay the salaries of departmental civil servants. But the Cáceres poll-tax lacked the material legitimacy of the earlier "indigenous contribution," which nominally guaranteed access to means of production, and it also lacked the political legitimacy that could follow from the articulation of local Andean social reproduction, and identity, with the authority of the central state and the legitimacy of the *patria*. By decentralizing state finances and designating that the poll-tax would pay for provincial government, Cáceres derailed any possibility of Indians making direct and patriotic "contributions" to the nation. Resistance would continue.

By 1888–89 the financial situation of the departmental administration in Huaraz was desperate. On 21 March 1889, Prefect Cavero wrote glibly to the Ministry of Finance in Lima:

> [It has been] impossible to collect the poll-tax from the Indians in this territory, despite all the efforts of the junta and the state authorities, who have seen their incessant propaganda ridiculed by the tenacious resistance of the Indians. It is thus no longer necessary to demonstrate with new arguments the need to take extraordinary measures in order that the Law [of Fiscal Decentralization] which created this tax be obeyed. [T]his is all the more important in light of the fact that the poll-tax constitutes the most considerable source of revenue in all of the departments [of the interior] and is, if I may say so, the very basis of fiscal decentralization, which can only be imaginary if the poll-tax is not made effective.[41]

Prefect Cavero could not have been more to the point. Without an effective poll-tax, the entire fiscal decentralization program was a cruel illusion. This being the case, the prefect continued, the Superior Court of Ancash had recently come up with a new proposal to make the poll-tax effective. Despite its apparently unconstitutional flavor, Prefect Cavero argued that it was worth considering given the tenacious resistance of the *indígena*, "who refused to meet his civil obligations."

The new proposal was written by Judge Pedro Cisneros on 27 April 1888—fully two months before the Chacas revolt—when he was chief justice and president of the reopened (but chronically underfunded) Superior Court of Ancash. The proposal had been sent to the Justice and Education Ministry in Lima, whose office, noting that the proposal contradicted "the exercise of rights declared by the Constitution," shuffled it off to the Ministry of Finance, where by 1892 it was looked upon favorably by the minister himself.[42]

Cisneros was a venerated lawyer, citizen, and *patriota ilustrado* who had fought against the Chileans in 1879.[43] His proposal is noteworthy in that it argued for a more explicit, and mandatory, republican compact between the state and the Indians. In Cisneros's plan, Indians would not be granted access to the courts that (in theory) protected their rights unless they first presented their poll-tax receipt. In short, Cisneros envisioned a poll-tax paid in exchange for access to the legal defense of Indian rights. That is to say, the justice dispensed by the liberal state would not be liberal, but rather openly conditional (which, in any case, it already was in practice). Since the ever besieged Indians were the ones with the greatest need to avail themselves of those judicial services, Cisneros reasoned, they would promptly pay the poll-tax. It was quite simple: Indians could not afford to forfeit their rights and interests in the courts.

There was a measurable dose of provincial realism in this proposal. It could be said, for example, that Justice Cisneros's proposal was not altogether new, since in some ways it was based on the earlier land-for-tribute pact upheld by the colonial Laws of the Indies. Cisneros had probably heard about, probably even read, the 1887 petition of the *alcaldes* of Huaraz. These were the rights Cisneros had in mind when he argued that Indians would "gladly contribute to the sustenance of the state in exchange for the protection of their laws." The problem with Cisneros's proposal, of course, was that the postcolonial state could not and probably would not be capable of upholding those colonial "rights" in practice. Flaccid nineteenth-century judicial procedures were a dim shadow of the dense paper trail left by more diligent, if excessively *oficialista* colonial courts (themselves frequently incapable, or unwilling, to uphold the much-abused *Leyes de Indias*).

Selected excerpts from this surprising proposal, which reached the central government and the national legislature of Peru (*Cámara de Diputados*), are illustrative of provincial thinking on the poll-tax problem and of the yawning budget gap that crippled departmental administration. Echoing Prefect Cavero, Judge Cisneros began by explaining that departmental budgets were illusory since the poll-tax could not be collected; the imbalance between expenditures and revenues produced chronic budget deficits. Cisneros noted that this deficit would soon put the Ancash court out of business, as it had in the past. This was most serious for Ancash, since it had a huge backlog of cases that had been sent to Lima during the war, when the court was in forced recess. As Prefect Noriega had argued in late 1884, so did Cisneros when he noted that the consolidation of the peace required that justice be enacted in convulsed regions like Huaylas-Ancash. In short, Ancash could not afford to close its court once again, but neither could it afford to operate it unless it "vanquished Indian resistance to the payment of the poll-tax." For Cisneros, "to renounce the poll-tax would be to renounce the food of life in this department and to establish the bases of her future social disorganization." Simply to defer its payment would merely postpone the moment of conflagration.

To employ coercive methods, he argued, would lead only to a repetition of the events of three years past. Moreover, since military force was no longer readily available, it was advisable to adopt measures "whose efficiency is beyond doubt, attending to the character and mode of being of the Indian, who spends the better part of his life tenaciously insistent at the door of the courts and state authorities, where he sacrifices in unauthorized expenses what his own right does not grant him." To clinch his point, Cisneros made a direct appeal to President Cáceres:

> Your Excellency the President knows [the Indian] well . . . for having contemplated [him] . . . during your glorious campaign in the central highlands of the Republic. An order of prevention imposed on all authorities and public functionaries, so that they may not receive or transmit any solicitation from those persons who are obligated to pay the poll-tax but have not fulfilled their obligation, would bring the result that, in addition to a considerable rise in revenues, the Indians would finally comprehend their obligation to contribute to the sustenance of the state in exchange for the protection of their laws.

The Departmental Junta of Ancash adopted the Cisneros proposal on 6 March 1889. It was then Prefect Cavero's duty to send the proposal on to Lima for authorization, which he did on 21 March. By 1892, Cisneros's proposal had been accepted by the minister of finance, who proposed the very same solution to the nation in his Annual Report, or *Memoria,* of that year.[44] But other political actors—in particular the Indian *alcaldes*—were at work in Huaylas-Ancash.

In September of 1889 Cavero resigned as prefect of Ancash to return to his former post as prefect of Cajamarca.[45] Only weeks before resigning, and one year after he had been asked to file a detailed report with the presidential commission on the abolition of community lands established by Cáceres, Prefect Cavero admitted the utter futility of surveying—let alone abolishing—the remaining "community lands" in Huaylas-Ancash:

> Lacking a decent land survey (*catastro*) or statistics . . . to complete the requested report, it was necessary to consult the *indígenas* themselves about the quantity and value of their community lands and production, with which a result completely contrary to the desired one was obtained. The *indígenas*, victims of tyranny and abuse at the hands of

the authorities and individuals of different race, look with the greatest distrust upon . . . them . . . and they studiously hide all that is of interest, fearful of being dispossessed or newly taxed, or of having their hopes deceived once again with the promises that are always made, but seldom kept.[46]

This was but the last in a long series of frustrations that Cavero faced in his attempt to resolve the department's vexing "Indian problem." It was also the last in the series of broken pledges that Cáceres had made to Atusparia in the meeting of 1 June 1886. Shortly after the Cáceres regime was overthrown by Piérola in 1895, Pedro Cisneros would be appointed prefect of Ancash. Although the illusory poll-tax had been rebuked by Piérola during the hostilities between *caceristas* and *coalicionistas* (an alliance of *pierolistas* and old *iglesistas*), by November 1895 Prefect Cisneros endeavored to reestablish the intent to collect what he now called the "merely suspended" poll-tax.[47] But once again the dogged effort to make the poll-tax effective would fail. Weeks later, a bill to legally abolish the poll-tax was introduced in Congress; by the end of December, abolition had been promulgated.

Alcalde Mediation after the Poll-Tax Abolition

After the abolition of the *contribución personal* in late 1895, the *alcaldes* remained as mediators of state–peasantry relations in Huaylas-Ancash. With the poll-tax gone, this mediation would now hinge more exclusively upon purveying "*la república*" (i.e., community labor brigades) for public-works projects. Nearly ten years later—and, indeed, well into the 1920s and Augusto Leguia's new "Ley Vial" (Road Law)—the *alcaldes* were still at the center of tensions between state and peasantry.

In January 1904 a revolt of the "comunidades de indios" of Huaraz, including Vicos (of Carhuaz) and Olleros (now of Recuay), was "discovered" and then apparently subdued when the "subversive" *caudillo* Manuel de la Vega was identified and captured on the streets of Huaraz. Predictably, Prefect Anselmo Huapaya first blamed everything on his political rival, Manuel de la Vega, who was then seeking election to Congress. But the prefect's correspondence with local officials, his local decrees, and to some extent his exchanges with Lima's ministries betray other causes and motives behind the near revolt of 1904. Most significant among these was the prefect's attempt to repress *varayoc* authority.

Prefect Huapaya noted that "the alarm in this capital has . . . been widespread, because the threat of an indigenous uprising has reminded [people] of the horrible acts committed by the Indian rabble in 1885." Following in the counterinsurgent, antilandlord footsteps of Prefect Noriega, Huapaya argued that subversive instigators—in this case, the would-be congressman Manuel de la Vega and the current leaselord of Hacienda Vicos, who was now a Señor Lostaunao—had driven the Indians of Vicos (among others) to revolt against his authority.[48] De la Vega had, in the prefect's conspiratorial (or paranoiac) view, urged the Indians of Vicos to defy the new *contribución rústica* (rural property tax). Apparently the *varayoc* had petitioned the prefecture for a reduction or exoneration of the tax, but when they did so they were violently abused by then president of the *junta departamental*, Don Pedro G. Villón. Pedro Villón had ugly precedents as an oligarch from Yungay whose brother, Manuel Rosas, was commander of the Urban Guard which had massacred Indians in the siege of 1885; Manuel paid with his life. In short, Villón was now the "José Collazos" (the governor who in 1885 ordered Atusparia's capture and torture) of 1904.

In 1904, however, unlike 1885, Prefect Huapaya took decisive preemptive measures to deter rebellion in Huaraz. He blocked a meeting of Indians at the plaza of La Soledad on the 17th of January, and the subprefect had all *chicherías* and liquor stores closed. The Urban Guard was called to duty, and all Indian assemblies were prohibited. The prefect then held a meeting with the Indian *alcaldes,* apparently persuading them to desist from their plans to revolt. He promised that the government would attend to their petition. Then Manuel de la Vega was captured. Still, the prefect wrote to Lima warning that the *alcaldes'* promise not to revolt could not be trusted and that a cavalry force would be required to maintain order.

But of greater interest than Huapaya's official account of the revolt— wherein he took credit for avoiding certain disaster—were the telegrams from distressed local officials in Carhuaz as well as some of the earlier correspondence between Prefect Huapaya and local officials. These communications reveal the pivotal mobilization roles of the *varayoc.* A January 2 telegram from the governor of Carhuaz, Luis B. Torres, advised the prefect:

> I have knowledge that the Indian rabble of this district [Carhuaz] are preparing to revolt. They only await word from the *alcaldes ordinarios* of [Huaraz]. . . . Indicate what measures are to be taken.

Upon being taken into custody, the accused Manuel de la Vega declared to his assistant that Huapaya's decree "that the chiefs of the indigenes not be recognized in the character of authorities, and that they be obliged not to carry the *vara,* which they consider to be a sign of authority and representation, was an injustice that called for violent measures."

In the prefect's counterinsurgent view, Manuel de la Vega was the sole author of the petitions signed by the *varayoc*. De la Vega had "made the *caciques* or *varas* meet to make hostile determinations and form petitions." Denying that the Indians were themselves capable of organized political protest, Huapaya proclaimed that the "horrible" events of 1885 would be repeated when, as he recounted it, "the brutal and savage . . . domination of the cities . . . converted each and every Indian into an authority without any organization or idea of administration . . . to exterminate all those who did not belong to the indigenous communities."[49]

The prefect's accusations against Manuel de la Vega were predictable: such accusations inevitably appear in every peasant revolt or near revolt in Ancash (most notably in 1854, 1885, 1887–88, and 1904). The politics of these official, counterinsurgent representations of the conflict were multifarious. On the one hand, the prefect was interested both in bolstering his image before his superiors in Lima and in defeating his local opponents in political battle. Taking energetic and diligent steps to avoid a conflagration, then nabbing the rebel leader, filled this bill. On the other hand, Andean peasants and their leaders were probably content to place the blame on a *misti caudillo*, since this deflected the repression that would inevitably follow.

Yet the nonrevolt of 1904 appears to have had an immediate cause not dissimilar to that which sparked the real revolt of 1885. This time the insults hurled at the *varayoc* (who, as in 1885, had ventured forth peacefully with a petition) came from the president of the *junta departamental* rather than from the district governor (in 1885, José Collazos). The injustice that nearly provoked violence was the proposed abolition of the *varayoc* themselves (concretely, the prefect's decree which prohibited them from carrying their *varas*, or staffs of office). Revolt was averted by negotiation with the *alcaldes*, and by the subsequent reversal of the abolition.

The centrality of the "*vara* question"[50] is confirmed by subsequent events recorded in the prefect's correspondence with Lima. Huapaya's liberal and anticlerical assault on Indian *vara* authority was made manifest in his note of 11 March to the Ministry of Government, where Huapaya accused the clergy of abusing Indians and of upholding—indeed, giving their blessing to—illegal *vara* authority. Huapaya informed Lima that he had abolished unpaid public-works labor and, with it, the *alcaldes* who purveyed it. Echoing Bolívar's 1825 decree, Huapaya declared that Indians and the clergy must recognize no other authorities "except those determined by the Constitution of the state." He ordered that parish priests stop "blessing the *varas* and taking oaths of office from the Indians as *alcaldes ordinarios* or *pedáneos*, because these offices are not recognized under the law." In his publicized broadside, the prefect expanded his attack on the *alcaldes* by resorting to the proven rhetorical tools of colonialism. As in the colonial crisis years of the 1570s, 1780s, and 1820s, Andean leaders were now labeled "despotic *caciques*" and "the worst exploiters of their kind," so as to justify their convenient removal (Bolívar was the last to do this). Indeed, the prefect would go so far as to claim that the "titular *alcaldes*" and their indigenous followers constituted an "independent state" within the department:

> [T]hose who have most abused the indigenes are the titular *alcaldes ordinarios* and *pedáneos* who dominate the communities and exercise all faculties in them, in effect making, if you will, an independent state of the indigenes in this department. With the object of correcting this evil, and to put an end to the titular *alcaldes'* continued exploitation of the indigenes . . . it is right . . . to suppress those selfsame authorities so that [the indigenes] submit to those authorities determined by law.[51]

This is the last we hear from Prefect Huapaya, but it was not the last word on the *alcaldes*. On 31 August the new prefect, Eulogio Saldías, notified the Ministry of Government that he had decided to recognize the offices of the *alcaldes* "for reasons of legality and practical prudence." The Indians, he continued, "have been exercising these offices since time immemorial; and apart from the fact that they are not expressly forbidden by law, they tend to be just one more set of agents who carry out the orders of the constituted authorities, thus consulting in the harmony and subordination of the classes that they represent."

Before re-recognizing the *vara* authorities, Prefect Saldías had solicited the legal opinion of a justice of the Superior Court of Ancash. The justice argued that by merely renaming the Andean authorities, the constitutional problem posed by their existence might be conveniently removed. Perhaps Saldías's error was in not accepting the judge's practical legal advice on the matter. In any case, Prefect Saldías retained and recognized the colonial *alcalde ordinario* title in his decree. The response from Lima should have been expected. According to the Ministry of Government, the *alcaldes ordinarios* had ceased to exist in 1821,[52] so recognizing them in 1904 was nothing short of folly. Prefect Saldías was informed by his superiors that the decree was void, "insubsistente."

Nevertheless, Saldías proceeded with the formal recognition of the Indian *alcaldes*. He did this out of fear that he would lose all measure of control over the communities and, more particularly, that he would not be able to procure the "la república" Indian labor he required to carry out planned public-works projects. He was right on both counts. Saldías noted that the *alcaldes* "have always had the object of contributing, with the prestige they efficiently exercise over their kind, to the realization of the orders decreed by the constituted authorities. [Moreover,] the suppression of said *alcaldes* may originate resentments that can be dangerous . . . and will also drive away the communities that are obliged to work on public works projects."

Prefect Saldías did not learn of the ministry's decision to reject his decree until a copy of the response—printed in a Lima newspaper—arrived in the mails. He responded to the ministry on 18 October, arguing once again that the *varayoc* were the key to a prudent form of republican indirect rule over the Indian communities (but now deleting the *ordinario* title in favor of *pedáneo*):

> By way of the newspapers of the capital of the Republic, which were received in yesterday's mail, has come the news that the Supreme Government has declared incompetent the decree made by this prefecture concerning the function of the *alcaldes pedáneos*. The circulation of this news has produced certain rumors that may bring very difficult complications. The *alcaldes pedáneos*—that is to say, the special authority exercised by qualified Indians over their communities, and which are the most populous in this department—apart from being a venerated custom not incompatible with the law, contribute to maintaining the indigenes within the reach of the respective authorities, subordinated to them as they are now, conciliatory and respectful in everything. But if they take the *vara* of *alcalde* away from them, which they exercise as a symbol of authority over all the communities, then it is not difficult to foresee what will happen, taking into consideration that the uprisings in the department have always obeyed the resentments and susceptibilities of these frightful people. This is why I have taken and take special care to grant all manner of guarantees, within the limits of the law, to them. And it is thus that they remain grateful, humble, and very obedient. I make these reflections so that the Supreme Government [may] take them into consideration. The contrary case may produce a cataclysm that administrative prudence advises us to prevent.[53]

The contrasting positions on the "*vara* question" held by Prefects Huapaya and Saldías in 1904 point to the resilience of Indian *alcalde* authorities some twenty years after the repression of the Atusparia insurgency. Although the abolition of the poll-tax in 1895 shifted the locus of the "Indian problem" away from the poll-tax to the corvée labor question (and later to the *enganche*, or "labor hooking," problem, which became a favorite target of the indigenists), the Indian *varayoc* authorities remained pivotal.[54] Without them, the "constituted" state authorities could not count on a labor supply for public works. With them, they could not have unimpeded access to atomized Indian citizens. In short, republican order depended upon the subaltern *alcalde* authorities.

Alcaldes and Nation

In her comparative analysis of regional responses to the Chilean occupation and civil war in Cajamarca and Junín—highland regions that lie directly north and south of Huaylas-Ancash—Florencia Mallon demonstrated that each of the two regions experienced the formation of peasant *montoneras* and multiethnic or multiclass coalitions. Only one particular microregion of Junín, centered around Comas, was able to develop an "authentic" peasant nationalism in the face of occupation and repression, however. In the Junín region, a "community tradition" underlay the particular viability of an alternative "peasant protonationalism," which emerged in the "defense of homeland" against Chilean invaders and rapacious Peruvian landlords. But in Cajamarca, the absence of such a community tradition undercut this historical possibility. Instead, an antistate (and anti-fiscal) coalition of landlords and their dependent peons formed around the *montoneras* of Puga and Becerra. Mallon concluded that

> while we would have to compare the Comasinos to peasants from more heavily indigenous regions in order to weigh the ethnic factor more completely, certainly the Andean tradition of reemerging protonationalism, in which the Comasinos also shared, provided a framework that facilitated the emergence of a certain nationalist perspective. In combination with the harshness of the Chilean invasion in the central highlands and the resilience of their own local communal institutions, the Andean tradition provided Comas peasants with the resources to fashion their own particular vision of the nation. . . . [T]he Comasinos envisioned a society in which local autonomy would nurture local prosperity, without landowner oppression or state exactions, and where a large confederation could handle commerce, infrastructure, and a common defense. It recognized the need for alliance with other classes, and for help from leaders who had a broader political preparation and vision. . . . Yet it is here that the development of nationalist consciousness [among the peasantry] came into conflict with the process of national unification. Once the war was over, the easiest and most viable class base for reconstruction was the landowning oligarchy. A peasant program for reform, for nation-building, was fundamentally at odds with such a base. Given the regionalization of class formation

and class conflict before the war, and the diverse wartime experiences of the various regions, there were no allies in other parts of the country who might have collaborated in constructing a different nation-building coalition.[55]

Mallon's comparative analysis raises many critical questions to which the Huaylas-Ancash experience may offer partial answers. Perhaps it is sufficient to note that the "federal state" declared by the Comasino peasant movement in 1888 probably would have found many allies in and around Huaraz. That the two, not-too-distant regions and peasantries did not connect is a telling consequence not only of the tragic history of misencounter which marked the Atusparia insurgency, but also of the particular legacy of "dislocation" and intensified regionalism that followed from Peru's late nineteenth-century fiscal politics.

Huaylas-Ancash, like Cajamarca and Junín, experienced a Chilean invasion and the formation of collaborationist and nationalist resistance forces. In Huaylas-Ancash, though, the nationalist resistance developed somewhat later than in Junín or Cajamarca, largely because an oppressive Chilean presence was insignificant before June 1883. The late timing of peasant mobilization gave it a particularly divisive character, since by this date the primary enemies of the peasantry in Huaylas-Ancash were no longer the Chileans but, rather, their Peruvian collaborators, the *iglesistas*, and the local social sectors that supported them. Among other misencounters, the critical absence of Puga, the phantom *caudillo* of 1885, and the poor timing of the meeting with the defeated Cáceres after Huamachuco in 1883 (see chapter 3 above) meant that the nationalist potential of Andean peasants in Huaylas-Ancash would be squandered.

Huaylas-Ancash had communities of a particular kind, but what was decisive for political mobilization and for the long-term formation of "republicano" political practice was the pan-communal system of subaltern authorities. In Huaylas-Ancash, the reemergent vitality of supracommunity, district-level linkages, sustained by the *alcalde* network, provided the base for regional peasant mobilization despite the presence of encroaching *haciendas*. District *varayoc* organizations, which could include blocks of up to twenty-four Indian hamlets, proved capable of building pan-district alliances with other *alcaldes*, as in the cases of Huaraz, Carhuaz, and Chacas in 1888, as well as with non-Indian *caceristas* of the nationalist resistance.

Although the evidence for wide peasant mobilization in Huaylas-Ancash is clear enough, the question of its flowering into a heightened or "accelerated" form of political consciousness remains elusive. Whereas in Comas

(Junín) a nationalist "federal state" was declared and defended, in Huaylas-Ancash a peasant federation of *alcaldes* already existed, albeit in subaltern relationship to the departmental state. None of the heroic *alcaldes*, such as Pedro Pablo Atusparia, would proclaim a semiautonomous "peasant federation" or "federal state." Rather, Atusparia and other *alcaldes*, in the spirit of what may be called a historically specific form of Andean peasant "republicanism," hailed General Cáceres, the symbolic and military leader of the resistance, as "The Great Republican." In Comas, the peasant federation was repressed and dissolved in 1902. In Huaraz, there was no "federation" to repress and pacify. Instead, the entire Indian political structure of "republicanos" and their *varayoc* authorities was now deemed threatening to the authoritative claims of the legally constituted state officials. Thus, the liberalizing Prefect Huapaya sought to abolish the "despotic" *alcaldes* in 1904. But Huapaya was impractical. His successor, Prefect Saldías, knew better. He prudently reinstated the *alcaldes*, despite strong objections from Lima's Ministry of Government.

The Modern Indigenization of Huaylas-Ancash

The pressing necessity, and active political presence, of subaltern *alcalde* mediation in the state–peasantry relations of postcolonial Huaylas-Ancash implicated an underlying social and demographic trend: the modern "indigenization" of the region in the late nineteenth and early twentieth centuries. Although savagely repressed, Andean peasant *republicanos* and their authorities, the *alcaldes*, were now a growing majority, and they employed the strength of their numbers to curb abuses, and to negotiate with the Peruvian state.

The official ratio of *castas* to *indígenas* in Huaylas-Ancash was balanced between 1791 and 1848–50 (51 percent indigenous, 48 percent nonindigenous). But after abolition of the early republican contribution, a marked "Indianization" or indigenization trend erased the earlier balance, and a new politics of race emerged in Huaylas-Ancash.[56] Between 1791 and 1876 much of Andean Peru recorded a gradual increase in the official indigenous population count. Still, the nineteenth-century Indianization of highland Peru did not occur everywhere, nor did it occur at the same rates in those regions which experienced an official rise in their Indian populations. Although Paul Gootenberg has demonstrated that this early nineteenth-century Indianization trend was not so accentuated as Kubler had maintained,[57] one cannot argue with Kubler's general assertion that "Indian Peru was more extensive in 1876 than in 1795, and it was growing faster than mestizo Peru in 1876."[58]

In 1876, Huaylas-Ancash's official census count yielded 57 percent indigenous, 33 percent *mestizo,* and 10 percent white. By 1940, however, 62 percent were classified as indigenous, and 38 percent fell into the combined "*mestizo*-white" category. In other words, between 1791 and 1940 the indigenous/nonindigenous ratio had shifted dramatically from nearly 1:1 to almost 2:1. The Callejón de Huaylas had looked far more *mestizo* and "integrated," or racially balanced, in 1791 or 1830 than it would after 1876. The national census for 1940 also revealed that most people in Huaylas were monolingual Quechua speakers, while 95 percent of the total population could speak Quechua. The latter figure suggests a high degree of bilingualism among *mestizos.* The same tendency was evident among Indian males, about one-third of whom were bilingual. This bilingualism, together with the pervasiveness of Quechua as the primary medium of social exchange, suggests that liberal modernization theory's expected tide of acculturation and Hispanization via *mestizaje* had not occurred. Another republican reality was in formation.

The relatively late indigenization of Huaylas-Ancash, however, was contrary to the aggregate national trend, which was driven by coastal population growth in and around the cities and which, after 1876, but most markedly around 1900, moved in the direction of official *mestizaje.*[59] Among Peruvian highland provinces, though, Huaylas-Huaraz was not alone in bucking the national trend. According to Kubler, significant percentage gains in the indigenous population between 1876 and 1940 were made in two large "ethnogeographical islands," one centered in the north around the Callejón de Huaylas, the other in the southern region stretching from Huancayo to Puno, in the zone known despectively as the *mancha india.* In other words, most of highland Peru, with the exception of the northern highlands (Piura, Cajamarca, La Libertad) and part of the north-central highlands (Huanuco, and the northern part of Junín), was now more "indigenous."[60]

According to the census, the classificatory language of which is manifestly subjective and historical,[61] the indigenization of much of the Peruvian sierra (and the Creolization of the coastal and *montaña,* or submontane, areas) is modern. As Kubler observed, "in the perspective of a century and a half [1790–1940], the sharp definition and geographical segregation of caste-identified territories (mestizo coast and *montaña* vs. Indian highlands) has become a political reality only in the years before 1940."[62] The heightened discourse of Peruvian dualism, which paradoxically essentialized and "othered" the Peruvian sierra as "natural" and "indigenous" as it refocused national discourse on "the Indian" as victimized subject, also dates from "the years before 1940," that is, the late nineteenth-century period of scientific racism followed by early twentieth-century indigenism.[63]

The "Race" without History

In the *El Comercio* edition of 29 May 1885, the editor Luis Carranza printed his long essay titled "The Intellectual and Physical Capacities of the Indigenous Race of Peru." The essay echoed the late nineteenth-century caricature of the Peruvian Indian as "indio manso" (cowed or docile Indian) then popular among the Creole elite. In the early stages of the war with Chile, Creole literati echoed these sentiments, as when Ricardo Palma contrasted the assumed docility of Peruvian Indians with the famed "bravura," or warriorlike qualities of the "Araucanian race" of Chile.[64] But Carranza, director of Peru's leading liberal newspaper, *El Comercio*, was from the highlands (Ayacucho), quite possibly of *mestizo* origin, and he had been Andrés Cáceres's "chief publicist while fighting with [the] legendary Andean *guerrillas*." He had become "a charter member of the . . . Society of Friends of the Indians (*Sociedad Amiga de los Indios*)," founded in the 1860s, and was also a congressman and "founder of the Partido Civil." And "after the war [he] created and led the prestigious *Sociedad Geográfica de Lima*, the new scientific beacon for greater Peruvian awareness."[65] Carranza was clearly a credentialed figure with experience and influence in powerful circles.

Gootenberg argues that one aim of Carranza's 1883 essay, "Consideraciones generales sobre el centro," written during the La Breña campaign, was "to herald 'the *raza indígena del Perú* [as] no inconvenience or fetter to national progress and greatness.'" In the 1883 essay, Carranza traces the "passivity" of Indians to "Peru's nineteenth-century commercial centralism, which enervated the Indian's natural 'activity' and stamina of Incan and Spanish times."[66] In short, Carranza here implicates Peru's postcolonial legacy of guano-age centralism and republican misrule as proximate causes of the Indian's "degradation." But in May 1885 Carranza would publish a very different essay on the "capacity" of the Peruvian Indian. The 29 May 1885 essay, printed on the very same page as Prefect Noriega's letter describing the violent events of the Atusparia insurgency, was far less optimistic about the "indigenous race of Peru"—indeed, it was irrevocably racist. Andeans were now irremediably mired in the compounded legacies of Inka and Spanish despotism, legacies which had been transmuted, in Lamarckian fashion, into biological traits: low foreheads, strong backs, an inherent absence of sensibility, brutishness, immobility. Why the shift? It is possible that Carranza discovered scientific racism in these years (further research is required), but it is also thinkable that the rapid shift in perspective reflected the new consensus among the *cacerista* elite, which now closed ranks with *iglesistas* in repressing "the indigenous race" and getting on with the task of ruling Peru. This rule and its racist discourse would not pass uncontested, however. A satirical reply, printed in the 30 May edition of *El Comercio* and anonymously signed "Un Mestizo," confirmed the conjunctural, historicist reading of Carranza's essay. For the anonymous "Mestizo," Carranza's reflections were an appropriate point of reference for raising the question of the Peruvian elite's compliance with a campaign of genocide.

Carranza's 1885 essay, which was later reprinted in the same collection of essays that included the 1883 piece,[67] included the following passages:

> The *indígena* of the cordillera is a robust being, strong to resist the fatigue of long journeys on foot, and capable of carrying heavy loads on his back for great distances. . . . In the eyes of a doctor he offers a lymphatic temperament, accentuated in his physical constitution as much as it is in the attributes of his character. His sad and severe physiognomy, with a certain strange mixture of malicious distraction, is that of a being who revels in a paralyzed intellect in the midst of a slow but certain progress. Craniologically, he belongs to those races in which the anterior lobes still have not reached the plenitude of their development.

Following this evolutionist physical anthropology concerning the "natural capacity" of the robust "indigenous race of Peru" for carrying heavy cargo on its back, and having noted the "underdeveloped frontal lobes" and inferior cranial capacity of that race, Carranza proceeded to establish the "artistic inferiority" of the Indian as well. Following his analysis of Indian aesthetics, or rather the lack thereof, Carranza argued—in the characteristically Lamarckian terms of late nineteenth-century Creole positivism—that the intellectual stasis of the "indigenous race of Peru" was caused by a historical event: the profound trauma of the Spanish Conquest.

> It is above all else necessary to keep in mind that the Indian of today is in intellectual capacity the same as [he was] in the age of the [Inka] Empire. The Conquest, far from communicating a new impulse to the intelligence of the Indian, actually paralyzed it. The spirit of this race appears to have suffered a trauma so profound that it left it immobile at a point in its progressive evolution, and since then it has remained in complete immutability, such that psychologically the Indian of our day is in the order of moral types what the mammoth preserved in the snows of the Siberian Sea is in the order of organic types.

Carranza then turned to yet another diagnostic theme of late nineteenth-century Creole discourse on the Indian, that of Indian passivity in the face of misfortune. The cowed Indians could not express, but only swallow, their rage:

> If at some time the sentiments of hate and revenge torment the soul of the Indian, he is not capable of giving himself over to the transcendence of virile fury, in which man finds in himself unknown strengths with which to challenge humanity and his destiny. . . . The idea of resistance, the sentiment of struggle, appears foreign to the character of the people dominated by the Inkas.

On the other hand, effective counterinsurgent propaganda and local, "white" racist images of "the indigenous race" in Huaylas-Ancash in 1885 contrasted sharply with Carranza's depiction of a passive and sullen people. The Indian in restless Huaraz was not the *indio manso* of the studied Creole imagination, but rather the *indio bravo* who, collectively, was known as "the savage horde" and "the barbarian" who now unleashed "race war" on whites. The Peruvian historian Nelson Manrique has argued that Chilean soldiers, influenced by their recent experience in Chile's genocidal "Indian wars" against the Araucanians, carried the *indio bravo* image with them to Peru. The result, says Manrique, was the brutal massacre of Peruvian Indian peasants in manifestly racist acts of excessive violence.[68] But the same could be said of the untimely repression suffered by the Atusparia insurgents at the hands of Peruvian "pacification forces." At the local commemoration ceremony of gratitude, held in Huaraz on 11 June 1885 and organized by local "notables" in honor of Prefect Iraola and his victorious pacification force, the "indigenous sublevation" was described as a contest between the "barbarism" of the "Indian rabble" and the "civilization" and "humanity" of the "decent people" of the towns. Iraola, echoing statements made in his correspondence with the *cacerista* prefect Manuel Mosquera at the bloody siege of Yungay, declared that his own battle and that of his brave soldiers had been "to defend a sacred principle of humanity." In his ceremonious eulogy to Iraola, the mayor of Huaraz compared the "blind masses . . . with the Barbarians of the North, adding that had the Indian rabble been victorious, it would have brought, in addition to barbarity, the reign of darkness."[69] Such rhetoric justified the massacre of the "blind masses" who, as the field commander put it, would be made to "pay very dearly for their temerity," and it implicitly waived aside the anticipated accusations of genocide.[70] No one knows exactly how many peasants died in Ancash in 1885, but the number was probably in the thousands.[71]

Although the Atusparia insurgency was not "race war," the persecution of *alcaldes* and the exemplary killing of "savage hordes" at the hands of "pacifying" and "civilizing" *iglesistas,* and the ready collaboration of significant segments of the town population, tipped the scales of political protest toward social and ethnic rage. In the end, *cacerista* and *iglesista* elites would, as William Stein argued, cut their losses and close ranks against the threat of social war from below. The "social war" would be subsumed as "race war" by elites of all persuasions. More than a convenient cover-up, however, the label of "race war" reflected deep paranoia harbored both by provincial and by national elites. Such fears were repeatedly expressed by worried prefects in the tense decades following 1885. Olívas Escudero's reflections on the Atusparia insurgency, written in 1887, revealed that the *indio manso* and *indio bravo* images could, at least in Huaraz, be the sobering poles of a single continuum that now haunted elite consciousness.[72] The learned Ancash priest wrote: "That . . . race war . . . a horrible picture splattered with blood and covered with hundreds of cadavers, and perpetually oscillating in our memory [might] give us lessons in prudence, justice, and discretion in our domestic and social relations with a race that, although noble and timid by nature, has the cleverness of a serpent and the ferocity of the savage whenever the limits of order are transgressed."[73] This "horrible picture" would endure.[74]

In his study of the events of 1885, Stein argued that the image of the Atusparia insurgency as "race war" was fabricated after the fact in the partisan pages of Lima's newspapers. There is little doubt that the race card was played both to deny the political intent of peasant actions and to relieve *cacerista* participants of responsibility "before history and the nation." But such denials of peasant political intent are common among elites everywhere. In this case, racist images of Indians in newsprint were by no means limited to ideologized depictions of the Atusparia insurgency, as Carranza's timely text illustrates. Notions of an inferior, passive race, well disposed to backbreaking work, lacking in intelligence, frozen in time by the Spanish Conquest as sentimental vestiges of Inka despotism, politically inept and without ambition for a higher destiny, contributed to the postwar elite consensus that, given this degraded state, "Peruvian Indians" were simply incapable of rising to the test of patriotism in the face of "wars of conquest" such as the one just suffered at the hands of the Chileans.

Yet this rationalized, Lamarckian racism that depicted Indians as sullen and immobile was itself haunted by a shadowy, historical fear of "race war." This fear was larger than the Atusparia insurgency, and it frequently found its way into newsprint in nineteenth-century Peru. It may be traceable to the Tupac Amaru II insurrection of 1780. The Atusparia insurgency—particularly the initial reports from *iglesistas* which appeared in Lima's newspapers—had fanned that flame, and reactionaries kept it stoked. The *pierolista* newspaper *El País*, which defended the uprising as understandable given the "extortions" and "abuses" of "certain authorities," noted on 7 May 1885 that "the simultaneity of the uprisings in the provinces and a certain mark of barbarism . . . have served as grounds for those who judge things based on appearances, who now affirm that the numerous bands spread all over the Department [of Ancash] are the race-hating legions of extermination, and [that] their chief [is] the Inka-King, another Tupac Amaru, restorer of the old empire. None of that is serious . . ." But it was serious for the *iglesista* newspaper, *El Campeón*, which attacked the *El País* editorial on 12 May 1885. Atusparia, *El Campeón* agreed, was no Inka (that claim was no longer serious), but he was certainly a "criminal" who wrought "race war" on whites, and he was also a "communist" for having led "the hordes" who pillaged and destroyed property. Those things were serious. An expedition would be sent and thousands would die for it.

But the last word, which was written in response to Carranza's essay, must go to the unnamed "Mestizo" who slyly responded to the editor in a letter printed in the 30 May edition of *El Comercio*. One may speculate that this anonymous "Mestizo" sympathized not only with the more radical elements of the *cacerista* cause, but also with the attention that Carranza's essay bestowed:

> We have much of the Indian [in us]: that is why we are grateful and faithful as a dog to those who love us and give us affection. The notes on our race published yesterday in *El Comercio*, which we read with much pleasure, commend our gratitude to the author, and we publicly manifest it here, discharging a sacred duty. It consoles the soul that while writers here generally occupy themselves with Russia, Turkey, or the Sudan, there is someone in Peru who is interested in the Peruvian Indians. We must acknowledge this exceptional preference of the author of these notes for the love it reveals for our race, and because today they brag about killing us by the thousands at the same time that they go to great lengths and expense to import a few hundred Chinese coolies because of a lack of manpower. How could we not be grateful to our incognito benefactor, when a few days ago one of those big capitalists,[75] overhearing someone read the military report from Huaraz

[printed on the same page], in which it was said that they had shot and killed 2,000 Indians, said: "All the better, there are too many Indians in Peru." Without the Indians, does this Señor think that Peru could govern itself, or defend itself from wars of conquest? If they kill us all, how many will remain of the other castes? You count them.
Un Mestizo.

CHAPTER 5

Republican Histories, Postcolonial Legacies

If Indians did count in Peru's republican history, what did their presence amount to? Mere cannon fodder for campaigning *caudillos*, or tax pesos for the national treasury? With enemies like "those big capitalists" and "friends" and "incognito benefactors" like Carranza, these certainly *were* important. But if we hesitate at elite claims to a monopoly on civilization, and upturn the discourses of counterinsurgency and race, then other questions emerge. The following, perhaps, is central: What kinds of political culture took shape among Peru's Andean peasantry between the repression of the insurgent "Inka Nationalism" of Tupac Amaru II in the 1780s and the rise of a radical but essentializing indigenism in the Peru of Mariátegui? The intervening nineteenth century—the foundational period of Peruvian nationbuilding—has all the signs of an Andean dystopia, of the Creole political imagination's misencounter with Andean aspirations. With momentary exceptions, the national community imagined by Peruvian Creoles elided the indigenous majority.[1] Yet the republican histories of Andean peasants in Huaylas-Ancash suggest that in the dark shadows cast by the "enlightened" discursive framework of the Creole national state, *un*imagined political communities coalesced in the redeployment of colonial "indigenous rights." This redeployment of indigenous or "republicano" rights constituted an avenue of political reinsertion in the postcolonial Republic and its history.

Republican Histories: Between "Inka Nationalism" and Indigenist Essentialism

In his classic essay on peasants and "modern" politics, Eric Hobsbawm remarked that "most of history is that of traditional peasants in traditional politics, but what [I am] chiefly concerned with is what happens when traditional peasants get involved in modern politics: a transitional situation, but one which for many parts of the world is of practical, and not merely of historical interest."[2] If "colonial" is substituted for "traditional," and "post-colonial" or "national" for "modern," then Hobsbawm's interest is shared by the present book. Ergo: What happened to the political worlds of Andean peasants in the transition from colonial to national rule, and from tributary to liberal fiscal regimes, and what did it mean for Peru's postcolonial nation-making process? Hobsbawm argued that, for peasants, the quintessential political problem posed by the development of a national state lies in the scale of peasant worlds. Peasants' horizons are, for Hobsbawm, "the parish pump or the universe," not the national state.[3] Translated (for the moment, ahistorically) into the case of Andean Peru—which also clearly informed Hobsbawm's essay—this might mean the *doctrina* (in our case, Huaraz), on the one hand, and Tawantinsuyo (the known universe of Quechua or *runa* peoples, the invoked "Inka realm") on the other. There are numerous historical examples of peasant rebellions and revolts in the Peruvian Andes which have been classified under one or the other of these spatial and political horizons.[4] The Andean historical experience, however, suggests that the critical question of the scale of peasant political worlds is not simply "structural," but culturally and historically contingent.[5]

In Peru's "Age of Andean Insurrection" (ca. 1742–82)[6] peasant rebellion occurred on a pan-regional scale (insurrection rocked central and southern Peru as well as Bolivia, and echoes were heard far beyond) and was made possible by at least three factors: (a) the articulating tributary relations of the colonial state; (b) the mercantile circuits traveled by Andean ethnic chiefs, or *kurakas;* and, perhaps most critical, (c) the emergence of "Inka nationalist" ideologies, which idealized (and prophesied the return of) Inka rule as an indigenous alternative to Spanish colonial administration.[7] However, the cultural and political repression of the colonial chiefs under the Bourbon *visitador* (viceregal inspector) Areche, the reformist intendancy regime, and finally Bolívar dealt historical blows to chiefly expressions of "Inka nationalism."[8] The so-called Andean utopia of Tupac Amaru II and other late colonial "Inka nationalists" would be displaced in the postcolonial period, only to be resurrected early in the twentieth century, albeit now under the auspices of radical (non-Indian) indigenist intellectuals.[9] In the early nineteenth century, the specter of another Tupac Amaru–like rebellion had made Peru's Creole elite more hesitant and practically guaranteed the ambivalent, nonnative flavor of Independence in Peru.[10]

In the postcolonial period, markets and politics became increasingly regionalized under *caudillo*-ridden regimes and, later, under the Lima-centered liberal state, dislocated.[11] Most nineteenth-century peasant uprisings in Peru would not spread beyond particular regions or even, in most cases, beyond local parishes. But some nineteenth-century peasant protests did reach beyond "the parish pump," connecting with regional movements and occasionally (although rarely effectively) with national leadership. The period of Creole national and civil wars in late nineteenth-century Peru (as in Bolivia and Ecuador)[12] produced just such a conjuncture of peasant political engagement. Yet this late-century engagement, which in the case of Huaylas-Ancash saw the Atusparia insurgency, did not appear suddenly out of a passive, disengaged past. As Platt and Mallon have argued,[13] it emerged through longer-term political relations between Andean peasants, provincial elites, and the national state.

As Andean peasants found themselves in the hybrid postcolonial predicament generated by the contradictions of making a national citizen-state in Peru, with its incomplete liberalization of individuals, lands, and taxation, they would deploy and reinvent an active "republicano" political culture of colonial origin. Yet it was not merely the paper existence of "Indian rights" in the *Leyes de Indias* that was reinscribed in postcolonial politics, but also the precedence of particular legal battles won in colonial courts (and upheld in early republican courts). In the discursive struggle to defend those "rights," peasants, via *alcalde* and legal mediators, engaged the dominant "discursive frameworks" of the courts and the liberal state in locally meaningful ways. In the process, peasants redefined their relationship to the larger political community subject to Peruvian law and destabilized exclusionary, official notions of "republican" citizenship.

Andean peasant "republics" (colonial or postcolonial) did not much resemble Plato's (or even Bolívar's), however. Although inhabited by Quechua language and localistic peasant political culture, Andean political communities were also articulated with wider church and state structures, and to national (and imperial) discourses. Village "republicans" could logically consider themselves to be "true citizens of the nation," although the dominant Creole political discourse rarely imagined them as such. In Huaylas-Ancash, peasant notions of "republicanism" could, by 1885, momentarily entertain General Cáceres, the hero of the nationalist resistance against Chilean occupation, as "El Gran Republicano"—and not as the messianic "Inka king" of indigenist lore.[14] The reverse, however, was not true: Creole elites had great difficulty imagining indigenous peasants as "great republicans."

In postcolonial Huaylas-Ancash, Andean peasant communities "continually engaged their political worlds,"[15] even as the terms of that engagement shifted over time. Central to this shifting engagement was the uneven mediation of the *alcaldes*. The Indian *varayoc* or staff-holding head-men, represented subaltern political organization, officially unrecognized by the liberal state (even though frequently indispensable to departmental and municipal government). The first *alcalde* posts were established in the early colonial period of the Toledan reforms (1560s–70s). One or two-year rotations filled by election, these posts were created to check the local power of chiefs, to serve the parish priests, and in general to provide the local police and judicial functions demanded by the neo-Mediterranean model of civil society known as *res publica* and, in this instance, as the *república de indios*. In practice, the early colonial *alcaldes* of Huaylas were literate, were chosen by consensus and prestige, were supporters of chiefly interests, and were drawn from the lesser native "nobility," known as *principales*. The *alcalde ordinario*, as opposed to the powerful *alcalde mayor*, who was drawn from the chiefly class, may have been less transculturated than the Hispanized chiefs.[16] Un-like the *alcaldes*, the colonial chiefs (*kurakas*) had been officially recognized as ethnic political authorities and subordinate colonial administrators of the "Indian republic." After 1783 the political role of the chiefs was curbed as *mestizo* "neo-*caciques*," who held the official posts of "governor" and "trib-ute collector," were often appointed to assume duties previously assigned to the chiefs. With the decline of chiefly functions in the late eighteenth century, the *alcaldes* would emerge in the 1790s and subsequent decades as representatives of Indian communities, often leading protests against ille-gitimate *caciques*. The *alcaldes* of the late Intendancy period became the primary purveyors of the new "contribution." After Independence, the re-maining hereditary chiefs of Huaylas were stripped of their titles and privi-leges as representatives of Indian communities.

In the post-Independence period, however, the *alcaldes* were subordi-nated to an array of petty *misti* (non-Indian) officials. Fiscal relations be-tween the state and the Andean peasantry become both more direct and increasingly entangled in petty clientage, and as a result the *alcaldes* receded as political mediators, despite their officially unrecognized role as local pur-veyors of the "contribution." With the "dislocation" of state–peasantry tributary relations under the fiscally autonomous "guano state" (ca. 1854–79) and increasingly so after the national disaster of the War of the Pacific (1879–83), the *alcaldes* reemerged as key political actors mediating state-peasantry relations. By the early twentieth century, their presence as indis-pensable mediators between departmental officials and the peasantry could be seen to threaten the "legally constituted authorities" of the national state, and could also effectively undermine the "national reconstruction" and liberal nationbuilding programs of the *cacerista* and *pierolista* military regimes (ca. 1886–1904).

The decline of the colonial chiefs and the emergence of an expedient, republican dependency on the *alcaldes* had profound political and cultural consequences for the modern history of Andean peoples. The shift from dual colonial republics toward a unitary liberal republic undermined the fragile logic of indirect rule, opening the gates to direct state domination over, and atomization of, Andean peasant societies. The colonial chiefs, who frequently held office by bloodright and for the duration of their adult lives, were usually literate in Spanish and well versed in Quechua language and culture. They had been the mediating "intellectuals" of colonial rule.[17] The postcolonial *alcaldes*, however, were local justices of the peace with tax-collection and policing roles, and they rotated into office for one year and then left. Most were either illiterate or semiliterate. They accumulated significant and legitimate prestige as respected figures in community politics, but they were rather less than the socially mediating intellectuals of colonial rule that the chiefs could be; thus, they were significantly more dependent on non-Indian intellectuals in their dealings with the state. The postcolonial leveling of Indian authority meant that Andean leaders more readily stepped forward from the middle peasant strata. Social and cultural gulfs within Andean society may have narrowed with the decline of the more acculturated chiefs, as Roger Rasnake has argued for the Yura case in Bolivia,[18] but this post-*kuraka* "peasantization" of Andean politics also implied that Indians would have to rely increasingly upon non-Indian intellectuals and literates for the realization of supralocal political goals and for the defense of their interests.

In the nineteenth century, critical mediatory roles were increasingly assumed from without by petty non-Indian intellectuals, bureaucrats, small-time lawyers (*tinterillos*), and by landlords (*gamonales*) with momentary partisan interests. The heightened role of *mistis* as go-betweens in state-peasantry relations was thus the historical product of a more direct state control over the Andean peasantry. Postcolonial mediation was inevitably riddled with the misrepresentation and exploitation born of ethnic and class antipathy and miscommunication and, ultimately, with a growing cultural alienation that would plague *misti* political programs toward Indians (including indigenism) to this day.[19] In 1885 the Andean leaders of peasant rebellion in Huaylas-Ancash were not historically positioned to become the intellectual authors of an insurrectionary program capable of finding its way into print (or, at least, into lampoon and manuscript). They could not do what the chiefs of southern Peru, the *tupamaros* and *tupakataris*, had done in the 1780s.[20] Instead, dissident *misti* "ventriloquists" (in this case, local *caceristas*) assumed the ideological leadership of the Atusparia insurgency. Republican state formation had produced a stratum of petty intermediaries potentially capable, but in reality often falling fall short of, linking peasant politics with the national politics of *caudillos* like Cáceres or, before him, Castilla. Thus, as republican nationbuilding in Peru "peasantized" Indian society, it deprived Andeans of "ethnic" or "organic" intellectuals. In the long run, a critical wellspring of ethnic reproduction was lost.

Was Atusparia "the Tupac Amaru II of the Republic"?[21]

Looking beyond the Huaylas-Ancash region to Peru at large, an instructive contrast may be drawn between two major Andean rebellions: the first was supraregional and colonial; the second, regional and postcolonial. These rebellions, separated by a century of political transfiguration, provide windows into the distinct political cultures and horizons of the late eighteenth-century chiefs of the south, on the one hand, and the late nineteenth-century *alcaldes* of the north-central highlands, on the other.

The "Royal Shining Serpent Insurrection" (1780–83), led by José Gabriel Condorcanqui Thupa Amaro (Tupac Amaru II) in Peru and by the Kataris in Upper Peru, or Bolivia, was led primarily by chiefs who, seeking to legitimate popular rebellion against corrupt colonial magistrates, claimed genealogical and, in some cases, mythical descent from the unjustly deposed Inkas.[22] The insurgent chiefs would be successful to the extent that an identifiable image of an Andean or Inka utopia could provide an imaginative counterpoint to, and thus a potential reversal of, the late colonial order.[23] The utopian vision of the chiefs included images of benign Inka rulers, and these images were cultivated and disseminated among Andean peasants in the ritual dramatizations of "Inka Atawalpa dances" which accompanied civic and religious festivities in the cities and villages.[24]

The insurrection of 1780–83 had a program and an ideology developed by literate Andean chiefs (some of whom, like Condorcanqui, were *mestizo*) and also by some imaginative Creole nationalist allies.[25] The subordinate Andean nobility of the late eighteenth century thus constituted a potentially dangerous class of dissidents, a political fact which was imminently clear to the viceregal inspector Areche, who adopted severe repressive measures against the *kuraka* class. In Spanish America, however, no concerted colonial effort had been made to reproduce or reinvent indigenous culture under titular chiefs, as British colonial administration attempted in Central Africa, for example. The colonial Andean chiefs were for the most part educated Christians with Hispanic tastes. The missionary zeal of early Spanish colonialism had dictated a profound religious transformation among the native elites toward Catholicism. Spanish rule in the Andes was nevertheless indirect, albeit in the more expedient and circumscribed political sense. Thus, the "Inka nationalist" movement of the colonial Andean elite, with its "aristocratic Andean utopia," grew in the logical political space of mediation left open by an indirect colonial rule which permitted the parallel (albeit subordinate) legal-political existence of the "Indian republic."[26]

Andean chiefs were the necessary and compromised dependents of the Spanish magistrates, or *corregidores*. But some chiefs, particularly in the south, accumulated wealth as independent mule traders and coca leaf merchants, thus bringing them into direct commercial competition with the magistrates, who redistributed similar goods under the statist *repartimiento de mercancías,* or coerced consumption program.[27] These chiefs were in a position to challenge the magistrates since they could draw on the support of Andean peasants, *and* claim legitimate political capital as entitled, hereditary chiefs recognized by the Crown.[28] They took advantage of this dual political legitimacy (Andean and Spanish) to mobilize tens of thousands of willing peasants. José Gabriel Condorcanqui Thupa Amaro (Tupac Amaru II) traced his descent to the last Inka (Tupac Amaru I) executed in 1572 by Spanish authorities. He would restore order where colonial disorder reigned; he would be the hybrid "Inka king" who would govern in Peru, but also remain loyal to the king of Spain.[29]

With the violent repression of "Inka nationalism" in 1780-81 by Inspector Areche, with the abolition of hereditary chiefship under the new intendency regime in 1783–84, and (more decisively in Huaylas-Ancash) with the Bolivarian decrees of the early 1820s, the colonial chiefs were displaced, and non-Indians of various shade and color began to fill the critical political and cultural space the chiefs had vacated. This political space itself was flattened and reworked, and the explicit intent of the Bolivarian decrees was to eliminate it altogether, thus bridging the two republics under a unitary administrative apparatus.

If the great Andean insurrection of 1780–83 could be called the "rebellion of the chiefs," then the Atusparia insurgency of 1885 might well be seen as the "rebellion of the *alcaldes.*" However, in nineteenth-century Huaylas-Ancash, *mistis* now filled much of the lettered, intellectual space once filled by the chiefs. When peasant rebellion broke out in early March 1885, Atusparia was recognized as its "natural" leader, for his post of *alcalde ordinario* of the District of La Independencia (in colonial times the chiefly Waranka Ychoc Huaraz) was, since the founding of the "republic of Indians" of San

Sebastián de Huaraz in the 1570s, numerically and politically dominant over La Restauración District (in colonial times the chiefly Waranka Allauca Huaraz). But with the ouster of the *iglesista* prefect Noriega in March 1885, dissident *caceristas* were appointed to the lettered positions of political leadership, including prefect, subprefect, and secretary. The late colonial alternative of Andean chiefly rule was no longer an option.

Manuel Mosquera, the *cacerista* prefect, was a small-time lawyer, professor, and provincial political representative to the *monterista* National Congress, held in Arequipa in 1883. Mosquera, as we saw above in chapter 3, was commander of rebel forces at the siege of Yungay, and his letters to the *iglesista* prefect and counterinsurgency commander José Iraola constitute one of the primary sources left by the rebels. These letters also betray Mosquera's unease with, and ultimate alienation from, the "savage hordes" he would command. The appointed *cacerista* secretary of the rebellion was a small-time newspaperman and self-styled intellectual with indigenist leanings: Luis Felipe Montestruque. In Ernesto Reyna's indigenist fictional drama retelling the rebellion, journalistically researched and written forty years after the event, Montestruque is depicted as the ideologue of the rebellion. In Reyna's account, Montestruque declares the *alcalde* Atusparia to be the "Inka" redeemer of "the indigenous race." But the indigenous leaders of rebellion—Atusparia, Cochachin, Granados, Guillén, Bambarén, etc.—were largely illiterate. They left little or no record of their agendas, and their motives were misrepresented by the dominant "prose of counterinsurgency" which related events for posterity. Only the postrebellion petitions, signed by the *alcaldes ordinarios* of Huaraz, provide clues about peasant motives behind the uprising. These remarkable petitions raise critical questions. Who were the "masked men" behind the pen? Radical Red *tinterillos* with long experience as defenders of Indians in the local courts? What was the process of translation and approbation? In what sense do these petitions speak for the subaltern who cannot speak in the juridical "republic of letters" for historical reasons of marginalization? The petitions of 1887 do suggest that not all *misti* intellectuals were "desubicados" or entirely removed from the history of peasant struggles in Huaylas-Ancash. At once claiming and displacing the representative voice of the authentic native, the shield or mask of anonymity and the defensive tactic of "ventriloquism" was also the product of postcolonial history and the ever-present threat of counterinsurgency. It was the means for subaltern history to reveal itself at a level of literary expression that would not detract from its authoritative value. They would not speak of "Inka-Kings" and vengeful messiahs, but of patient engagement and a suffered, and in many ways criminal, postcolonial history. The petitions would be debated, and they would have political effects.

It is possible that, Pedro Pablo Atusparia, following nineteenth-century custom, was named the honorable ritual sponsor, or symbolic "Inka," at the fiesta or victory celebration that, according to Reyna, took place in rebel Huaraz. Perhaps Atusparia, then wounded, was elected "Inka" for the upcoming patron saint festival of Huaraz, El Señor de la Soledad, which takes place in early May.[30] Such chosen "Inka" sponsors (akin to *mayordomos*) were expected to generously provide drink, food, and music for the fiesta's many celebrants. Perhaps the rebel "banquet" that Reyna depicts, and over which Atusparia presides, moved in the dangerous poetic space between customary fiesta and uncustomary revolt. Atusparia, however, could not have been an "Inka" in the sense that the literate, well-heeled chief of Tinta, José Gabriel Condorcanqui Thupa Amaro (Tupac Amaru II), was in 1780. An otherwise smallholding peasant residing in a humble hamlet of *forasteros* outside Huaraz, Atusparia would necessarily vacate his rotating post of *alcalde ordinario* at year's end. He only learned to sign his name, and even then very shakily, as part of his legal duties as *alcalde* around 1885.[31] Such an "Inka" could only be invented by a skilled ventriloquist of the likes of Montestruque (or, rather, Reyna). Atusparia's hypothetical ritual role as "Inka" was not comparable to the long-term prestige politics of hereditary colonial Andean chiefship. And it was Reyna, not Montestruque, who popularized the "Inka" and "amauta" images of Atusparia in the heyday of indigenism within Lima's leftist literary circles.

It was in such twentieth-century *misti* intellectual circles, both in Lima and in the south (particularly Cuzco and Puno), that the "Andean utopia" was reinvented by those who now wished to radically transform, and mediate, state-peasantry relations. Indeed, the rise of *indigenista* discourse in Peru may have coincided with the decline of *alcalde* mediation, which was officially abolished (but widely unobserved) by the officialist indigenism of the dictatorial Leguía regime (1919 30). It appears that leftist intellectuals, including such luminaries as José Carlos Mariátegui, followed in the well-worn, liberal footsteps of Ancash's Prefect Huapaya, of Simón Bolívar, and of the viceregal inspector Areche, all of whom saw the so-called Indian *caciques* as ruthless "despots" and "the worst" exploiters of their own people, thereby justifying their convenient removal.

The insurrection led by the *tupamaros* and *tupakataris* of Peru and Upper Peru in the 1780s was therefore historically and politically distinct from the regional uprising led by the *varayoc* of Huaylas-Ancash under the political and ideological command of *caceristas* in the 1880s. The contrast between the two events illustrates the profound historical transformations that occurred within the peasantry, its ethnic leadership, and the Peruvian state in the space of one critical century. William Stein has pointed out interesting "structural" parallels between the Tupac Amaru insurrection and the Atusparia uprising.[32] In contrast, my discussion has emphasized the profound historical gulf that separated the two movements, and the colonial and postcolonial histories they contested.

Postcolonial Legacies

In his preface to Ernesto Reyna's indigenist "crónica novelada" of the Atusparia insurgency, *El amauta Atusparia*, published circa 1930, José Carlos Mariátegui noted that "Peru's republican history has usually, and almost invariably, been written as political history, in the most narrow and Creole sense of the term."[33] Reyna's journalistic and popularized fictional drama, noted Mariátegui, was not critical history—which was still unavailable in Peru—but, given the backward state of "professional history" in the "aristocratic republic" of the 1920s, Reyna's "novelized history" was at least an inspiring first step in the new generation's revolutionary task of writing the social history of Peru's excluded masses. Mariátegui, however, like Reyna, was also the product (and producer) of Peruvian intellectual history, particularly of the new fusion of indigenism and socialism in Lima's radical intellectual circles. Although urban indigenists and socialists of the period strove to include the Andean masses in their writings, they usually portrayed them as backward victims oppressed by highland "feudalism," or as noble savages far removed from the historical and political forces shaping modern Peruvian life in and around the coastal cities. Thus, in his remarkable *Seven Interpretive Essays on Peruvian Reality*, the heroic founder of Peruvian socialism could write: "The dualism of the Peruvian soul and of Peruvian history in our age is defined by a conflict between the historical form elaborated on the coast, and the indigenous sentiment that survives in the sierra, deeply rooted in nature. Peru today is a coastal formation."[34]

Mariátegui, of course, was not alone in this sentiment. Fernand Braudel's Mediterranean "law of history" states that mountain regions "are as a rule a world apart from civilizations, which are an urban and lowland achievement. Their history is to have none, to remain almost always on the fringe of the great waves of civilization, even the longest and most persistent."[35] But Braudel's "law" walks on its hands in the Americas. In the early sixteenth century, wayward European lowlanders stumbled upon high civilizations at spectacular elevations. In Peru, Pizarro first encountered Inka civilization on the high plateau of Cajamarca, and from there the conquistadors advanced along the stone-paved Inka Way through Huaylas, and on to Pachacamac and imperial Cuzco.[36] Europeans would later come to understand that the history of civilization in Mesoamerica and the Andes was made in mountain regions like Huaylas-Ancash, and that mountain peoples would not cease to make history with the sudden arrival of the Spanish conquistadors.

Yet a mere glance at any modern map of Peru appears to confirm Braudel's Mediterranean maxim. Between 1530 and, say, 1930, the tables had turned. Is civilization's home not the modern urban centers of the coastal lowlands? Are the Andean highlands not, as Mariátegui insisted, the proverbial "world apart" from this lowland achievement? It has long been fashionable (since at least the late eighteenth century), both in Lima and abroad, to describe Peru in such binary terms. The cliché has been that there are two Perus: the "Perú profundo" of the "Indian" and "natural" Andean sierra, and the "modern Peru" of the "civilized," Westernized Creole coast. The alleged duality is incessantly evoked as evidence for an unvanquished "colonial heritage" or "colonial legacy" in Peru, whose life was prolonged (for some, up to the present) by "neocolonial" feudalism in the sierra.[37] These apparent truisms and dualisms, however, do not hold up very well in the case of the colonial and postcolonial history of Huaylas-Ancash.

Although the long colonial process of inversion (from mountain to coastal civilization) began with Francisco Pizarro's fateful decision to remove his Spanish capital from highland Xauxa (Jauja) to coastal Lima in 1534,[38] contemporary manifestations of Peruvian dualism may be readily traced to nineteenth-century historical forces.[39] Chief among these postcolonial historical forces was the Peruvian linkage to the Atlantic world system of export-led capitalist growth and the gradual, but uneven, development of a centralizing national state anchored in coastal Lima.[40] In addition, underappreciated demographic and ideological shifts (see chap. 4) were critical to the formation of contemporary images of Peruvian dualism.

This book has plotted the fragmentary republican histories of unimagined political communities in one region of postcolonial Andean Peru. These histories reveal the political engagement of the indigenous peasantry with the state and the nation, and they subvert those accounts of Peru's (and Latin America's) republican history which deny historical subjectivity to "ethnic" subalterns by placing them, intentionally or not, outside history. The modern creed of Peruvian dualism, which tended to dehistoricize Andean Peru, has had the effect of denying the republican historical agency of Andean subalterns. By insisting on the long and traumatic shadow of the Conquest and the always vaguely defined "colonial legacy," the postcolonial legacy which recast (and reinvented) that earlier legacy was passed over, often under the convenient rubric of "neocolonialism."

Nevertheless, and contrary to the backward-looking, "neocolonial" characterization of the nineteenth century so common in *dependentista* historiography, the republican ideal—although clearly not yet fully "liberal capitalist"—was still essentially "modernist" in its nationbuilding telos. Víctor Peralta, writing on early republican Cuzco, has persuasively critiqued the "presentist," a posteriori interpretation that reduced Peru's nineteenth-century history to prologue (as merely the frustrated period of capitalist development). Yet Peralta appears to fall victim to the equally anachronistic trap of characterizing the postcolonial period as essentially "maintaining a respect and permanent return to the past" and to the so-called *mancomunidad nacional* of the colonial period.[41] On the contrary, the postcolonial republican political project was an ambivalent metamorphosis of the late colonial project of Bourbon reformism, which produced new fragmentations. The deep contradictions of this incomplete, contested metamorphosis cast a long and enduring shadow across Peru's twentieth century. The classical liberal-republican ideal of propertied citizenship and unmediated rule was bracketed by the expedient politics of the postcolonial predicament: countless caudillisms, liberal dystopias, positivist racisms, destabilizing subaltern readings. These brackets were new, and enduring.

This history, then, does not easily yield to the "modernization" or "dependency" paradigms that have often circumscribed the Latin Americanist historical imagination on the post-Independence period.[42] The republican histories of Andean peasants engaged in the postcolonial political world of Peru do not support either (a) the view that emphasizes the imminent demise of the ancien régime in the irresistible rise of the liberal nation-state, or (b) the view that, in the diagnostically negative tone of (neomarxist) *dependentista* discourse, dismisses political and cultural shifts (Independence was a nonevent) and reduces the post-Independence period to a colonial curtain call followed by an inevitable "neocolonial" dependency.[43]

Early liberal-republican discourse negated the language and legacy of colonial "despotism," proclaiming the end of "Indians" and the decolonizing liberation of "Peruvians." Subsequently, "enlightened" discourses and fiscal compromises conspired with *caudillo* politics to produce a hybrid republican disorder in which Andean peasants regenerated a "republicano" political culture of colonial origin, albeit now with notable postcolonial resonance: this was the paradoxical postcolonial order. By the middle of the nineteenth century, the guano-age "dislocation" of this disordered order would produce not the liberal utopia of free trade and individualized state-society relations, but the postcolonial dystopia of Peruvian dualism. Some Creole elites would now argue that the Indian's "degradation" was a consequence of republican failures. According to Manuel del Río, Peru's treasury minister, the "national problem" of the Peruvian state, more than the colonial legacy, was republican misrule.[44] The frequent and unwise changes in tax policy which followed from the political instability of caudillism, and the fiscal autonomy afforded by the guano bonanza, would produce an irreversible *dislocación* between the country's taxpayers, who were primarily indigenous contributors, and the Lima state. Such an erosion was evident in Huaylas-Ancash by the 1870s. In the postwar decade (1886–95) this dislocation doomed the liberal poll-tax (and, with it, Cáceres's experimental postwar plan for national integration via fiscal decentralization) to insolvency and failure. By the late nineteenth century liberal-positivist, Lamarckian ideas about the "desgraciada raza indígena" would again assign the irredeemable "Peruvian indigenous race"—as Luis Carranza did in the midst of the Atusparia insurgency—to the dustbin of history, a victim of the Spanish Conquest and Inka despotism.

In this sense, then, we may identify several complex postcolonial legacies —rather than the amorphous and dehistoricized "colonial legacy" that appears like a mantra in nearly all Latin American history textbooks—shaping twentieth-century events and political discourse. Perhaps the most critical of these legacies for the present study are subaltern readings and translations of postcolonial history. The petition that the *alcaldes* of Huaraz directed to President Cáceres in 1887 depicted the colonial period in more favorable terms than the postcolonial. This was not, in an absolute sense, an accurate reading: the colonial period—particularly in the eighteenth century, when chiefs and communities in Huaylas witnessed the alienation of significant extensions of land—was no utopia. But in the face of weak, *caudillo*-ridden postcolonial regimes, liberal reforms, and landlord encroachment, colonial "indigenous rights" became the bulwark of legal defense.

Indeed, the *alcaldes* had little or nothing good to say about the postcolonial state. Their "indigenous rights," colonial in origin, had been disregarded by the warring *caudillos* who had, again and again, "kidnapped" them for "some criminal project." The critical deployment of the precedent of protective colonial law, combined with the political agency of Indian *republicano* authorities, the *alcaldes,* would generate a powerful (albeit suppressed) critique of the *caudillo*-ridden, postcolonial state. This historical critique raised (and raises) the possibility of an alternative "history of indigenous rights and property" that countered the official historicity of national progress but partook necessarily of its historical rhetoric. In the process, it raised the specter of the postcolonial legacy. In their petition for the suspension of poll-tax collection, the *alcaldes* of Huaraz had declared to President Cáceres that

> Every regime that has fought to sustain itself in power, and every *caudillo* [faction] that has worked to overthrow it, has availed itself by decree or by force to draft free men by yanking them from their homes . . . to incorporate them by force under pain of death . . . to serve . . . what are almost always criminal projects[.] [N]ot having any other means of avoiding this noxious kidnapping than the money or goods with which we have bought our liberty. . . . This is the history of indigenous liberty in its relations with the military politics of the country, and this is the protection that the state and the regimes and the rebel [*caudillos*] have dispensed. . . . Has this ill been remedied in Peru, Your Excellency? We are not yet sure. . . . In respect to indigenous property rights what shall we say, Your Excellency? Since Independence the exiguous goods of our fortune, fruit of the sweat of our brow, the few animals we have raised for our subsistence and for plowing, all have been inhumanely stripped from us by the disturbers of order and by its pseudodefenders, without there being one single *caudillo* or one single president who has taken pity on our fate. Such is the history, traced in broad strokes, of indigenous property in its relations with regimes and the enemies of those regimes. . . . [A]nd such has been the protection that one or the other has dispensed.[45]

By speaking in the liberal tongue that the state wanted to hear, this petition's anonymous editor in the employ of the *alcaldes* of Huaraz subtly recast notions of "indigenous commons" and "indigenous rights" in the language of "liberty" and "property." But this petition would go so far as to speak of the republican "history of indigenous liberty" and "the history of indigenous property rights." Indigenous subalterns, it would seem, could also employ the skilled rhetoric (and legal defense) of liberalism to weave a counterhegemonic historical narrative. But the authors seemed unaware that the deeper contradiction of this "history" was that it had refractory colonial origins; it was therefore unsavory to nationalists and liberals alike. In this case no measure of liberalism could negate the historical presence of the colonial: the only land titles and rights the *alcaldes* could claim were written on colonial paper.

Although Cáceres would choose to overlook the deeper claims, after three years of tenacious resistance he finally did grant a temporary reduction of the poll-tax, personally requested by Atusparia in 1886, for the Indians of Huaraz. But, like so many other such instances in postcolonial history, this "temporary" measure turned out to be permanent. What made it permanent was the massive Indian show of force in 1885 and the sly threat that, if "liberties" and "property" were not respected, such terrible force might be brought to bear once again (as in the open threats of 1888 and 1904). So long as this specter loomed in elite minds, and so long as the "indigenous" population of Huaylas continued to grow at what for elites were alarming rates, the possibility of an alternative republican history could be broached.

In another context, closer to our own political predicament, Milan Kundera wrote that "the struggle . . . against power is the struggle of memory against forgetting,"[46] but "forgetting" is also a primary instrument of domination in the employ of the postcolonial nationalist imagination, which must negate aspects of the ever-near colonial past.[47] In Peru, Creoles negated the near Indian past (which lay under the shadow of the Black Legend) and revived the distant Inka past. For to do otherwise raised the specter of an alternative "republic" with a colonial political history. Creoles thus selectively imagined a political community that could not imagine the majorities as political agents. Sadly, the notion of "prepolitical" peasants has lived on in twentieth-century historiography. But an Andean *republicano* politics informed by the struggle to make the postcolonial state recall its colonial obligations was present, and it "inverted the relationship between past and present advanced by the official logic of progress."[48] At a minimum, the recovery of this struggle should urge a rethinking of our tired textbook notions of the "colonial legacy" in light of the postcolonial-nationalist legacy that reinvented it. This rethinking is part of the task of "provincializing European history"[49] and historicizing the postcolonial by focusing historical narratives on the existential political predicaments and cultural initiatives of subalterns in the Americas.[50]

But there is another, more particularly Peruvian, legacy that needs to be rethought in light of the argument presented here. After the national debacle of the War of the Pacific (1879–83), the ensuing civil war between *caceristas* and *iglesistas,* and the Atusparia insurgency (1885), Creole intellectuals would increasingly blame the unresolved "Indian problem" for Peru's woes, arguing that the Andean masses were insufficiently integrated into the life of the nation. But as the Junín case studied by Nelson Manrique and Florencia Mallon strongly suggests,[51] and the present case of Huaylas-Ancash confirms, the supposed lack of nationalist support emanating from the Andean peasantry was *not* the problem. The problem was that most of the elite (including, eventually, Cáceres himself) could not accept the challenge of patriotic and, let it be said, *republicano* peasants. It was a question of class and race, among other things.

Perhaps the most enduring legacy of the postwar Peruvian misreading was this: the negation of the historical agency of republican Indians opened an ideological space that would be filled by an early twentieth-century indigenism which ultimately essentialized Indians as prepolitical, indeed prehistorical. The uplifting of the previously "degraded race" was championed so that "the Indian" might assume his rightful place in a national pantheon where he had already stood—only to be thrown out. But, like the *alcaldes* of Huaraz after the Atusparia insurgency, "the Indian" would nevertheless remain more than a specter: the postcolonial predicament of Andean peasants would continue to mean integration on separate terms, inclusion on the excluded fringes, disenfranchisement in the franchise. From this subaltern predicament, however, there also emerged the promise of an unrealized solution to the problem of the fragmented Peruvian nation. This solution would entail, among other things, imagining the unimagined communities of the postcolonial Andes as political communities with colonial and republican histories.

NOTES

1. Historicizing the Postcolonial Andean Predicament

1 For an introduction to the problems of nation-state formation in the Andes, see Jean Paul Deler and Yves Saint-Geours, eds., *Estados y naciones en los Andes* (Lima, 1986), Heraclio Bonilla, "Comunidades indígenas y estado nación en el Perú," in Alberto Flores Galindo, ed., *Comunidades campesinas: Cambios y permanencias* (Lima, 1987), pp. 13-27, and Bonilla, ed., *Los Andes en la encrucijada: Indios, comunidades y estado en el siglo XIX* (Quito, 1991).

2 Benedict Anderson, *Imagined Communities: Reflections on the Origin and Spread of Nationalism* (London and New York, 1991).

3 On "national" novels in postcolonial Latin America, see Doris Sommers, *Foundational Fictions: The National Romances of Latin America* (Berkeley, 1991).

4 Eric Hobsbawm, *Nations and Nationalism since 1780: Programme, Myth, Reality* (Cambridge, 1990).

5 On "primordialist" versus "modernist" positions on nations and nationalism, see Anthony D. Smith, *The Ethnic Origins of Nations* (Oxford, 1986).

6 Thomas E. Skidmore and Peter H. Smith, *Modern Latin America* (New York and Oxford, 1992), p. 6.

7 Anderson, *Imagined Communities*.

8 In now classical essays on the uses of anthropology for the study of political culture, Geertz characterized the "new states" of ethnographic Africa and Asia as, to paraphrase, neither the indigenous "peasant states" of the precolonial past nor the unmediated reproductions of "modern" European nation-states. See Clifford Geertz, *The Interpretation of Cultures* (New York, 1973), pp. 338-40.

9 Clifford Geertz, ed., *Old Societies and New States* (New York, 1963).

10 Anderson draws too sharp a contrast between the ethnic and linguistic makeup of the American Creole republics and the postcolonial "new states" of Africa and Asia by misleadingly generalizing the relatively more homogeneous cultural and linguistic composition of modern Argentina and Venezuela to all the American republics.

11 Anderson, *Imagined Communities* (1983), pp. 50-65. In the revised edition of *Imagined Communities* (1991), Anderson, in a move designed to emphasize the early nature of American states, changed the chapter title "Old Empires, New Nations" to "Creole Pioneers."

12 Anderson, *Imagined Communities* (1991), p. 52. Masur, *Simón Bolívar* (Albuquerque, 1948), p. 678. Still, Anderson and Masur do not have it quite right. In Spanish South America, the boundaries of the new Creole republics did not so neatly correspond to the wider jurisdictions of the long and foundational Habs-

burg period (ca. 1550–1700), nor did they correspond to any ethnic or linguistic frontiers. Rather, as the ethnohistorian John H. Rowe has pointed out, the new republics were carved from the new administrative units quite recently drawn by the "enlightened" and reformist Bourbon dynasty which ruled Spanish America during the eighteenth century. Creole republics were considerably narrower in scope and vision than the huge, plurinational polities of the protocolonial and early colonial periods. The new republics were fragments of larger colonial spaces, and they experienced the chronic border conflicts with neighboring new states that young and contested frontiers readily incite. Thus, the more accurate formulation of the question is, Why were the late colonial jurisdictions largely maintained or further fragmented in the early Republican period? The Andean historian's answer to this query is terse: the Creole state was in many ways an extention of the late colonial project of Bourbon administrative reform, albeit with a postcolonial nationalist twist. The colonial-postcolonial metamorphosis of Spanish America was thus complicated by the intervening "neocolonial" period of Bourbon reform (ca. 1750–1820) which nurtured the rise of "enlightened liberalism" and Creole nationalism.

13 *Imagined Communities* (1991), p. 52.

14 Anderson resurrects Victor Turner's plastic concept of how meaning is molded in journeys, suggesting that in the perambulations of a Creole official's career the colonial administrative unit could be imagined as a nation. Travel to the metropolis, it is claimed, was infrequent among American-born "Spaniards" (although not, it seems, for the political elite of the likes of Simón Bolívar), who were thus confined to an American experience that kindled an antimetropolitan envy. In the late eighteenth-century period of expanding commercial opportunities for Latin America, this invidious consciousness would eventually find its way into the incendiary pamphlets of patriotic "Creole printmen." Anderson's Creole journeys are at least imaginable, even if less frequent than one might imagine (Creole elites preferred to tour Europe, and peninsular officials probably did American tours rather more often). In any case, such journeys do little to explain the disturbing political fact that most Creoles in Lima apparently remained loyal to the "mother fatherland" (*madre patria*) of Spain.

15 On the ambivalence of postcolonial nationalism, see Partha Chatterjee, *Nationalist Thought and the Colonial World: A Derivative Discourse?* (London and Delhi, 1986) and *The Nation and Its Fragments: Colonial and Postcolonial Histories* (Princeton, 1993); also see Homi K. Bhabha, "Introduction: Narrating the Nation," in Bhabha, ed., *Nation and Narration* (London, 1990).

16 Gyan Prakash, "Subaltern Studies as Postcolonial Criticism," *American Historical Review* 99:5 (1994), p. 1481.

17 Anderson, *Imagined Communities* (1991), p. 48, emphasis in the original.

18 David Brading, *The First America: The Spanish Monarchy, Creole Patriots, and the Liberal State, 1492–1867* (Cambridge, 1991), p. 484.

19 Ibid., p. 646.

20 John Lynch, *The Spanish American Revolutions, 1808–1826* (New York, 1986), pp. 341–56.

21 Ibid.; Brading, *The First America;* George Reid Andrews, "No Revolution in the Historiography of the Revolution," *Radical History Review* 27 (1983), pp. 174–84.

22 Anderson, *Imagined Communities* (1991), p. 48.

23 Lynch, *The Spanish American Revolutions;* Cecilia Méndez, "Los campesinos, la Independencia y la iniciación de la República: El caso de los iquichanos realistas," in Henrique Urbano, ed. *Poder y violencia en los Andes* (Lima, 1991), pp. 165–88.

24 Heraclio Bonilla and Karen Spalding, "La Independencia en el Perú: Las palabras y los hechos," in Heraclio Bonilla et al., *La Independencia en el Perú* (Lima, 1981), pp. 70–113.

25 Brading, *The First America.*

26 Quoted in Lynch, *The Spanish American Revolutions,* p. 25.

27 Bernard S. Cohn, "From Indian Status to British Contract," in Cohn, *An Anthropologist among the Historians and Other Essays* (Delhi, 1987), p. 463.

28 The phrase is from Anthony Giddens, *The Nation-State and Violence. A Contemporary Critique of Historical Materialism* (Berkeley, 1985), although he uses it in very different contexts.

29 Hobsbawm, *Nations and Nationalism,* pp. 14–15.

30 Ibid., pp. 14 and 18–19.

31 The notion of a political-territorial nation—rather than an ancestral or ethnolinguistic one—was clearly manifested in early Latin American constitutions. In the founding Peruvian Constitution of 1822, we find that "all the provinces of Peru reunited in one body form the Peruvian nation" (*todas las provincias del Perú reunidas en un sólo cuerpo forman la Nación Peruana*), and that "the nation shall be named the Peruvian Republic" (*La Nación se denominará República Peruana*). Although at first glance this rings of a Tawantinsuyo-style union of provincial social spaces, the territorial emphasis actually reflected the pressing conjunctural need to incorporate by constitutional fiat those provinces (Junín, Huamanga) still occupied by loyalist forces. By the Constitution of 1827–28 the Independence Wars were over, however, and it is then that the "Peruvian nation" takes on its characteristic citizen-state definition. Thus, in 1827–28 "the Peruvian nation is the political association of all the citizens of Peru" (*la nación peruana es la asociación política de todos los ciudadanos del Perú*). This unmistakably political definition of nation is repeated in subsequent constitutions until 1867, when a renewed but brief war with the Spanish fleet off the coast of Peru occasioned the return of additional territorial language in the definition. The next Peruvian constitution, composed in 1920, resumed the 1828 citizen-state notion. See Emilio Dancuart, *Crónicas parlamentarias del Perú,* 13 vols. (Lima, 1906–55); also J. V. Ugarte de Pino, *Historia de las constituciones del Perú* (Lima, 1978).

32 In the official dictionary of the imperial Real Academia of 1726–37, *república* was glossed as follows: (a) "el gobierno del público," be it under the form of monarchy,

aristocracy, or democracy; (b) "la causa pública, el común o su utilidad"; and (c) "por extensión se llaman también algunos Pueblos." These meanings implicated each other at the various levels of Spanish colonial political organization, including the political practice of governance within the local "Indian republics" (*pueblos de indios*). See Mark Thurner, "From Two Nations to One Divided: The Contradictions of Nation-Building in Andean Peru" (Ph.D. diss., University of Wisconsin-Madison, 1993), chap. 2.

33 Serge Gruzinski's interpretation of the colonial Nahua *pueblos* of central Mexico in some ways parallels the Huaylas case: "At the same time that ethnic and regional solidarity was breaking up, the pueblo or town was becoming a fallback zone, a zone of resistance and adjustment to the colonial regime. In that haven the Indians managed to maintain or create a collective religious, economic, and even juridical identity, which they were able to safeguard from the ravages of a brutal deculturation." Gruzinski, *Man-Gods in the Mexican Highlands: Indian Power and Colonial Society, 1520–1800* (Stanford, 1989), p. 17. For the southern Andes, Tristan Platt describes a process of ethnic continuity and ethnogenesis under the colonial reduction regime. See Platt, *Estado boliviano y ayllu andino: Tierra y tributo en el norte de Potosí* (Lima, 1982), pp. 26–27. On the long history of fragmentation in the Andes, see John V. Murra, Nathan Wachtel, and Jacques Revel, eds., *Anthropological History of Andean Polities* (Cambridge, 1985).

34 See Steve Stern, *Peru's Indian Peoples and the Challenge of Spanish Conquest: Huamanga to 1640* (Madison, 1982), which challenged Nathan Wachtel's influential notion of "destructuration." For the view that "Indian" identity was formed in resistance and opposition to Spanish colonialism, see Irene Silverblatt, "Becoming Indian in the Central Andes of Seventeenth-Century Peru," in Gyan Prakash, ed., *After Colonialism: Imperial Histories and Postcolonial Displacements* (Princeton, 1995), pp. 279–88.

35 Walter Mignolo, "Editor's Introduction," special issue of *Poetics Today* 15 (Winter 1994), pp. 505–21, "Loci of Enunciation and Imaginary Constructions: The Case of (Latin) America."

36 See Noble David Cook, *Demographic Collapse: Indian Peru, 1520–1620* (Cambridge, 1981); Thurner, "From Two Nations," chap. 2.

37 Frederic Cooper and Ann Stoler, "Introduction. Tensions of Empire: Colonial Control and Visions of Rule," *American Ethnologist* 16:4 (1989), pp. 609–21.

38 Brading, *The First America*, pp. 582–636. Nevertheless, nineteenth-century Creole liberals and conservatives alike usually traced the origins of the Mexican nation to the Spanish conquistador Hernán Cortés. The influential liberal José María Luís Mora, for example, consistently denied the existence of Indians in postcolonial Mexico. See Charles Hale, *Mexican Liberalism in the Age of Mora, 1821–1853* (New Haven, 1968).

39 The exiled Peruvian and Jesuit priest Juan Pablo Viscardo y Guzmán did invent such a common national history wherein the Creoles would become legitimate heirs to Tawantinsuyu, but his program apparently failed to generate wide sup-

port. See Anthony Pagden, *Spanish Imperialism and the Political Imagination* (New Haven, 1990), pp. 117-32.

40 See "Los Ideólogos," vols. 1-3 of the *Colección documental de la Independencia del Perú*, 27 vols., (Lima, 1971-75). Such *indigenismo liberal* rhetoric can also be found in early editorials of the Lima newspaper *El Comercio*. Also see Enrique Tord, *El indio en los ensayistas peruanos, 1848-1948* (Lima, 1978) and Efraín Kristal, *The Andes Viewed from the City: Literary and Political Discourse on the Indian, 1848-1930* (New York, 1987) on the mid-nineteenth-century literary precedents of early twentieth-century indigenist discourse in Peru.

41 Brading, *The First America*, p. 420.

42 Of course, some nineteenth-century Creoles were inclined to reinvent Tawantinsuyu. For two notable examples, see Alberto Flores Galindo, *Buscando un inca: Identidad y utopía en los Andes* (Lima, 1987) and Pagden, *Spanish Imperialism.*

43 In *The First America*, Brading notes that "in effect, if the creole elite were slow to lay claim to Inca history, it was because it was not a distant past, shrouded in myth, but rather a living presence, to be observed proudly parading through the streets, the cultural property of a subordinate but rival elite" (p. 342). Such parading, however, was explicitly forbidden when the viceregal inspector Juan Antonio de Areche outlawed the cultural symbols of Inka nationalism following the capture and execution of José Gabriel Condorcanqui Thupa Amaro in 1780. See John Rowe, "El movimiento nacional inca del siglo XVIII," *Revista Universitaria* (Cuzco) 107 (1954), pp. 17-47.

44 See Rowe, "El movimiento"; Jan Szeminski, *La utopía tupamarista* (Lima, 1984) and "Why Kill the Spaniard? New Perspectives on Andean Insurrectionary Ideology in the 18th Century," in Steve J. Stern, ed., *Resistance, Rebellion, and Consciousness in the Andean Peasant World, 18th to 20th Centuries* (Madison, 1987), pp. 166-92; Flores Galindo, *Buscando un inca*; Steve J. Stern, "The Age of Andean Insurrection, 1742-1782: A Reappraisal," in Stern, ed. *Resistance, Rebellion, and Consciousness*, pp. 34-93; and Mark Thurner, "Guerra andina y política campesina en el sitio de La Paz, 1781," in Urbano, ed., *Poder y violencia*, pp. 93-124.

45 Szeminski, "Why Kill the Spaniard?"

46 See John Phelan, *The People and the King: The Comunero Revolution in Colombia, 1781* (Madison, 1978).

47 Pagden, *Spanish Imperialism*, p. 3.

48 Ibid., pp. 119-32.

49 Monarchist projects did survive in nineteenth-century Mexico and Brazil, however.

50 Pagden, *Spanish Imperialism*, p. 134.

51 Ibid., p. 138.

52 The phrase "buscando un inca" (searching for an Inka) is from Flores Galindo (n. 42 above). Although Bolívar was not searching for an Inka, Tristan Platt has argued that in Bolivia Andean peasants may have seen him as one. See Platt, "Simón Bolívar, the Sun of Justice and the Amerindian Virgin: Andean Conceptions of

the *Patria* in Nineteenth-Century Potosí," *Journal of Latin American Studies* 25:1 (1993), pp. 159–85.

53   Commentary by Frank Safford on Charles Walker's paper presented to the Andean Studies Committee Meeting, "Ideological Transformations in the Post-Colonial Andes," Conference on Latin American History, American Historical Association Annual Meetings, Chicago, 29 December 1991.

54   Mary Louise Pratt, *Imperial Eyes: Travel Writing and Transculturation* (London and New York, 1992).

55   Brading, *The First America*, p. 490; see Jorge Juan and Antonio de Ulloa, *Discourse and Political Reflections on the Kingdoms of Peru* [1749], trans. John T. Tepaske and Besse A. Clement (Norman, 1978), pp. 143–44.

56   Manuel Burga, *Nacimiento de una utopía: Muerte y resurrección de los incas* (Lima, 1988).

57   Pagden, *Spanish Imperialism*, p. 103.

58   In his landmark *History of the Conquest of Peru* (1847), Prescott characterized the Inca Empire as " 'pure and unmitigated despotism' comparable to the regimes that dominated east Asia. If no one starved in ancient Peru, there was no possibility of progress since 'ambition, avarice, the love of change, the morbid spirit of discontent . . . found no place in the bosom of the Peruvian.' " Brading, *The First America*, p. 633.

59   Tristan Platt, "Liberalism and Ethnocide in the Southern Andes," *History Workshop Journal* 17 (1984), pp. 3–18.

60   This modernist Creole dismissal of contemporary Andean peoples was steeped in a reinvented *leyenda negra*. The Black Legend of Spanish misrule, which was accentuated and spread by Spain's colonial rivals, the British and the Dutch, was convenient for Creoles who blamed the "tyranny" of Spanish colonialism for every imaginable social ill afflicting postcolonial society. The Creole dismissal was superseded by the more radical indigenism of the early twentieth century which, in its struggle to correct the nineteenth-century negation, generated an image of the Indian that lent itself to the denial of Andean cultural contemporaneity. Under this revived indigenist ideology, the timeless association of the contemporary Indian community with an invented precolonial past, intended to elevate Indians, in effect negated the historicity of Andean peoples and cultures. In this sense, the medicine of certain strains of more radical, early twentieth-century indigenism was not dissimilar to the disease it had hoped to cure. To undo the violent silence of nineteenth-century Creole discourse, it was necessary to exalt Indianness.

61   Nineteenth-century travel writers in search of Andean civilization—like the twentieth-century anthropologists and streams of international tourists that have followed them—would sojourn to Cuzco (and not to places like Huaylas-Ancash, which then as now attracts natural scientists and mountaineers), the former capital of the Inka Empire, where they could admire the monolithic ruins of a "lost civilization" and, if their itinerary allowed, seek out its living but degraded vestiges. Typically, our nineteenth-century travel writer would momentarily reflect (in

print) on how it was possible that such ragged, illiterate Indians could possibly have descended from the glorious monumentality of Inka civilization.

62 Kristal, *The Andes Viewed,* pp. 141, 209.

63 Anderson, *Imagined Communities.*

64 Chatterjee, *The Nation and Its Fragments,* p. 158.

65 See Cecilia Méndez, "República sin indios: La comunidad imaginada del Perú," in Henrique Urbano, ed., *Tradición y modernidad en los Andes* (Lima, 1993), pp. 15–41.

66 Gilbert Joseph and Daniel Nugent, eds., *Everyday Forms of State Formation: Revolution and the Negotiation of Rule in Modern Mexico* (Durham, 1994).

67 For an insightful discussion of the creative potential of this tension, see Florencia Mallon, "The Promise and Dilemma of Subaltern Studies: Perspectives from Latin American History," *American Historical Review* 99:5 (1994), pp. 1491–1515.

68 On "discursive frameworks" and the "grammar of politics," see William Roseberry, "Hegemony and the Language of Contention," in Joseph and Nugent, eds., *Everyday Forms of State Formation,* pp. 355–66, and Philip Corrigan, "State Formation," ibid., pp. xvii–xix. On recent approaches to the question of subaltern subjectivity, see Prakash, "Subaltern Studies," pp. 1482–83.

69 The major problem for this and other archival studies of the postcolonial Andean experience is the absolute paucity of documentary sources written in Quechua. The official language was Spanish, and court bilinguals most probably strategized their translations to make them more intelligible and acceptable to the scribe and the judge. Yet the Quechua of Huaylas was also laden with Hispanisms by the nineteenth century, especially where there were no clear Quechua equivalents for Spanish juridical and political concepts. One such Spanish term without a precise Quechua equivalent appears to have been *república.*

70 David Warren Sabean, *Property, Production, and Family in Neckerhausen, 1700–1870* (Cambridge, 1990), p. 79.

71 I am not suggesting that the local archive is exempt from the structurations and tropes of the dominant discourses housed in state institutions and in canonized literary texts. The difference, it seems to me, is that the politics of the local archive are more readily visible in their specific social location.

72 Ranajit Guha, *Elementary Aspects of Peasant Insurgency in Colonial India* (Delhi, 1983).

73 Frank Salomon, "Andean Ethnology in the 1970s: A Retrospective," *Latin American Research Review* 17:2 (1982), pp. 75–128.

74 George Kubler, *The Indian Caste of Peru, 1795–1940: A Population Study Based upon Tax Records and Census Reports* (Washington, D.C., 1952), p. 1.

75 Florencia Mallon, "Introduction," *Latin American Perspectives* 48 (1986), pp. 3–17.

76 See Bernard S. Cohn, "Anthropology and History in the 1980s: Toward a Rapprochement," *Journal of Interdisciplinary History* 12:2 (1981), pp. 227–52.

77 Ibid., p. 233; Salomon, "Andean Ethnology," pp. 101–2.

78 See Frederic Cooper et al., *Confronting Historical Paradigms: Peasants, Labor, and the Capitalist World System in Africa and Latin America* (Madison, 1993). Also see

the "AHR Forum on Subaltern Studies" in the December 1994 issue of the *American Historical Review*. On the Latin Americanist trend in regional historical studies informed by anthropology, see William B. Taylor, "Between Global Process and Local Knowledge: An Inquiry into Early Latin American Social History, 1500–1900," in Olivier Zunz, ed., *Reliving the Past: The Worlds of Social History* (Chapel Hill, 1985), pp. 115–90, and William Roseberry, "Beyond the Agrarian Question in Latin America," in Cooper et al., *Confronting Historical Paradigms,* pp. 318–68.

79 On the notion of "contemporaneity" and its frequent denial to anthropological Others, see Johannes Fabian, *Time and the Other: How Anthropology Makes Its Object* (Cambridge, 1983).

80 Raúl Rivera Serna, *Los guerrilleros del centro en la emancipación peruana* (Lima, 1958).

81 Bonilla and Spalding, "La Independencia"; Lynch, *The Spanish American Revolutions.*

82 Platt, *Estado boliviano,* p. 17; Bonilla and Spalding, "La Independencia," pp. 112–13.

83 Platt, "Simón Bolívar," p. 168.

84 The precolonial ethnic polities of Chayanta appear to have been reproduced without severe fragmentation under the colonial tributary regime. The Bolivian treasury was also more heavily dependent on the Indian tribute than was the "guano state" of Peru, which helped foster the postcolonial reproduction of indirect rule.

85 Tristan Platt, "The Andean Experience of Bolivian Liberalism, 1825–1900: Roots of Rebellion in 19th-Century Chayanta (Potosí)," in Stern, ed., *Resistance, Rebellion, and Consciousness,* pp. 318–19.

86 Platt, "Simón Bolívar," p. 168.

87 Platt, *Estado boliviano* and "Liberalism and Ethnocide."

88 Platt, "Liberalism and Ethnocide."

89 On the "normalization" of subaltern aspirations in postcolonial nationalist projects, see Chatterjee, *The Nation and Its Fragments,* and Prakash, "Subaltern Studies," p. 1481. On Mexican nationmaking, see Florencia Mallon, *Peasant and Nation: The Making of Postcolonial Mexico and Peru* (Berkeley, 1995) and Joseph and Nugent, eds., *Everyday Forms of State Formation.*

90 On the "guano age" centralization of the Lima-based Peruvian State in the 1840s–80s, see Paul Gootenberg, *Between Silver and Guano: Commercial Policy and the State in Postindependence Peru* (Princeton, 1989) and *Imagining Development: Economic Ideas in Peru's "Fictitious Prosperity" of Guano, 1840–1880* (Berkeley, 1993).

91 Archivo General de la Nación, Peru (AGN), Archivo del Ministerio del Interior, Legajo 95, Mesa de Partes 73.

92 AGN, Ministerio del Interior, Legajo 95, Mesa de Partes 424.

2. Unimagined Communities

1   Biblioteca Nacional del Perú, Sala de Investigaciones (BNP/SI), D11680, Copia de Documentos relativos a acuerdos sobre la continuación del pago de tributos, que fue suspendido por las Cortes, 20 November 1813.

2   Archivo Departamental de Ancash, Huaraz (ADA), Fondo Notarial Valerio, Legajo 3, Autos seguidos por Gregoria Gonzáles contra el Peruano Manuel Jesús Barreto sobre el cobro de arrendamiento de las tierras trigueras de Marcac, 1823.

3   ADA, Fondo Notarial Valerio, Civiles, Legajo 12, Expediente que le pertenece a José María Chacpi, Manuel Aniceto y María Sevastián Chacpi de los terrenos de repartición que se le ha adjudicado de orden Superior, fols. 28-29, 12-16 May 1846.

4   John Lynch, *The Spanish American Revolutions, 1808-1826* (New York, 1986).

5   J. V. Ugarte de Pino, *Historia de las constituciones del Perú* (Lima, 1978), pp. 23, 29-30. Ugarte de Pino appears to be one of the few Peruvian historians to note the modular significance of the Spanish Constitution of 1812 for independent Peru's republican constitutions.

6   BNP/SI, D11680, Copia de Documentos relativos a acuerdos sobre la continuación del pago de tributos, que fué suspendido por las Cortes, 20 November 1813.

7   BNP/SI, D9738, Expediente sobre aseptar la espontánea Voluntad de los Yndios de las principales Provincias del Reyno que ofrecen pagar los tributos, 16 November 1812. Also see BNP/SI D11670, Reunión promovida por las principales autoridades del Virreynato viendo la conveniencia de continuar cobrando los tributos, frente a la grave amenaza que se cierne sobre las colonias como consecuencia de los movimientos separatistas que se intentan realizar, Lima, 11 July 1812.

8   BNP/SI D11670, Reunión promovida por las principales autoridades del Virreynato, 11 July 1812.

9   The "neo-*cacique*" tribute collectors appear after 1783, when some, but not all, hereditary *kurakas* were removed from tribute-collection duties. In some cases the *kurakas* were allowed to continue as nominal *caciques*, but not as *recaudadores de reales tributos* or *gobernadores*. The separation of chiefship from the tribute-collection function and the office of governor did irreparable damage to the power and authority of the remaining *kurakas* in late colonial Huaylas. See Thurner, "From Two Nations," chap. 2.

10 Tristan Platt, "Liberalism and Ethnocide in the Southern Andes," *History Workshop Journal* 17 (1984), pp. 3-18.

11 BNP/SI, D9738, Expediente sobre aseptar la espontánea Voluntad, 16 November 1812.

12 BNP/SI, D6183, Expediente y providencias para la creación de alcaldes [de españoles] en las Doctrinas del Partido de Huaylas, Lima, 22 June 1820.

13 BNP/SI, C3493, Autos seguidos de oficio por la real justicia contra la sedición de varios individuos vecinos del Pueblo de Huaraz, Caraz, 1 April 1797.

14 BNP/SI, D6183, Expediente . . . para la creación de alcaldes en las Doctrinas del Partido de Huaylas. The words are Yrigoyen's, dated in Lima, 22 June 1820.

15   On the ceremonial attire of republican officials in the provinces—prefects, subprefects, and governors—see Emilio Dancuart, *Anales de la Hacienda Pública del Perú* (Lima, 1902-26), vol. 5, pp. 143-48.

16   For colonial transformations see Mark Thurner, "From Two Nations to One Divided: The Contradictions of Nation-Building in Andean Peru" (Ph.D. diss., University of Wisconsin–Madison, 1993), chap. 2.

17   Delivered in Lima, 27 August 1821. For the text of San Martín's decree, see Dancuart, *Anales,* vol. 1, p. 239.

18   Decree given in Cuzco on 4 July 1825. For the text, see ibid., vol. 1, p. 272.

19   For Gregoria's full name and lineage, see ADA, Fondo Notarial Valerio, Civiles, Legajo 5, Testamento de Gregoria Palma Gonzáles y Rimaicochachin, 27 March 1830.

20   ADA, Fondo Notarial Valerio, Legajo 3, Autos seguidos por Gregoria Gonzáles contra el Peruano Manuel Jesús Barreto sobre el cobro de arrendamiento de las tierras trigueras de Marcac, 1823.

21   The Constitution of 1812, drawn up by the liberal Cortes de Cadiz, was approbated in public assemblies throughout Huaylas. See Félix Alvarez-Brun, *Ancash: Una historia regional peruana* (Lima, 1970).

22   Toribio Luzurriaga, who with San Martín campaigned in La Plata (i.e., Argentina), was the first president of the liberated Department of Huaylas, which then included most of the north-central highlands and coast, including Huanuco. See ibid.

23   ADA, Fondo Notarial Valerio, Legajo 3, Autos seguidos por Gregoria Gonzáles contra el Peruano Manuel Jesús Barreto sobre el cobro de arrendamiento de las tierras trigueras de Marcac, 1823.

24   The *ex-cacica* Doña Gregoria found ways to retain considerable influence in post-colonial Huaylas. In her last will and testament of 1830, she explained that she had donated "some quantities" of pesos to the bankrupt departmental treasury and that "in compensation" the authorities had, in classic colonial style, granted her continued dominion over half of the *cacicazgo* lands of Huaraz. This was her "service to the *patria.*" Thus, in this case, the diminished post-Independence leverage of a *kuraka* was accommodated in the fiscal pressures of the early republican moment. The *ex-cacica*'s testament revealed that she and her *mestizo* husband still held considerable properties.

25   The term "indígenas" remains the contemporary emblem of progressive consciousness about "Native Americans" (yet another historical oxymoron). Its origins, however, lie in the Creole nationalist distaste for terms colonial. In many ways, moreover, "indio" or "Indian" was more generous, since it recognized cultural origins and national identity distinct from Europe and prior to the newly invented nation-state. As the Peruvian congressman and political economist Pedro de Rojas y Briones observed, in his explicatory amendment to the Constitution of 1828, "To change their title from Indian to Peruvian, and after that to indigene, seems like a great injury to so heroic a nation; do they think it honorable to change the proper

title of one's origin, when he who is born in Spain, France, or England considers it an honor to be called Spanish, French, or English?" The unequal exchange of "Indian" nationhood for dubious "native" or "indigene" status at the bottom of the national racial hierarchy served only to mark the great distance over which any Indian had to travel to reach the apex occupied by the Creole elite. See Rojas y Briones, *Proyectos de economía política, que en favor de la República Peruana ha formado el ciudadano Pedro de Rojas y Briones, diputado del soberano congreso nombrado por la Provincia de Cajamarca* (Lima, 1828), fols. 22 23.

26 See Thurner, "From Two Nations," chap. 2.

27 ADA, Fondo Notarial Valerio, Civiles, Legajo 12, Expediente que le pertenece a José María Chacpi, Manuel Aniceto y María Sevastián Chacpi de los terrenos de repartición que se le ha adjudicado de orden Superior, 12–16 May 1846.

28 In late colonial Huaylas, the *waranka* (Quechua = thousand) was not the equivalent of an Inka censual unit of 1000, but was rather a multi-community moiety under an ethnic chief, or *waranka kuraka* (Spanish, *cacique de guaranga* or *cacique principal*). These chiefly moieties contained peasant communities or hamlets grouped together in *pachaca* (Quechua = hundred) units, which were also not groups of 100 in the same sense that *waranka* were not units of 1000; that is to say, *pachaca* were peasant communities, or *ayllu* (ancestor-focused kin groups), and often multi-*ayllu* communities of peasants. In the postcolonial period, the chiefly *waranka* (Spanish, *guaranga*) are officially renamed and reconstituted as *distritos* (districts) under non-Indian officials called *gobernadores* (governors), who in turn held jurisdiction over the Indian *alcaldes*. The nominations *pachaca* and *ayllu* largely disappear in the postcolonial period, when hamlets are identified as *estancias*.

29 Twentieth-century ethnographies indicate that "la república" referred both to festive community labor brigade (*minka*) and corvée labor service. Those who took part in *la república* labor were known as *republicanos*. Paul Doughty notes, however, that usage of "republicano" was more widespread in the district of Atun Huaylas than elsewhere in the Callejón de Huaylas when he did fieldwork there in the 1960s (personal communication, 1994). See Doughty, *Huaylas: An Andean District in Search of Progress* (Ithaca, 1968), and William Stein, *Hualcan: Life in the Highlands of Peru* (Ithaca, 1961).

30 ADA, Fondo Notarial Valerio, Civiles, Legajo 19, Expediente del Yndígena Manuel Resurrección con Juan de Mato sobre división y partición de bienes, 1854.

31 On the alienation of lands and the decline of the tributary population in colonial Huaylas, see Thurner, "From Two Nations," chap. 2.

32 This and following passages are from ADA, Fondo Notarial Valerio, Civiles, Legajo 15, Estéban Ramírez con María Santos y otros sobre las tierras de Cuyuc-Rumi en la estancia de Llactas, 1850–51.

33 Tristan Platt, *Estado boliviano y ayllu andino: Tierra y tributo en el norte de Potosí* (Lima, 1982).

34 Jean Piel, "The Place of the Peasantry in the National Life of Peru in the Nineteenth Century," *Past and Present* 46 (1970), pp. 108–33.

35 Dancuart, *Anales*, vol. 4, pp. 94–96; also see Heraclio Bonilla, "Continuidad y cambio en la organización política del estado en el Perú independiente," in Alberto Flores Galindo, ed., *Independencia y revolución, 1780–1840* (Lima, 1987), p. 285.

36 George Kubler, *The Indian Caste of Peru, 1795–1940* (Washington, D.C., 1952); Carlos Contreras, "Estado republicano y tributo indígena en la sierra central en la post-Independencia," *Histórica* 13:1 (1989), pp. 9–44.

37 Kubler, *The Indian Caste*, p. 2.

38 The grab-bag "castas" category was abolished in 1854, however. The first national census (1876) — perhaps reflecting the heightened racialist consciousness of Creoles — restored the "white" category by distinguishing it from "mestizos," although neither were any longer linked to fiscal or tax status. In the second national census (1940), "whites" return to the fold and are counted together in a "mestizo-white" category. On the postcolonial tax system, see Thurner, "From Two Nations," chap. 3.

39 For one such case, see ADA, Fondo Notarial Valerio, Juicios Civiles Republicanos, Legajo 6, Autos criminales seguidos contra Don Gabriel Gomero sobre estorciones que hizo en Jangas, 1836. On the general trend, see Bonilla, "Continuidad y cambio."

40 See Felipe Guaman Poma, *El primer nueva coronica i buen gobierno* [1936] (Mexico, 1980), pp. 738–51, and Roger Rasnake, *Domination and Cultural Resistance: Authority and Power among an Andean People* (Durham and London, 1988), pp. 9–14 and 215–22. Still, Rasnake's reading of the detailed drawings of *kurakas* in hispanic garb (as evidence for acculturation) may overlook the corresponding illustrations of *alcaldes* in the *justicia* section of the *Nueva coronica*. The *alcaldes* are depicted in Andean or Inka attire, while the *principales* are clothed in hispanic robes. Since the *Nueva coronica* states that certain *alcaldes* are *principales*, i.e., the *camachicoc* or *pachaca* authorities, one may assume that the author wishes to present two (situational?) images/poses of the same personages at different functions. No such dual wardrobe is found in the closets that were assigned to the *capac apu* or *waranka kuraka* of the early colonial period, however. In the eighteenth century, however, powerful *kurakas* were portrayed in ceremonial Andean and Hispanic robes by painters and colonial inspectors.

41 In Huaylas until the early 1780s, most hereditary chiefs (*kurakas*) or *caciques principales* held three functions or powers invested in three titles or posts: (a) *cacique*, or chief, which was an honorary title; (b) *gobernador*, or governor, which was a political office; and (c) *recaudador de real tributo*, or royal tribute collector, whose responsibility it was to collect tribute from his Indian subjects. The three together lent considerable prestige and power to the position of chief. After 1783, many *caciques* in Huaylas held only the honorary title while the real power, invested in the positions of governor and tribute collector, was assigned by the magistrate to *mestizo* governors and collectors, who also adopted the title of *cacique* but were much disliked by native communities. See Thurner, "From Two Nations," chap. 2.

42 The appointment of *mestizo* tribute collectors was protested and litigated by Indian

alcaldes and others in the name of their communities in the most important *cacicaz-gos* of the Huaylas region, including Lurin Huaylas, Yungay, and Huaraz in 1775–90. See Archivo General de la Nación, Peru (AGN), Derecho Indígena, Legajo 21, Cuaderno 362; BNP/SI, C2806, Petición de Don Clemente Alba al Real Hacienda, 1785; BNP/SI, C3040, Expediente promovido por Don Domingo Ramos Huerta y Julián Guerrero yndios del Pueblo de Yungay . . . a nombre de su comunidad solicitando la separación del cargo de Cobrador de Tributos a José Gonzáles Olivera, 7 January 1789; and BNP/SI, C3636, Provisión real ordenanza de diligencias de cacicazgos, dirigida al Subdelegado del Partido de Huaylas, 1792.

43   BNP/SI, C3490, Alcaldes de Indios de Huaraz al Subdelegado del Partido de Huaylas, 1790.

44   In colonial and postcolonial Huaylas, the *alcaldes'* staffs were blessed by the parish priest each year at the office rotation, which occurred on the Feast of the Magi in early January. On the symbolism of the staff in Yura, Bolivia, see Rasnake, *Domination and Cultural Resistance*, pp. 215–22.

45   BNP/SI, D5875, Expediente de Visita del Partido de Huaylas, 1817.

46   In 1813 the *alcaldes,* not the hereditary chiefs or appointed *caciques,* collected tribute in Atun Huailas. Archivo Arzobispal de Lima (AAL), Capítulos, Legajo 41, Expediente VI, 1813.

47   AGN, O.L. 357-66, Prefecto Joaquín Gonzáles al Señor Ministro de Estado en el Despacho de Gobierno, Huaraz, 18 February 1850. Gonzáles wrote that the *alcaldes de campo,* were named by the *gobernadores* to collect tribute in the hamlets, or *estancias,* and that they did this "by custom, without pay." When in 1849 a law was passed making such unpaid service illegal, the prefect saw that without the *alcaldes* it might be very difficult to find "volunteers" who would collect the tribute for a *premio* of a mere 2 percent. The solution was to name the *alcaldes* as collectors when a paid "volunteer" could not be found.

48   Andrés Guerrero (personal communication, 1992) has pointed out that this was not necessarily Bolívar's intention. In New Granada, *alcaldes ordinarios* and *pedáneos* were recognized in 1821 as "jueces de primera instancia" at the county and parish level. I have not located comparable republican legislation on *alcaldes* in Peru. *Alcaldes pedáneos* were recognized in Peru in 1855, but as municipal authorities. In 1904, however, the Peruvian state maintained that the Indian *alcaldes* were colonial authorities and, as such, had been abolished with Independence. The problem in 1904 had more to do with *alcalde ordinario* political authority, and with the role priests had in blessing the *vara,* than with the municipal office of *alcalde pedáneo.*

49   ADA, Fondo Notarial Valerio, Civiles, Legajo 17, Civil seguido por el Alcalde Pedáneo de Quillo contra los Yndígenas que han enajenado sus topos sin saber leer ni escribir, con infracción de la ley de 27 de Marzo de 1828, 1853.

50   *Polylepis* was the major source of cooking fuel until the eucalyptus tree was imported and propagated in sufficient numbers, which appears not to have occurred in Huaylas until the twentieth century. Eucalyptus, however, is a lower-elevation, planted tree which is usually privately owned.

51   AGN, H-4-1832, Sección Contribuciones, Matrícula de Yndígenas de la Provincia de Huaylas, Tomo II, Observaciones generales, 1842.

52   Of course, identical arguments were made by colonial officials in defense of the *reparto de mercancías* and other tributary obligations.

53   ADA, Fondo Notarial Valerio, Causas Civiles, República, Legajo 12, Manuel Ysidro y otros sobre exoneración de tributos, Huaraz, 4 January 1846, fols. 1-1v.

54   ADA, Fondo Notarial Valerio, Causas Civiles, República, Legajo 12, Manuel Ysidro y otros sobre exoneración de tributos, Huaraz, 4 January 1846, fols. 1v-2.

55   Thurner, "From Two Nations," chap. 2.

56   Karen Spalding, "Hacienda–Village Relations in Andean Society to 1830," *Latin American Perspectives* 4 (1975), pp. 107-21.

57   ADA, Fondo Notarial Valerio, Causas Civiles, República, Legajo 12, Manuel Ysidro y otros sobre exoneración de tributos, Huaraz, 4 January 1846, fols. 5-5v.

58   ADA, Fondo Notarial Valerio, Civiles, Legajo 20, Benito Vincenti vecino de Huaraz y hacendado de Lucma, contra indígenas de la estancia de Pampa Huahin, fols. 19-19v, 1855-56.

59   *El Comercio*, 12 January 1855.

60   BNP/SI, D2090, Decreto expedido por . . . Ramón Castilla, 26 June 1855.

61   An interesting treatise in support of Castilla's liberal revolution and highly critical of the National Convention, which blocked many of the proposed reforms, was written by the liberal priest Gavino Uribe of Huarmey, Ancash. See the 17 February 1855 edition of *El Comercio*.

62   See Paul Gootenberg, *Between Silver and Guano: Commercial Policy and the State in Postindependence Peru* (Princeton, 1989).

63   Paul Gootenberg, *Imagining Development: Economic Ideas in Peru's "Fictitious Prosperity" of Guano, 1840-1880* (Berkeley, 1993).

64   Gootenberg argues for this hands-off scenario, albeit with different implications, in "Population and Ethnicity in Early Republican Peru: Some Revisions," *Latin American Research Review* 26:3 (1991), pp. 109-57.

65   "Memoria del Ministro de Hacienda, Sr. D. Manuel del Río, presentada á las Cámaras reunidas en sesiones extraordinarias, 1849," in Dancuart, *Anales*, vol. 4, pp. 190-93.

66   Nelson Manrique makes this last point in *Campesinado y nación: Las guerrillas indígenas en la guerra con Chile* (Lima, 1981).

67   This point has sometimes been lost on the historiography. There are two traditional views, each equally misleading when applied to the Huaylas-Ancash case, concerning the meaning of Castilla's abolition. The first is that it was a "sincere" abolition; that is to say, Indians thereafter were completely free of tribute obligations, since the liberal guano state no longer required tribute of them. Castilla himself realized that guano income made this fiscally possible, but only in the short run. He realized that guano was a temporary and "extraordinary" resource and that more stable forms of revenue had to be found, but also that new forms were inherently unstable and difficult to establish. He was not interested in "liber-

ating" Indians from the contribution but, rather, in replacing it with the universal citizen poll-tax. This, of course, has the whiff of 1812. The second view holds that Castilla's abolition was meaningless—that "neocolonial" tribute continued to be paid in the provinces until 1895, when Piérola abolished it. This view was also held by numerous Lima intellectuals in the late nineteenth century who agonized over the defeated, illiberal state of affairs in postwar Peru. But such a view is untenable in the Huaylas-Ancash case for two reasons. First, the *contribución personal* was a sporadic and essentially uncollectable war-tax and, in the Cáceres period, a phantom of departmental budget projections. In contrast, the tributary *contribución de indígenas* was eminently collectable in Huaylas from at least 1830 to 1848.

68 Platt, *Estado boliviano.*

69 See Gavin Smith, *Livelihood and Resistance: Peasants and the Politics of Land in Peru* (Berkeley, 1989), pp. 66–67, for an interesting footnote to the Castilla campaign near Huancayo.

70 In the pages of the Lima newspaper *El Comercio* for 23 November 1854, diagnostic descriptions of disease symptoms were given by a physician sent to Huaylas. The examining physician argued that the epidemic was not yellow fever but, rather, some unknown disease that killed with striking rapidity in the Indian *estancias*, where, he noted, hygiene was poor. Further correspondence on the epidemic in Huaylas appeared in *El Comercio* editions of 30 July, 7 September, and 9 October 1855. Typhoid or yellow fever was suggested in the correspondence of priests with the Lima archbishopric. From the letters of parish priests it is clear that the epidemic spread up from subtropical Santa to Macate as early as 1851 and into Conchucos in 1853 before reaching Yungay and the Callejón de Huaylas in 1854. See AAL, Comunicaciones Oficiales y de Curas, Legajo 18, 1855. The descriptions of the symptoms agree with those of *verruga peruana*, or Carrión's disease. This Peruvian measles, native to the subtropical valleys, would not be identified until the late nineteenth century when, in a medical experiment, David Carrión injected himself with some infected tissue. Carrión died as a result of his experiment. I thank Raúl Osorio, M.D., for pointing out to me that the clinical symptoms of *verruga peruana* correspond to those of the 1854 descriptions.

71 *El Comercio,* 19 January 1855. See article under the heading "Indíjenas y Esclavos."

72 On the 1854 revolt and the epidemic in Huaraz, see *El Comercio,* 20 February; 8, 11, 13, 14, 18, 23, and 27 March; 8, 18 April; 8 May; and 29 June 1854. Also see Moisés Octavio Haro F., *Actuación de Ancash en la revolución nacional de 1854* (Lima, 1940). The revolt was limited to Huaraz and environs. Yungay-Caraz and the rest of Huaylas-Ancash appear to have supported the incumbent regime. On the exuberance in Huaraz after Castilla's victory, see the 23 January 1854 edition of *El Comercio.*

73 AGN, Derecho Indígena, Legajo 20, Cuaderno 210, Manuel Morales, *Síndico* of Cochabamba, to President Ramón Castilla via the Subprefect of Huaylas, 1856.

74 The recomposition of lands in Peru had been ordered by the Crown in the late seventeenth century, but the royal land delegation did not reach Huaylas until 1712.

The recomposition was ordered in response to the fragmentation of Indian hold-ings, Indian tributary population decline, and the many illegal, unauthorized, or untitled land transfers that had transpired in the preceding period. In addition, it was a moneymaking venture for the Crown and its officials. On this last aspect, see Dancuart, *Anales,* vol. 1, pp. 67–71.

75 See Joanne Rappaport, *The Politics of Memory: Native Historical Interpretation in the Andes* (Cambridge, 1990) for an insightful discussion of the role of early colo-nial titles in struggles for ethnic and territorial identity in Colombia.

76 Jürgen Golte, *La racionalidad de la organización andina* (Lima, 1980).

77 In 1593 the number of tributaries in greater Huaylas was judged to be some 5,799. By 1602–4 the reported tributary population had fallen to 5,005 and the total Indian population was set at 28,779. The next relatively complete set of figures we have for Indian tributaries is for 1726, after the epidemic of bubonic plague in 1719–20 (for 1619–25 we have incomplete figures). The partial figures for Huaraz given in the Recomposition of 1712 reveal the drop in the *originario* (native landed peasant) population of Huaraz in 1726 to have been about 30 percent, from 132 in 1712 to 95 in 1726. When compared with the figures for Huaraz from the *visita* of 1558, the 1712 figures reveal a long decline in Huaraz's tributary population, from 596 to 132 *tributarios originarios.* The 1726 figures also reveal a deep decline in the tributary Indian population of Huaylas since 1593, probably sustained over the dis-astrous seventeenth century, which, according to Sánchez-Albornoz, was a period of demographic decline across highland Indian South America. In 1726 a total of only 3,173 tributaries were counted—or little more than half the number in 1593— and about half of these were *forasteros.* By 1754, the number of tributaries edged upward to 3,857 and the total number of Indians was set at 12,541—a drastic de-cline from the 28,779 of 1602–4. See Thurner, "From Two Nations," chap. 2. For general trends in Peru and Latin America, see Noble David Cook, *Demographic Collapse: Indian Peru, 1520–1620* (Cambridge, 1981) and Nicolás Sánchez-Albornoz, *The Population of Latin America: A History* (Berkeley, 1974).

78 See Thurner, "From Two Nations," chap. 2.

79 In 1594 the *kurakas* of Huaraz purchased 110 *fanegadas* (1 *fanegada* is approximately 10 acres) "for the Indians of our *warankas.*" This expanse was greater than the total repartition lands (95 *fanegadas*) granted to the Indians of both *warankas* of Huaraz in 1712. See Thurner, "From Two Nations," chap. 2.

80 Platt, *Estado boliviano,* p. 20.

81 Not all of the composition lands purchased by *kurakas* in 1594 or 1712 were inherited by the Indian communities, though. Besides those sold by *kurakas* as noted above, some late eighteenth-century chiefs sought to claim composition lands as their own private property, arguing that the lands did not belong to the *común.* See, for ex-ample, BNP/SI, C2780, Autos que sigue Don Carlos Gonzáles Rimay Cochachin, Cazique y Gobernador de la Parcialidad de Ychoc Huaraz . . . con Diego de Cáceres sobre las tierras de repartición nombradas Picop, 1786. In this dispute, one side ar-gued that the lands in question were repartition lands and therefore belonged to

the community; the other side argued that they were composition lands purchased by their ancestors in 1594 and therefore the private property of the chief's lineage.

82   *El Comercio,* 17 February 1855.

83   ADA, Fondo Notarial Valerio, Civiles, Legajos 20 and 23.

84   See ADA, Fondo Notarial Valerio, Civiles, Legajos 25-35, passim. On the general trend, Florencia Mallon, *The Defense of Community in Peru's Central Highlands: Peasant Struggle and Capitalist Transition, 1860–1940* (Princeton, 1983).

85   ADA, Fondo Notarial Valerio, Civiles, Legajo 36, Civil seguido por Ysidro Reyes y Julián Espada con Manuel Robles, sobre despojo de unas tierras denominadas Cajacay, 1871.

3. Republicans at War

1   Biblioteca Nacional del Perú, Sala de Investigaciones (BNP/SI), D7041, Expediente organizado con motivo de pretender la H. Municipalidad de esta Capital ingerirse en asunto de conscripción, Huaraz, 30 December 1883. Also see C. A. Alba Herrera, *Atusparia y la revolución campesina de 1885 en Ancash* (Lima, 1985), pp. 25-26.

2   Archivo Histórico Militar, Lima (AHM), Estado Mayor General del Ejército, Legajo 0.1885.6.

3   Emphasis in original: "General Cáceres EL GRAN REPUBLICANO, como ellos lo llaman."

4   William Stein repeats Ernesto Reyna's error when he states that Atusparia was "alcalde pedáneo of the barrio of La Restauración, one of the two subdivisions in which the district of Huaraz is and was divided" (*El levantamiento de Atusparia,* Lima, 1988, p. 65). Atusparia was *alcalde ordinario* of the "first" district of La Independencia (to which Marian belonged), Guillén was his *segundo* or counterpart in Huaraz's "second" district of La Restauración — neither were "barrio" organizations and Huaraz was not a district. The dual asymmetry of political organization in postcolonial Huaraz had its colonial origins in the late sixteenth-century reduction of the Indian population of the region into the chiefly moieties or *guarangas* of Ychoc and Allauca Huaraz. Ychoc was the "originario" or *llacta* chieftaincy, and it was always dominant over the smaller Allauca chieftaincy, which was considered the "forastero" or *llachuaz* congregation. Most of the ethnohistorical literature on Huaraz and Huaylas has likewise mismapped the dual colonial organization of the region by simply assuming that Ychoc (which means "left" in Quechua) corresponded to the left (west) bank or Cordillera Negra side of the Upper Santa River, and that Allauca (which means "right" in Quechua) corresponded to the right (east) bank, or Cordillera Blanca side of the river. Colonial land titles and related documentation demonstrate that the *ayllus* and *pachacas* of Ychoc were located on both sides of the Santa River, as were those of Allauca. The spatial division, which was diffuse, was not centered on the river, but rather on the reduction or *pueblo* of Huaraz. The relationship of the dual *warankas* was low/high or, in this case, north/south of the center of town. The *ayllus* of Ychoc were situated in the lands to the north of the center of the reduction, or downriver from Huaraz, whereas

Allauca was situated south or upriver. It is also clear that the postcolonial districts correspond to the colonial *warankas*. Ychoc, which remained dominant, became Huaraz's "first district" of La Independencia, whereas Allauca became Huaraz's "second district" of La Restauración (the *ayllus* and *pachacas* would come to be called *estancias*). The *alcalde ordinario* of La Independencia district, like his Ychoc *kuraka* predecessor, was the leading Indian authority in the province of Huaraz (and, by extension, in the entire Huaylas region). Likewise, the non-Indian district governor of La Independencia was invested with more authority and power than his counterpart in La Restauración. The procedure for registering taxpayers and collecting the contribution began with the La Independencia governor and his district, then proceeded to the La Restauración district. This is probably why Atusparia and his *varayoc* were implicated and jailed first, and later Guillén appeared with his *alcaldes*. In the 1840s La Independencia district included the urban *barrios* of San Francisco and Huarupampa, and the Indian *estancias* of Picup, Pongor, Marcac, Chontayoc, Huanja, Huantallon, Antahuran, Unchuc, Catoc, Ssancayan, Curhuas, Cantu, Marian, Huanchac, Paria, Uquia, Chiqiuao, Acovichay, Aclla, Matcor, and Ssecsecpampa (and possibly Atupa, Chaquiyacu, Sanja, and Lucma as well). La Restauración included the *barrios* of Belen and Cercado, and the Indian *estancias* of Toclla, Huallcor, Aco, Jauna, Huamarin, Quechcap, Purucuta, Macasca, Coyllur, Lloclla, and Ssanssa. See Mark Thurner, "From Two Nations to One Divided: Contradictions of Nation-Building in Andean Peru," Ph.D. Diss., University of Wisconsin-Madison, 1993, chap. 2. Also see Archivo General de la Nación (AGN), H-4-1813, Expediente de actuación de la matrícula de indígenas de la provincia de Huaylas, 1841, fols. 9, 23–24, 30v, 35–35v, AGN H-4-1863, Libro de matrícula de indígenas de la provincia de Huaylas, Tomo I, 1845 [sic: 1842], and AGN H-6-0401, Censo de la ciudad de Huaraz, 1907.

5   Although this petition has not been preserved, rough descriptions of it were given in the newspaper reports of the day, including the 22 June 1885 edition of *El Comercio*. From these descriptions, it is clear that the petition closely resembled surviving petitions presented by the *alcaldes ordinarios* of Huaraz in 1887. For the latter petitions, see Chapter 4 below.

6   See *El Comercio*, 9 April 1885.

7   Although the historiography claims that Atusparia signed with an "X" because he supposedly could not sign his name (Stein, *El levantamiento*, p. 74), he had in fact learned to do so by early 1886. Although usually illiterate and unschooled, postcolonial *alcaldes* in Huaylas had to sign for legal purposes, however shakily. That Atusparia could not sign in 1879 (see ADA, Fondo Notarial Valerio, Civiles, Legajo 44, Don Pedro Pablo Atusparia con Don Francisco Huayané sobre propiedad de los terrenos de Huanchacpampa, 1879) but did in early 1886 suggests as much. Atusparia's scratchy signature appears in ADA, Fondo Notarial Valerio, Civiles, Legajo 48, Juicios Verbales, fol. 1v, 4 February 1886.

8   On braids and Andean authority, see Stein, *El levantamiento*, pp. 327–29, who cites Karen Spalding, *Huarochiri: An Andean Society under Inca and Spanish Rule* (Stan-

ford, 1984), p. 256. Today the preferred male hairstyle among the Ancash peasantry is a military-style crew cut.

9 Newspaper reports give in one case twelve *alcaldes*, and in the other twenty-four or twenty-five. Since La Independencia District had about twenty-four *estancias*, and since Atusparia, *alcalde ordinario* of that district had been imprisoned, it is safe to assume that the twenty-four *estancia alcaldes* who were imprisoned corresponded only to his district, not to all of Huaraz. Moreover, Collazos was governor of the district. Another report gives close to fifty *alcaldes* in all Huaraz, which was probably close to the true number; an 1887 petition signed by all the *alcaldes* of both districts of Huaraz included fifty-two signatures.

10 The point about cutting braids appears in newspaper accounts of the day. It has also become firmly lodged in the memory of the event. There is considerable disagreement about how many *alcaldes* lost their braids, with accounts ranging from one to all (including *alcaldes* in Carhuaz and elsewhere outside Huaraz). It is not clear if this sort of punishment was a last straw type of measure. It is also unclear whether all the *alcaldes* in Huaylas wore braids at the time although the *costumbrista* writer and Huamachuco native Abelardo Gamarra, who apparently passed through the Callejón de Huaylas in 1883, wrote that "the *varayos* [sic] . . . always carry a staff about one and a half yards long, full of decorative silver rings and with a handknob of the same material, and they all wear braids like those of the Chinese." See Gamarra, *Costumbres del interior* (Lima, 1888), pp. 4–5.

11 For this 2 March encounter, reports range from 400 to 2,000 Indians at the protest in Huaraz. The lower figure appears more likely.

12 According to the Census of 1876, the total male Indian population of the two districts of Huaraz was 4,504, while the female population was slightly larger, for a combined total of 9,145.

13 See letter signed by "Los Vecinos de Huaras" in *El Comercio* 29 April 1885.

14 *El Comercio*, 2 May 1885, "Ancash. Correspondencia para *El Comercio*," dated in Huaraz, 24 April 1885.

15 On the nationalist potential of the highland peasantry in the War of the Pacific, see Nelson Manrique, *Campesinado y nación: Las guerrillas indígenas en la guerra con Chile* (Lima, 1981); Florencia Mallon, "Nationalist and Anti-State Coalitions in the War of the Pacific: Junín and Cajamarca, 1879–1902," in Steve J. Stern, ed., *Resistance, Rebellion, and Consciousness in the Andean Peasant World, 18th to 20th Centuries* (Madison, 1987), pp. 232–79; and Mallon, *Peasant and Nation: The Making of Postcolonial Mexico and Peru* (Berkeley, 1995).

16 See Maurice Zeitlin, *The Civil Wars in Chile (or the bourgeois revolutions that never were)* (Princeton, 1984).

17 The Magdalena government was so called because it was based in the suburban barrio of Lima known as La Magdalena. The "neutral zone" was established by international agreement between Chile, the United States, and the García Calderón regime.

18 Manuel Reina Loli, *Ancash y la guerra con Chile* (Huaraz, 1981). Also see AHM, Ar-

chivo Recavarren, Cuaderno 10, Arturo Derteano to Isaac Recavarren, Hacienda Puente, fols. 34–39, June 1883.

19   AHM, Archivo Recavarren, Cuaderno 7, Tadeo Terry to Isaac Recavarren, fols. 11–12, Huaraz, 30 June 1882; AHM, Prefecturas, Ancash, Legajo 0.1879.4, Prefect Meneses to the Señor Director de Policía, Huaraz, 16 September 1879.

20   BNP/SI, Archivo Piérola, Caja 86, *Sirius,* nos. 1–13, 10 May to 27 September 1882.

21   Most of these recruits were labeled "vagos"—essentially, underemployed Indians—and not "hombres laboriosos," or elites, according to the recruitment orders of Prefect Meneses in 1879. Reina Loli (see n. 18 above) finds the Ancash case similar to that of Junín, where Indians apparently made up about half of the recruits at the Defense of Lima. On Junín and Lima, see Manrique, *Campesinado y nación,* pp. 61–71. Several patriotic members of Ancash's landed elite, including Pedro Cisneros (see below chap. 4), did respond to the call to arms for Lima's defense, however.

22   Reina Loli, *Ancash y la guerra,* p. 22.

23   Ibid., p. 24; Manrique, *Campesinado y nación,* p. 78.

24   García Calderón had written to Terry, asking for his support in achieving a swift end to Chilean occupation and to "the destruction of private property." In response, Terry firmly reprimanded García Calderón for "placing his private interests above those of the nation." Moreover, Terry exhorted García Calderón to resist paying Chilean "occupation taxes" and instead to donate the funds to the highland resistance. García Calderón's response was Isaac Recavarren's expeditionary force. See Reina Loli, *Ancash y la guerra,* p. 38.

25   On this effort, see Manrique, *Campesinado y nación,* pp. 76–78, 120–21. At the same time, an expedition was sent to Huarochiri. The Huarochiri expedition met a similar fate, with large desertions to Cáceres and the resistance.

26   Reina Loli, *Ancash y la guerra,* p. 36; also AHM, Archivo Recavarren, Cuaderno 7, War Minister Carrillo to Colonel Ysaac Recavarren, fols. 2–3, La Magdalena, 4–5 May 1881.

27   See Manrique, *Campesinado y nación,* p. 78.

28   Yungay boasted a small landed elite of its own with colonial and early republican roots. Moreover, the Yungay labor market was more directly connected with the coastal plantation and guano-extraction economy than other highland towns in the Callejón de Huaylas, and this juncture linked Yungay's landed elite with its coastal counterpart. Indian and *mestizo* "enganche" or bonded labor recruited in Yungay for the guano-producing islands and coastal plantations was considerable. On the latter, see Mario Vázquez, "Los braceros de las islas guaneras del Perú," in José R. Sabogal Wiesse, ed., *La comunidad andina* (Mexico, 1969), pp. 257–72.

29   Manrique, in *Campesinado y nación,* citing Cáceres, claims a couple hundred, but Recavarren's own archive affirms a number closer to a hundred.

30   Olívas Escudero, a native of the Pomabamba (Conchucos) region to the east of Yungay, was a central figure in provincial life, and he played a key role in the pacification of the Atusparia uprising; later he rose to become bishop of Ayacucho. In a serious political blunder, Prefect Gonzáles had Olívas Escudero forcibly removed

from his popular ministry in Huaraz. Editor of Huaraz's Catholic artisan news-paper, *El Obrero de Ancash*, the priest had both a personal vendetta and the social position to punish the *calderonistas* for their repressive actions.

31   AHM, Archivo Recavarren, Libro de Recortes de Periódicos, *El Obrero de Ancash*, 29 June 1881.

32   AHM, Archivo Recavarren, Cuaderno 17, D252, Recavarren to Olívas Escudero, fol. 69v, 20 May 1883.

33   I follow Manrique's distinction between semi-independent peasant *guerrillas* operating under the auspices of the La Breña command, and the multiclass *montoneras* made up primarily of forced recruits. This usage has the advantage of agreeing with the language of the campaign itself.

34   Cáceres was offered the second vice-presidency under Calderón but declined in order to dedicate himself to military matters. His spouse, Antonia Moreno de Cáceres, may have influenced the general's decision to adhere to the Calderón-Montero government, which he did officially on 24 January 1882.

35   Recavarren, who was Calderón's brother-in-law, could now maintain loyalty both to the Constitution and his family.

36   Montero apparently chose Huaraz because it was close enough to Lima to permit negotiations with foreign emissaries who sought to mediate a negotiated peace treaty with the Chileans, but far enough away from the Chilean command in Lima to ensure a semblance of independence. The U.S. envoy Prescott met with Montero in Huaraz on 9 May but failed to persuade him to accept Chilean terms for peace.

37   Reina Loli, *Ancash y la guerra*, p. 48.

38   Ibid., p. 53.

39   AHM, Archivo Recavarren, Cuaderno 8, Cáceres to Recavarren, Canta, fols. 3-6, 1 March 1883. After the failed mission to Huaraz in 1881, the colonel made his way back to his native Arequipa, where his aristocratic family owned a large estate. His political and military career was still far from over, however. A hero of the Defense of Pisagua, where he defended Peruvian and Bolivian batteries against overwhelming Chilean naval firepower, Recavarren had gained a reputation among Chilean and Peruvian officers alike for his gutsy courage and leadership. It was this reputation earned in the Southern Campaign that prompted Cáceres to call on him later that year. Between August and December, Recavarren corresponded with Cáceres, who was then commander-in-chief of the Central Army headquartered in Tarma (Junín). They exchanged views on such matters as the viability of Piérola's dictatorship, on the National Congress to be held in Arequipa, and on the problem of the traitorous rebellion of General Iglesias in Cajamarca, who had defected in late August; they also discussed the need to secure arms. See AHM, Archivo Recavarren, Cuaderno 7, Cáceres to Recavarren, fols. 14-22v, Tarma, 31 August, 15 November, and 29 December 1882.

40   Recavarren set off from Junín with a force of only 194 men ("without military instruction or discipline, dressed in rags") drawn from the Pucará Battalion of Cáceres's Central Army and armed with "187 broken rifles." They were short of

munitions and had only two small artillery pieces, one of which Recavarren had personally lugged all the way from his native Arequipa. See AHM, Archivo Recavarren, Cuaderno 10, Cáceres to Recavarren, fols. 2–3, Tarma, 20 February 1883; AHM, Archivo Recavarren, Cuaderno 10, Recavarren to Cáceres, fols. 106–8v, Carhuaz, 23 May 1883.

41 Cáceres considered Iglesias to be weak and vulnerable to attack, and he reasoned that Recavarren's small contingent, if joined with the nationalist forces of José Mercedes Puga and Manuel Becerra in Cajamarca, would be sufficient to subdue Iglesias. This inaccurate perception of the threat posed by Iglesias was in large part owing to Becerra's and Puga's consistent exaggerations of their own strength. Positioned between the two, Recavarren recognized a measure of patriotic breast-beating in this, and his military strategy took into account the numerous blind spots in the correspondence between the nationalist *caudillos* of north and center. See AHM, Archivo Recavarren, passim. On the Puga and Becerra *montoneras* in Cajamarca, see Mallon, "Nationalist and Anti-State Coalitions."

42 In 1883, these seven provinces were Cajatambo, Santa, Huaylas, Huaraz, Huari, Pallasca, and Pomabamba.

43 The northern departments (Ancash, Huanuco, La Libertad, Cajamarca, Lambayeque, Piura) were also ordered to support Cáceres's Central Army with monthly quotas, since the "*pueblos* [of the north] [we]re relatively virgin compared with th[o]se [of the central highlands] that c[ould] no longer support us materially." See AHM, Archivo Recavarren, Cuaderno 10, Cáceres to Recavarren, fols. 8–10, Canta, 29 March 1883.

44 AHM, Archivo Recavarren, Cuaderno 17, Document 17, Recavarren to the commanding officers of the Huallaga and Pisagua battalions, fols. 7–9, Huaraz, 15 April 1883; also Document 20, Recavarren to Commanding Officer of Pisagua, Huaraz, 20 April 1883. On accounting, see Document 91, Recavarren to Benavides, fols. 27v–28, Sayan, 18 March 1883. An example of Recavarren's persuasive rhetoric appears in Document 117, a circular issued from Copa on 4 April 1883.

45 See AHM, Archivo Recavarren, Cuaderno 17, Documents 19, 20, 24, 26, 33, 47, 48, 50, 52, 64, 65, 68, 74, 103, and 106, Recavarren to various officials, 29 March to 10 June 1883.

46 On *guerrillas* in Ancash, see AHM, Archivo Recavarren, Cuaderno 17, Documents 228–49, Recavarren to various officials and *jefes de guerrillas,* fols. 65–69, Huaraz, 15–19 May 1883.

47 Ministerio de Guerra, Comisión Permanente de Historia del Ejército del Perú, *La Guerra del Pacífico. La Resistencia de La Breña: Huamachuco y el alma nacional (1882–1884)* (Lima, 1983), tomo 3, vol. 1, p. 320. Ministerio sources are the reports of Stephan to Lynch, Casma, 23 July 1883, and Lynch to War Ministry, Lima, 25 July 1883.

48 See Atusparia's interview with Cáceres in Lima (chapter 4 below).

49 Manrique, *Campesinado y nación,* p. 284.

50 Ibid., p. 199.

51   AHM, Archivo Recavarren, Cuaderno 10, Elías to Recavarren, Chilia, fols. 48-43v, 29 July 1883.

52   Manrique, *Campesinado y nación,* p. 284.

53   AHM, Archivo Recavarren, Cuaderno 10, Elías to Recavarren, Chilia, 29 July 1883.

54   AHM, Archivo Recavarren, Cuaderno 10, Cisneros to Recavarren, Chancos, fol. 53, 17 September 1883.

55   AHM, Archivo Recavarren, Cuaderno 10, A. C. Vidal to Pedro Tocas, fols. 118-22v, Vilcasagra, 20 September 1883.

56   AHM, Archivo Recavarren, Cuaderno 10, Cisneros to Recavarren, fols. 54-54v, Chancos, 10 October 1883. Also see BNP/SI, Prefecturas, Ancash, Prefect Vargas to Ministry of Government, Huaraz, 4 and 8 November 1884. Another repressive move by the *iglesista* regime was the closing of the Corte Superior of Ancash in February 1884. The regime justified the measure in economic terms, eliminating both the Piura and the Ancash court and ordering their archives be shipped to Lima. See *El Peruano,* Boletín Oficial, Semestre 1, no. 5, Decreto del Presidente de la República Miguel Yglesias, 2 February 1884.

57   Prefect Vargas was ordered to send 500 recruits to Lima in late October 1883. In January 1884 he sent 420 recruits from Huaraz to the port at Casma for passage by steamer to Lima. See AHM, Prefecturas, Ancash, Legajo o.1884.6., Vargas to the War Ministry, Huaraz, 7 January 1884.

58   Nevertheless, Vargas did order that the poll-tax be collected in Huaylas-Ancash. It was resisted in Macate, Pomabamba, and elsewhere, though. See BNP/SI, Prefecturas, Ancash, 1884 (II), Governor of Macate Gómez to Prefect Vargas, Macate, 27 March 1884. The newspaper accounts of 1885 that placed the blame on Prefect Noriega for being "the first prefect to collect the *contribución personal* in recent years" were inaccurate. For one such false accusation, see *El Comercio,* 29 April 1885, letter signed by "Los Vecinos de Huaras," Huaraz, 24 April 1885.

59   BNP/SI, D7041, Provincial Mayor Vidal to Prefect Vargas, Huaraz, 17 December 1883. Also see Alba Herrera, *Atusparia,* pp. 25-26.

60   On the dependency of *alcaldes* on municipalities in Tarma, see Archivo General de la Nación, Peru (AGN), Ministerio del Interior, Legajo 9, Mesa de Partes 101, Reclamo ante el Supremo Gobierno sobre servicios de las Comunidades del Distrito, 1889. Huasicancha appears to have been an exception. On the latter, see Gavin Smith, *Livelihood and Resistance: Peasants and the Politics of Land in Peru* (Berkeley, 1989).

61   BNP/SI, Prefecturas, Ancash, Prefect Vargas to the Ministry of Government, Huaraz, 18-19 May 1884.

62   BNP/SI, Prefecturas, Ancash, Prefect Vargas to the Ministry of Government, Huaraz, 15 June 1884.

63   BNP/SI, Prefecturas, Ancash, Prefect Vargas to the War Ministry, Casma, 29 June 1884.

64   According to the ex-subprefect of Huari, the *iglesista* Juan Miguel Esparza, Puga attacked Huaraz with "350 asiáticos prófugos y 40-50 peruanos vagos." See BNP/SI,

D8276, Subprefect Esparza to the Minister of State, 22 September 1884. Esparza's estimate left out the 200–300 seasoned *montoneros* who were the heart of Puga's force, but who seem not to have participated directly in the sack of Huaraz. The matriculation of Chinese bonded laborers, ordered by the Iglesias regime in December 1883, may have contributed to the flight of coolies to Puga's force. On 10 May, Prefect Vargas received a bulletin from Lima noting that only contracted rural and urban Chinese laborers were subject to the matriculation, not unemployed Chinese or those engaged in commerce. See BNP/SI, Prefecturas, Ancash, Prefect Vargas to the Ministry of Government, Huaraz, 24 May 1884.

65 BNP/SI, D4382, Prefect Porturas to the Subprefect of Huari, Sihuas, 22 October 1884.

66 AHM, Legajo o.1884.2, Echenique to War Ministry, Chimbote, 31 October 1884, and Echenique to War Ministry, n.d. [6 November?]. Echenique reported five companies of the Batallón Callao with 294 men, and 43 men with Noriega's escort.

67 BNP/SI, Prefecturas, Ancash, 1884 (IV), Noriega to Ministry of Government, Huaraz, 7 November 1884.

68 BNP/SI, Prefecturas, Ancash, Noriega to Ministry of Government, Huaraz, 21 November 1884.

69 *El Peruano,* Boletín Oficial, Semestre 2, 1884, no. 20, 3 December 1884, Ministro de Justicia Juan Sánchez al Señor Prefecto del Departamento de Ancash, Lima, 28 November 1884.

70 Prior to Noriega's arrival, however, most *puguista* officials had been removed from state posts. Delfín Araña assumed the prefecture after the Collazos-led coup, and Collazos assumed the subprefecture of the Province of Huaraz, displacing Justo Solís. Noriega had Collazos promoted to "teniente coronel" for having "captured the *cabecillas* of the *montonera*" and for leading "the reaction" in Huaraz. See BNP/SI, Prefecturas, Ancash, 1884 (IV), Prefect Araña to Ministry of Government, Huaraz, 25 October 1884; BNP/SI, Prefecturas, Ancash, 1884 (IV), Prefect Araña to Ministry of Government, Huaraz, 18 October 1884; *El Peruano,* Boletín Oficial, Semestre 2, 1884, no. 13, 25 October 1884, Nombramiento de Justo Solís como Subprefecto del Cercado de Huaraz, Lima, 6 October 1884; and AHM, Prefecturas, Ancash, Noriega to Ministry of Government, Huaraz, 6 December 1884.

71 BNP/SI, Prefecturas, Ancash, Noriega to Ministry of Government, Huaraz, 6 December 1884. After officially appointing Collazos as subprefect of Huaraz (he had occupied that post since the coup of 9 October), Lima informed Noriega that all subprefectures had been suppressed. Collazos had held the position of governor of La Independencia District under Prefect Vargas. Under Noriega, he was the unofficial subprefect of Huaraz as well as governor of La Independencia District, having direct jurisdiction over the *alcalde ordinario,* who in 1885 was Atusparia.

72 *El Comercio,* 2 May 1885, "Ancash. Correspondencia para *El Comercio,*" Huaraz, 24 April 1885 (see n. 14 above).

73 Archivo Departamental de Ancash, Huaraz (ADA), Libros Republicanos Varios,

Libro Copiador de Oficios de la H. Municipalidad de Huaraz 1884-85, fols. 1-1v, 29 October 1884.

74 *El Comercio,* 2 May 1885, Ancash. Correspondencia para *El Comercio,* Huaraz, 24 April 1885.

75 *El Peruano,* Boletín Oficial, Semestre 2, 1884, no. 6, Ministerio de Gobierno, Segundo Bringas to the Prefect of Ancash, 15 November 1884.

76 See *El Comercio,* 9-10 April 1885. The fabricated accusations against Noriega, which depicted him as the archvillain who single-handedly, and illegally, implemented the poll-tax, have unfortunately been picked up in the historiography. In implementing the poll-tax, Prefect Noriega acted legally and with the approval of the central government, and he had the full support of the departamental *junta de notables.*

77 BNP/SI, Prefecturas, Ancash, 1884 (IV), Prefect Noriega to Ministry of Government, Huaraz, 6 December 1884.

78 AGN, Ministerio de Hacienda, O.L.-559-81/559-88, Prefect Noriega to the Ministerio de Hacienda y Comercio, Huaraz, 2 January and 12 February 1885.

79 AGN, Ministerio de Hacienda, O.L.-559-92, Prefect Noriega to the Ministerio de Hacienda y Comercio, Huaraz, 21 February 1885.

80 AHM, Prefecturas, Ancash, Legajo o.1884.6, Noriega to the War Ministry, 18 November 1884.

81 BNP/SI, Prefecturas, Ancash, 1884 (IV), Prefect Noriega to the Ministry of Government, Huaraz, 18 November 1884. On the Chilean confiscation of the telegraph equipment in Casma, see BNP/SI, Prefecturas, Ancash, 1883 (I), Prefect Vargas to Ministry of Government, Huaraz, 27 October 1883.

82 AHM, Prefecturas, Ancash, Legajo o.1884.6, Prefect Noriega to the War Ministry, Huaraz, 5 December 1884.

83 AHM, Prefecturas, Ancash, Legajo o.1885.1, Prefect Noriega to the War Ministry, Huaraz, 21 February 1885.

84 BNP/SI, Prefecturas, Ancash, 1885 (I), Prefect Noriega to the Ministry of Government, Huaraz, 21 February 1885.

85 BNP/SI, Prefecturas, Ancash, Prefect Noriega to the Chief of Police in the Ministry of Government, Huaraz, 27 February 1885.

86 AHM, Correspondencia General, Legajo o.1885.7, Parte de la Comandancia del 1er Cuerpo de Policía (Manuel de la F. Mazuelos) al Sor. Coronel Comandante General de la División Expedicionaria de Huaras, Casma, 3 April 1885. For further discussion of the ill-fated Gonzáles expedition, see Stein, *El levantamiento,* pp. 338-43.

87 In the colonial period, Ecash Waranka (*guaranga de ecas*) was one of two moieties (Rupas was the other half) of the *pueblo* of Carhuaz. Together they now formed one postcolonial district, and thus their twin *alcaldes* held the title of *pedáneo* and not the higher rank of *ordinario,* which, in Huaylas-Ancash, was reserved for district-level *alcaldes,* as in Huaraz's La Independencia and La Restauración districts.

88 The source on Cochachin's experience as *alcalde pedáneo* is an oral account in Stein, *El levantamiento*, pp. 245–48.

89 It is also unclear whether Pedro Cochachin elicited any name recognition as carrier of an aristocratic Indian surname. The Cochachins were a powerful line of *kurakas* in both Carhuaz and Huaraz throughout the colonial period. Atusparia also had some colonial precedents of Indian leadership associated with his surname. Early in the eighteenth century, an Atusparia was both an *indio principal* and *alcalde*, with tribute-collection responsibility in the Waranka Allauca Huaraz. Pedro Atusparia was the *alcalde* of La Independencia District, however, which corresponded to the colonial Ychoc Huaraz.

90 The source is an oral account in Stein, *El levantamiento*, pp. 282–84.

91 On the revolts in Macate and Atun Huaylas, see AHM, Correspondencia General, Legajo o.1885.7, Telegrama Oficial no. 1, L. Haza to the Prefect, Chimbote, 3 April 1885. Also see Alba Herrera, *Atusparia*.

92 The first alarm appeared in AHM, Correspondencia General, Legajo o.1885.7, Subprefect J. Yandavere to Prefect Noriega, Caraz, 1 April 1885.

93 Mosquera was a marginal *misti* intellectual—in popular Andean parlance, a provincial "letrado" or "doctor." He appears to have been a professor, a lawyer, and a representative of Huaraz to Montero's National Congress held in Arequipa during April–July 1883. He was thus notably absent during Recavarren's Northern La Breña Campaign and the march to Huamachuco in 1883.

94 It is not unthinkable that while Mosquera was in Yungay, the Indian soldier Pedro Manuel Granados assumed a leadership role in Huaraz. A pro-Noriega source in Huaraz reported on 10 April that "having deposed the prefect whom they initially named, a Doctor Mosquera, the Indians have replaced him with one of their own chiefs, the Indian Pedro Granados, an old soldier of the gendarmes, who has let his braids grow long and has returned to wearing the national costume" (i.e., a poncho). Clearly an alarmist source, but nevertheless of historical interest. Pedro Granados does appear to have exercised military command. He made his mark during the rebellion in Huaraz, where he repelled *iglesista* attacks from *guerrilla* positions in Pumacayán. On the latter, see an anonymous letter dated in Huaraz on 26 May and printed in *El Comercio* on 22 June 1885. Granados's role is corroborated by another source, printed in *El País* on 11 April (see below). These sources, though, predictably confused the dual structure of command, which was both *cacerista* and *alcalde*.

95 AHM, Correspondencia General, Legajo o.1885.7, Subprefect Yandavere to the Prefect of Ancash, Caraz, 1 April 1885.

96 *El Comercio*, 23 April 1885: "Chimbote: Extracto de la correspondencia de *La Opinión Pública*," 19 April 1885.

97 The aging aristocrat Figueroa was named prefect of Ancash shortly after Noriega's defeat, but declined, he said, owing to ill health. Having received no help from Figueroa, Gonzáles requested that Lima appoint another prefect "so that we can resolve the difficult situation which has enveloped this department." Colonel José

Iraola was the choice. See AHM, Ministerio de Guerra, Correspondencia General, Legajo o.1885.7, Comandancia General de la División de Operaciones a Huaraz al Ministerio de Guerra, Casma, 4 April 1885.

98 AHM, Prefecturas, Ancash, Prefect Iraola to the War Ministry, Yungay, 29 April 1885. Part of the ultimatum was transcribed and printed in *El Comercio* 20 April 1885, and is also reproduced in Stein, *El levantamiento,* pp. 166-68.

99 *El País,* 11 April 1885, César Murga to Elías Malpartida, 9 April 1885. Reproduced in part in Stein, *El levantamiento,* pp. 82-89.

100 BNP/SI, Prefecturas, Ancash, 1885 (I), Prefect Iraola to the Ministry of Government, Lima, 8 April 1885.

101 AHM, Prefecturas, Ancash, José Iraola to the War Ministry, Puerto de Casma, 13 April 1885.

102 Indeed, Iraola's new field commander may well have been responsible for Puga's assassination. After the war, Puga's widow accused Colonel Callirgos Quiroga of murdering her husband. Callirgos Quiroga was later sentenced to prison as the commanding officer responsible for the assassination. See Alba Herrera, *Atusparia,* pp. 203-5.

103 Iraola's pacification force consisted of the remains of Gonzáles's force (two companies of "Policía" or "Celadores de Lima," the diminished "Artesanos de Lima" Battalion, and a small cavalry unit) plus the Batallón Canta and two artillery brigades. This force numbered between 600 and 800 men. An additional cavalry force, commanded by Sergeant Nickels, was sent from Pacasmayo with a large munitions shipment. Nickels's cavalry force did not reach the theater of battle until after Iraola had taken Huaraz, however. On the composition of these forces, see AHM, Estado Mayor del Ejército, Legajo o.1885.6, and Correspondencia General, Legajo o.1885.7. On Nickels's late arrival, see AHM, Correspondencia General, Legajo o.1885.7, Callirgos to War Ministry, Huaraz, 27 May 1885. Also see Manuel Valladares and Jean Piel, "Sublevación de Atusparia," in Wilfredo Kapsoli, ed., *Los movimientos campesinos en el Perú* (Lima, 1977), p. 160.

104 AHM, Estado Mayor General del Ejército, Legajo o.1885.6, Callirgos Quiroga to the Peruvian Central Command, Yungay, 27 April 1885.

105 AHM, Prefecturas, Ancash, Prefect Iraola to the War Ministry, Yungay, 29 April 1885.

106 Ibid.

107 Ibid.

108 Ibid.

109 On 1 May, Iraola had called his officers together in "junta de guerra" to decide on a course of action. All officers present voted to remain in Yungay and wait for a shipment of munitions and machine guns expected from Lima. But Iraola promptly vetoed their timidity, taking all responsibility upon himself for the success of the march on the rebel stronghold in Huaraz. See AHM, Prefecturas, Ancash, Legajo o.1885.1, Yungay, 22 April 1885.

110 AHM, Prefecturas, Ancash, Legajo o.1885.1, Prefect Iraola to War Ministry,

Huaraz, 7 May 1885; AHM, Estado Mayor General, Legajo o.1885.6, Parte del Estado Mayor de la División (Salazar) to Prefect Iraola, Huaraz, 3 May 1885.

111   AHM, Estado Mayor del Ejército, Legajo o.1885.6, Callirgos to Estado Mayor General, Huaraz, 8 May 1885.

112   *El Comercio*, 28 May 1885: Ancash (del *Boletín Oficial*), Prefect Iraola to the People of Ancash, 12 May 1885.

113   AHM, Prefecturas, Ancash, Legajo o.1885.1, Prefect Iraola to the War Ministry, Huaraz, 20 May 1885.

114   AHM, Prefecturas, Ancash, Legajo o.1885.1, Isidro Salazar to the Commander of the Northern Expeditionary Operation, Huaraz, 12 May 1885.

115   See Ranajit Guha, "The Prose of Counter-Insurgency," *Subaltern Studies II* (Delhi, 1983).

116   *El Comercio*, 9 October 1885.

117   Jorge Basadre, *La multitud, la ciudad, y el campo en la historia del Perú* (Lima, 1980), p. 223.

118   In *El levantamiento*, Stein writes: "La fecha del nombramiento [de Cochachin] nos es desconocida; puede haber sido dado antes del levantamiento, durante él, o puede haber sido enviado despúes de fracasar en sus ataques sobre Huaraz. Es posible que haya sido traído a Ancash por el coronel Manuel Armando Zamudio, asignado por Cáceres como jefe político y militar del norte" (pp. 96–97). Stein based his assertion on an article appearing in *El Comercio* on 9 October 1885, which reported that Cochachin had been appointed "por insinuación del doctor don Manuel Mosquera, ex-prefecto de los indios y de Justo Solís; que despúes continuó por haber recibido del General Cáceres y por conducto del Coronel Zamudio, los depachos del Comandante General de los guerrilleros de Ancash."

Nevertheless, at the same time Zamudio was named by Cáceres as "Jefe Superior," Tomás Romero y Flores also claimed that title as heir to Puga. Indeed, Romero y Flores would continue to assert his claim to the title and command as "Jefe Superior del Norte" even beyond the armistice signed between Cáceres and Iglesias. I am inclined to think that Cochachin was recognized by Romero y Flores because they operated in adjacent regions. Cáceres and Zamudio were very distant from Cochachin, apparently unaware of his actions. Moreover, in July 1885, Cáceres was no longer interested in allying himself with Indian *guerrillas* against the landed class he sought to win over. Zamudio's mission to Ancash was to "guarantee order," not to begin a campaign of *guerrilla* warfare. See AHM, Prefecturas, Cajamarca, Legajo o.1885.1, and Prefectura, La Libertad, Legajo o.1885.1, various communications, October–December 1885.

119   On the movements of Romero y Flores during March–May 1885, see BNP/SI, D3797, Prefect Relayze to the Ministry of Government, Trujillo, 9 May 1885; BNP/SI, D3710, Relayze to the Ministry of Government, Trujillo, 29 March 1885; and BNP/SI, D4362, Relayze to the Ministry of State, 17 May 1885.

120   Sources on events surrounding Puga's assassination include BNP/SI, D3710, Pre-

fect Relayze to the Ministry of Government, Trujillo, 29 March 1885; and BNP/SI, D4362, Relayze to the Ministry of State, 17 May 1885.

121   AGN, O.L.-560-13, Mariano José Madueño Comandante General de la División del Ejército del Norte to the War Ministry, Lima, 4 April 1885. To my knowledge no historian has claimed that Puga was on his way to Huaraz in March of 1885, nor is the document filed under AGN O.L.-560-13 anywhere cited in the literature.

122   Puga would have brought between 500 and 600 *montoneros* with him, most of whom carried firearms taken from the *iglesistas* at Huamachuco. It is noteworthy that an anonymous letter appearing in the Lima newspaper *El País* on 3 June 1885, stated that "had the Indians had about five hundred well-munitioned rifles [at the siege of Yungay] success in combat would have been theirs: valor and decision were in no short supply."

123   Manrique, *Campesinado y nación*, pp. 356–73.

124   See ibid., and Stein, *El levantamiento*.

125   For the Iraola–Zamudio correspondence, see AHM, Prefecturas, Ancash, 29 July to 7 August 1885.

126   Zamudio, the former subprefect of Santa, had occupied Huari (in Conchucos), but in the Callejón de Huaylas he failed to garner support.

127   *El Bien Público*, 10 September, 1885. Reproduced in Stein, *El levantamiento*, pp. 232–33.

128   *El Comercio*, 9 October 1885.

129   See *El Comercio*, 22 June 1885. As in the Mantaro Valley, Indians apparently knew the collaborationist enemy as "argollas" or "argollistas." These terms were originally applied to the *calderonistas* who sought peace with Chile after the fall of Lima in 1881.

130   This last objective is less clear. Jorge Basadre argues (*Historia de la República del Perú* [Lima, 1968] v. 8, p. 320) that the Chinese merchants of Lima were ransacked in January 1881 because certain Chinese had collaborated with the Chilean invaders. In Huaraz in 1885 the attacks on Chinese merchants were probably a response to the high prices of basic goods, but the attacks may also have had something to do with *puguista* reprimands. Some urban Chinese had joined Puga in Cajamarca, and Puga took Huaraz in June 1884 with a force of Chinese coolies freed from the plantations situated between Trujillo and Santa. It is possible, although undocumented, that the urban Chinese merchants of Huaraz, which numbered only three or four, resisted Puga or collaborated with the *iglesistas*. On the other hand, it is not unlikely that Chinese merchants' goods were considered neutral, and therefore "fair game" as sustenance for hungry rebels.

131   *El Comercio*, 9 April 1885.

132   See *El Comercio*, 29 April 1885. The pro-Noriega side of the debate claimed that the rebels, supposedly egged-on by delinquent landlords, had burned the *escribanías públicas* in order to destroy documents which purportedly demonstrated that they had usurped state lands. The anti-Noriega forces countered that only the Caja Fis-

cal archive had been burned; the latter were correct. The public notary registers, or *Protocolos* for the pre-1885 period are about 75 percent complete and show no signs of fire damage, and most are now deposited in the ADA. Likewise, the "Indian mob" was also accused of robbing the departmental treasury, but it is clear that there was nothing there to rob. Both Prefect Noriega and the *cajero fiscal* declared that no monies were kept in the safe, since all funds were drawn daily to support the troops. See Archivo General de la Nación (AGN) O.L. 561-416, Expediente relativo al incendio del archivo de la Caja Fiscal del Departamento de Ancash, 1885–86. In addition to the Prefectural Archives, it appears that some personal property records, kept in the sacked homes of suspected *iglesistas*, were also lost in the fray.

133   The complete contents of this archive as it stood in March 1885 is uncertain, but the general nature of the collection is clear. For an inventory of the Caja Fiscal archive as it stood in 1881, see ADA, Fondo Notarial Valerio, Legajo 45, Expediente de inventario de las existencias de la Caja Fiscal del Departamento de Ancash, 22 Junio 1881. The 1881 inventory included *padroncillos, matrículas de contribuyentes*, and an *archivo de oficios de la Prefectura*, among other things. Also see AGN, O.L. 639-53, and other prefectural correspondence to the Finance Ministry reporting the destruction of the prefectural secretary's archive, including the *libros copiadores* which contained copies of all prefectural correspondence.

134   See Kapsoli, ed., *Los movimientos campesinos.*

135   Stein, *El levantamiento,* p. 73.

136   James C. Scott, *Weapons of the Weak: Everyday Forms of Peasant Resistance* (New Haven, 1985). Stein (*El levantamiento,* pp. 72–73) does suggest that the Atusparia uprising happened in 1885 and not later because the Indians' "urban patrons" wanted it to. Clearly the uprising of 1885 was part of the civil war; but in 1888 no civil war was necessary for the Chacas revolt to occur. Moreover, factions of the "urban elite" of Huaraz, according to Prefect Huapaya, tried to instigate revolt in 1904, but they failed to mobilize the Indians *en masse* (see below, chapter 4). Indeed, we may upend the recycled argument about peasants' inability to lead their own revolts: parasitic "urban patrons" in provincial Peru could not succeed in carrying off a rebellion, nor could they win a civil war (not to mention a "war of conquest" like that suffered at the hands of the Chileans) without the decisive support of the *varayoc*, who mediated access to the necessary legions of Andean peasants.

137   Of the considerable Peruvian literature on the Atusparia uprising, Alba Herrera, *Atusparia*, is the best researched. The Peruvian historiography includes, but is certainly not limited to, the following works: Santiago Antúnez de Mayolo, *La sublevación de los indios del Callejón de Huaylas* (Lima, 1957); José Santiago Maguiña Chauca, *La revolución indígena de 1885* (Huaraz, 1974) and *La sublevación de Atusparia, Versión oral* (Huaraz, 1984); Ladislao Meza, *Dictadura Atusparia* (Huaraz, 1928); Fidel Olívas Escudero, "Sublevación indígena de 1885," in *Geografía del Perú* (Lima, 1887); Alfonso Ponte González, *Por la senda: Breve ensayo histórico biográfico* (Lima, 1945); Aníbal Quijano, *Problema agrario y movimientos campesinos* (Lima, 1979); Manuel Reina Loli, "Causas del movimiento campesino de 1885," *Revista*

Campesina no. 2 (Lima, 1969), pp. 31–47, and *Pedro Pablo Atusparia* (Lima, 1987); Ernesto Reyna, *El amauta Atusparia* (Lima, 1932); and José Ruíz Huídobro, "La revolución indígena de Ancash," *Ancash* nos. 7 and 11–12 (Lima, 1936), pp. 2–4 and pp. 2–8. Many of these accounts are used in Jeffrey Klaiber, *Religion and Revolution in Peru, 1824–1976* (Notre Dame, 1977) and in Stein, *El levantamiento*, which is the most complete account to date and in which is incorporated Stein's earlier material, previously published in English (among which see especially "Myth and Ideology in a Nineteenth-Century Peruvian Peasant Uprising," *Ethnohistory* 29 [1982] pp. 237–64).

138   Manrique, *Campesinado y nación*.

139   On Aloys Schreiber's public life, see ADA, Libros Republicanos Varios, 1884–95. Also see Stein, *El levantamiento*, pp. 332–34, where Schreiber's obituary is reproduced.

140   ADA, Libros Republicanos Varios, Libro de Correspondencia de la Junta Departamental de Ancachs con los Subprefectos y Apoderados Fiscales, 1890–95.

141   Stein, *El levantamiento*, pp. 103–58, offers an exhaustive treatment of these newspaper debates.

142   Guha, "The Prose of Counter-Insurgency" and *Elementary Aspects of Peasant Insurgency in Colonial India* (Delhi, 1983); also see Gyan Prakash, "Subaltern Studies as Postcolonial Criticism," *American Historical Review* 99:5 (1994), p. 1479.

143   AGN, O.L. 639-53, Informe sobre la Hacienda Jimbe, Prefect Noriega to the Juez de Primera Instancia, fols. 26–26v, Huaraz, 25 January 1885.

144   AGN, O.L. 639-53, Informe sobre la Hacienda Jimbe, Prefect Iraola to the Finance Ministry, fol. 39, 22 July 1885.

145   AGN, O.L. 561-416, Expediente relativo al incendio del archivo de la Caja Fiscal, 1885–86.

146   Florencia Mallon, *The Defense of Community: Peasant Struggle and Capitalist Transition, 1860–1940* (Princeton, 1983); Manrique, *Campesinado y nación* and *Yawar Mayu: Sociedades terratenientes serranas, 1879–1910* (Lima, 1988).

147   AGN, O.L. 639-53, Informe sobre Hacienda Jimbe, fols. 44–44v, 1885–98.

148   BNP/SI, D3688, Expediente iniciado por Alonzo P. Cartland, 1885–87.

149   For the *hacienda*'s boundaries, see AGN, O.L. 639-53, Informe sobre Hacienda Jimbe, fols. 100–103, 1885–98.

150   AGN, O.L. 639-53, Informe sobre Hacienda Jimbe, fols. 34–62, 1885–98.

151   BNP/SI, D4285, Prefect Noriega to the Ministry of Government, 21 February 1885.

152   Subsequent to this attack, Cartland demanded action from Prefect Iraola and let the *iglesista* official know that, as a U.S. citizen, he was also contacting the U.S. representative in Lima as well as the minister of state. Iraola did not catch up with Cochachin until September, though.

153   Other statements also contradicted Cartland's version of events. Carlos Wenceslao Nieto, *alcalde municipal* of the Cáceres del Perú District, argued that Cartland was a mere sharecropper who "became administrator of the lucrative Hacienda San José, leaving Jimbe *al partir* at 30 percent for the *comuneros*" and that he made

no improvements in Jimbe. Moreover: the sugar mill was in Nepeña, not Jimbe; the Chileans had burned the *pueblo*'s homes, not Cartland's; and Castro had been Cartland's friend, but Cartland had merely used Castro, leading the Chileans to Jimbe to capture him, and thus he had betrayed Castro, and for this reason Castro turned on him.

154   A decade later, Jimbe was still a major preoccupation of Ancash's scrambling prefects. See AGN, O.L. 619-161, various communications between Prefect Pedro Cisneros and diverse authorities, 21 December 1895; AGN, O.L. 639-53, Informe sobre Hacienda Jimbe, 1898.

155   *El Comercio*, 29 May 1885. Reproduced in Stein, *El levantamiento*, pp. 141-46.

156   If we use the Census of 1876 as a comparative rather than an absolute measure, then the relative independence of Huaylas's Indian population in terms of land tenure was greater than that of Junín. Citing the 1876 census, Florencia Mallon states that about 30 percent of the population resided on estates in both Cajamarca and Junín. According to the same census taken in Huaylas (provinces of Huaylas and Huaraz), only 7 percent of the total and 11 percent of the rural population resided on *haciendas;* nearly 90 percent of the rural population resided in peasant *estancias* or hamlets. It is significant that Prefect Noriega used the same Census of 1876 to draw up tax registers in 1885. Thus, *hacendados* could have had only a tiny percentage of Indians on their respective lists. The *alcaldes* would have had the rest. I do not wish to suggest here, however, that Huaylas's peasantry exercised greater autonomy than Junín's. Junín's greater market dynamics and the presence of a large mining industry amplified peasant options there. In Junín, moreover, *haciendas* controlled less land than in Ancash or Cajamarca, where landlord control over access to resources did not require that peasants actually reside within the *hacienda*. See Mallon, "Nationalist and Anti-State Coalitions," p. 252.

157   "Voting with one's feet" is a familiar peasant tactic and one that is particularly well suited to avoiding the abuses of military conscription. See Scott, *Weapons of the Weak*.

158   Evidence for this preference of peasants for *guerrilla* over *soldado de línea* service comes from Corongo, Pallasca, and Atun Huaylas. See AHM, Archivo Recavarren, Cuaderno 9, Lazúrtegui to Recavarren, Corongo, 11 June 1883, and Cuaderno 17, D228-248, Recavarren to various officials and Jefes de Guerrillas, fols. 65-69, Huaraz, 17-19 May 1883.

159   *El Comercio*, 9 April 1885.

160   According to an opinion expressed in *El Comercio*, Cáceres was collecting the polltax in the central highlands at the time. Cáceres had suspended the poll-tax for Indians who were enlisted in patriotic *guerrillas* in the departments of Junín and Huancavelica, but not in Ancash. The suspension forgave unpaid taxes in 1882 and waved payment of the 1883 poll-tax. See Manrique, *Campesinado y nación*, p. 206.

161   AHM, Estado Mayor General del Ejército, Legajo 0.1885.6, Callirgos Quiroga to the Peruvian Central Command, Yungay, 27 April 1885.

162   Guha, *Elementary Aspects*.

163   Reyna, "El Amauta Atusparia," *Amauta* 27 (1929), pp. 30 and 39.

164   Stein, *El levantamiento*, p. 91.

165   The cavalry unit, commanded by Sergeant Nickels (also Nichols), did not reach the Callejón de Huaylas until after Iraola took Huaraz. Nickels had been given false information concerning the positions of Indian *guerrillas* in the *quebradas* leading up to the Callejón. See AHM, Correspondencia General, Legajo o.1885.7, Callirgos to War Ministry Dispatch, Huaraz, 27 May 1885; AHM, Prefecturas, Ancash, Legajo o.1885.1, Nickels to War Ministry, Casma, 11–12 and 17 May 1885.

166   On the 22 April vote of Iraola's *junta de guerra* over whether to remain in Yungay, march on Huaraz, or countermarch to the coast, see AHM, Prefecturas, Ancash, Legajo o.1885.1, Iraola to War Ministry Dispatch, 20 May 1885. Iraola overrode the opinions of his officers and ordered his troops to march on Huaraz immediately. Also see AHM, Estado Mayor del Ejército, Legajo o.1885.6, Callirgos Quiroga to the Estado Mayor, Huaraz, 8 May 1885, where Callirgos reports that he expected to confront a force of at least 15,000 *guerrilleros* in Huaraz, and that his officers had agreed to wait eight days in Yungay and then retire to the coast to await instructions, munitions, and a cavalry reinforcement from Lima.

167   Víctor Manuel Izaguirre, "Fiesta del barrio" [1885], in Mauro G. Mendoza, ed., *Ancash: Tradiciones y cuentos* (Lima, 1958).

168   Observations on recent El Señor de la Soledad festival practices were gathered in a series of interviews with informants in Huaraz during May 1990.

169   Archivo Arzobispal de Lima (AAL), Visitas Pastorales, Visita Pastoral de Ancash, Legajo 6, Expediente XXIX, Razón de las yglesias, capillas, y oratorios visitados . . . y las fiestas que en ellos se celebran, 1848.

170   Such an orchestration of religious procession in support of a peasant siege is not unknown in Andean history. Tupac Katari capitalized on the redirected religious processions of peasants and patron saints to bolster his rebel camp at the siege of La Paz in 1781. See Mark Thurner, "Guerra andina y política campesina en el sitio de La Paz, 1781: Aproximaciones etnohistóricas a la práctica insurreccional a través de las fuentes editadas," in Henrique Urbano, ed., *Poder y violencia en los Andes* (Lima, 1991), pp. 93–124.

171   Also reproduced in Stein, *El levantamiento*, pp. 84–95.

172   Ibid., pp. 66 and 195–97.

173   Although he is critical of their interpretations, Stein relies on Alfonso Ponte Gonzáles and Ernesto Reyna (see n. 137 above) for evidence of the clergy's pacification role as leaders of processions and other rituals that had the effect of "calming" the Indians. Yet there is little or no corroborating evidence for the scenarios invented by these writers, despite their claims that they based their accounts on oral testimony. In *El levantamiento*, pp. 186–87, Stein cites Ponte Gonzáles's account of Olívas Escudero "appearing like a ray of hope in the iciest moment, when irremediable things were about to happen . . ." leading a solemn procession in Huaraz on 4 March. According to Ponte, this procession "carried the idea of the Supreme Being to the revolutionaries, and vanquished from the Indian's mind fatal thoughts

of extermination." Unfortunately, Olívas Escudero was not in Huaraz on 4 March,
but rather in Aija with Prefect Noriega. Olívas Escudero himself claimed that he
returned to Huaraz on 5 March. See AGN, O.L. 561-416, Información de testigos
acerca del robo e incendio del archivo de la Caja Fiscal de Ancash, fol. 5, 1885-86.

174   Heraclio Bonilla, "The Indian Peasantry and 'Peru' during the War with Chile,"
in Stern, ed., *Resistance, Rebellion, and Consciousness*, pp. 219-31.

175   Mallon, "Nationalist and Anti-State Coalitions."

176   Tristan Platt, "Simón Bolívar, the Sun of Justice and the Amerindian Virgin:
Andean Conceptions of the *Patria* in Nineteenth-Century Potosí," *Journal of Latin
American Studies* 25:1 (1993), pp. 159-85, and "The Andean Experience of Bolivian
Liberalism, 1825-1900: Roots of Rebellion in 19th-Century Chayanta (Potosí),"
in Stern, ed., *Resistance, Rebellion, and Consciousness*, pp. 280-323.

4. Atusparia's Specter

1   Archivo General de la Nación (AGN), O.L. 571-240, Expediente iniciado por los
Alcaldes Ordinarios de los Distritos de Restauración y Independencia de Huaraz,
1 June 1887, emphasis in original.

2   AGN, O.L. 609-852, Prefect Rodríguez to the Finance Ministry, 20 October 1893.

3   AGN, Archivo del Ministerio del Interior, Legajo 95, Mesa de Partes 73, Prefect
Huapaya to the Ministry of Government, 5 April 1904.

4   *El Nacional*, 1 June 1886; *El Comercio*, 2 June 1886. The texts of these newspaper reports are reproduced in William Stein, *El levantamiento de Atusparia* (Lima, 1988),
pp. 272-76.

5   Ernesto Reyna noted in 1930 that "the painter Palas made a portrait of Atusparia
in which he appeared with a rifle in his hand, ready to attack" and that "they also
took a photograph of him together with the President." See Reyna, "El Amauta
Atusparia," *Amauta* 28 (1930), p. 43.

6   Use of the -*mi* suffix in Quechua, or, for native speakers, *Runa Simi* (in some areas
of Huaylas-Ancash, *Nuna Shimi*) indicates that the speaker has eyewitness valida-
tion of an event. It implies certainty, and it may have been precisely this certainty
that Atusparia sought.

7   Jean Piel employed the concept of "reserva andina" in "Las articulaciones de la reserva andina al estado y al mercado desde 1820 hasta 1950," in Jean Paul Deler and
Yves Saint-Geours, eds., *Estados y naciones en los Andes* (Lima, 1986), pp. 323-36.

8   This new correlation of forces also obtained in the Comas region of Junín, where
a sustained resistance was carried on into the early twentieth century, just as it was
in Huaraz. On the former, see Nelson Manrique, *Campesinado y nación: Las guerrillas indígenas en la guerra con Chile* (Lima, 1981), p. 371. For the opposite, and
in my opinion unfounded, view that the post-1885 period was unfavorable to the
peasantry, see Stein, *El levantamiento*, p. 312.

9   Heraclio Bonilla first noted this trend in "The War of the Pacific and the National
and Colonial Problem in Peru," *Past and Present* 81 (November 1978), pp. 92-118.

10   On the commission to abolish community lands, see Biblioteca Nacional del Perú, Sala de Investigaciones (BNP/SI), D12842, Proyecto de ley sobre repartición de las tierras de comunidad, Tarma, 11 July 1889.

11   For notes on Atusparia's son, see C. A. Alba Herrera, *Atusparia y la revolución campesina de 1885 en Ancash* (Lima, 1985), and Reyna, "El Amauta," *Amauta* 28, pp. 46-47.

12   Much of Atusparia's posthumous fame can be traced to Ernesto Reyna's thin book *El amauta Atusparia* (Lima, 1932), which first appeared in the pages of José Carlos Mariátegui's literary and political journal *Amauta* 26-28 (1929-30). In most of the accounts written prior to the 1920s, Atusparia is typically portrayed as (a) an ignorant, carnivalesque despot or (b) as the peace-seeking proponent of negotiation, honored by the local bourgeoisie for having saved them from "the savage hordes." Although both accounts share commonalities with later indigenist versions, they are typical of the late nineteenth-century racist views of local whites.

13   There is little evidence to support the hoarding of contributions by unscrupulous governors, as occurred in early republican Puno. The evidence here suggests that the poll-tax simply could not be collected. The fact that it was very difficult to find potential collectors, and that the percentage cut had to be increased, lends further credibility to the many voices that pointed to Indian resistance to payment. On Puno, see Christine Hünefeldt, "Poder y contribuciones: Puno, 1825-45," *Revista Andina* 14 (1989), pp. 367-407.

14   Stein, *El levantamiento,* p. 312.

15   Jorge Basadre, *Historia de la República del Perú* (Lima, 1968), vol. 10, p. 221.

16   Budget figures given in Emilio Dancuart, *Anales de la Hacienda Publica del Perú,* vol. 23, pp. 511A-12A, for 1891 agree with the figures cited by Basadre for 1893. According to Ancash's departmental treasury, the 1891 projected amount of *contribución personal* was exactly 96,486 soles, the same amount reported in Basadre's sources. According to this source, however, the total projected budget for 1891 was actually somewhat higher than that indicated in Basadre for 1893. The actual 1891 figure reported by the Ancash treasury was 138,207.60 soles. See AGN, O.L. 603-1114, 1891.

17   AGN, O.L. 603-1114, 1891.

18   Archivo Departamental de Ancash, Huaraz (ADA), Libros Republicanos Varios, Libro Corriente de Contribuciones, 1895-96.

19   AGN, O.L. 609-852, Prefect Rodríguez to the Finance Ministry, 20 October 1893.

20   AGN, Archivo del Ministerio del Interior, Legajo 19, Mesa de Partes 141, Prefect Portal to the Ministry of Government, 3 May 1891.

21   AGN, O.L. 609-852, Prefect Alarco to the Ministry of Government, 1891.

22   ADA, Libros Republicanos Varios, Libros de Contribuciones, 1885-95.

23   AGN, O.L. 579-1178, 1888.

24   ADA, Libro de Correspondencia con varios Ministros, Junta Departamental de Ancash, fol. 271, 1887-90.

25   BNP/SI, D8075, Petición de los Alcaldes Ordinarios de Huaraz al Sor. General
      Cáceres, Presidente de la República, 24 March 1887. See ministry annotations by
      Solar, fols. I–IV, 21 April 1887.

26   This is probably an allusion to the 1839 Battle of Ancachs (Yungay), where the
      Cuzco *caudillo* Agustín Gamarra, with his largely Chilean contingent, defeated
      "the foreign domination" of Andrés de Santa Cruz, the Protector of the Peru-
      Bolivia Confederation (1835–39). Although further research is required, local mili-
      tia units were apparently recruited to fight with Gamarra; it is unclear which seg-
      ments of the local population supported Santa Cruz. The event became enshrined
      in national and regional consciousness when, in commemoration of the battle, the
      Department of Huaylas was rechristened "Department of Ancachs" (later stan-
      dardized as "Ancash").

27   BNP/SI, D8075, Petición de los Alcaldes Ordinarios de Huaraz al Sor. General
      Cáceres, Presidente de la República, Huaraz, 24 March 1887.

28   AGN, Archivo del Ministerio del Interior, Legajo 4, Mesa de Partes 476, Prefect
      Carrión to the Minister of State in the Government Dispatch, 6 April 1887.

29   AGN, Archivo del Ministerio del Interior, Legajo 4, Enrique Caravedo of the Min-
      istry of Government to the Prefect of Ancash, 19 April 1887.

30   ADA, Protocolos Notariales, República, Libro 3, Escribano Vicente Figueroa, fols.
      277v–78, 11 July 1828.

31   Experts for each side produced contrasting sketch-maps of the lands. Particular
      wankas, or stone boundary markers, were assigned different names so as to match
      the particular party's claims vis-à-vis eighteenth-century titles, which gave place
      names only. The sketch-maps are inserted in the "Auto de deslinde" in ADA,
      Fondo Notarial Valerio, Juicios Civiles, Legajo 55, Juan Torres y compartes, agricultores y
      indígenas de la estancia de Marian . . . piden que se practique un deslinde . . . de
      siete fanegadas de tierras, Huaraz, 20 March 1890.

32   ADA, Fondo Notarial Valerio, Juicios Civiles, Legajo 55, Juan Torres y compartes,
      agricultores y indígenas de la estancia de Marian . . . piden que se practique un
      deslinde . . . de siete fanegadas de tierras, Huaraz, fol. 224v, 20 March 1890.

33   The testimonies of witnesses on this point are contradictory. See ADA, Fondo
      Notarial Valerio, Juicios Civiles, Legajo 55, Juan Torres y compartes, agricultores y
      indígenas de la estancia de Marian . . . piden que se practique un deslinde . . . de
      siete fanegadas de tierras, Huaraz, 20 March 1890.

34   ADA, Fondo Notarial Valerio, Juicios Civiles, Legajo 55, Juan Torres y compartes,
      agricultores y indígenas de la estancia de Marian . . . piden que se practique un
      deslinde . . . de siete fanegadas de tierras, Huaraz, 20 March 1890. See testimony
      of Manuel Alzamora, fols. 192–93.

35   One observer in Huaraz wrote, in the 22 June 1885 edition of *El Comercio,* that
      "little by little the Indians are turning over their arms, but they remain distrustful
      and do not come down into town, and as a result there is a scarcity of many articles
      of primary necessity, and among these firewood, which one cannot buy even for 20
      soles per load." Reproduced in Stein, *El levantamiento,* p. 94.

36   David Brading, *The First America: The Spanish Monarchy, Creole Patriots, and the Liberal State, 1492–1867* (Cambridge, 1991), pp. 213–27.

37   ADA, Libro de Actas de la H. Junta Departamental, 1887–89, Solicitud de Justo C. Solís haciendo presente que no tiene por ahora en su poder sus titulos de la quebrada de "Shallap," 30 July 1887.

38   See the extraordinary session of the *junta departamental* of 11 May 1887, Acting Prefect José María B. Sevilla presiding, in ADA, Libro de Actas de la H. Junta Departamental, 1887–89, fols. 14–14v and 31v–32.

39   AGN, O.L. 571-240, Expediente iniciado por los Alcaldes Ordinarios de Huaraz, 1 June 1887. See the resolution of the *junta departamental*, fols. 5–5v, 7 August 1887.

40   AGN, Archivo del Ministerio del Interior, Legajo 6, Mesa de Partes 398, Prefect Cavero to the Ministry of Government, 30 June 1888.

41   AGN, O.L. 583-171, Prefect Cavero to the Finance Ministry, Huaraz, 21 March 1889.

42   AGN, O.L. 580-3, Pedro Cisneros to the Minister of State in the Department of Justice, 27 April 1888.

43   See AGN, Corte Superior de Ancash, Legajo 3, Cisneros to the President of the Superior Court of Ancash, Huaraz, 15 and 17 December 1879.

44   Dancuart, *Anales*, vol. 5, p. 67A.

45   BNP/SI, Prefecturas, Ancash (V), Prefect Cavero to the Ministry of Government, Huaraz, 13 September 1889.

46   BNP/SI, Prefecturas, Ancash (V), Prefect Cavero to the Ministry of Government, 16 August 1889.

47   AGN, O.L. 619-160a, Prefect Cisneros to the Finance Ministry, Huaraz, 7 November 1895.

48   The Vicos episode is noteworthy because similar charges were made in 1885. In 1904, a dispute arose when the leaselord of Vicos, Señor Lostaunao, was accused by his peons of forcing them to work for other landlords on distant *haciendas*. The peons presented an eminently reasonable petition in which they declared that all they wanted was for the *patrón* to respect traditional paternalist codes of behavior. Lostaunao apparently overreacted (some say for premeditated political reasons) and alarmed the population by having an article published in *La Prensa de Huailas* in which he announced an imminent revolt by the peons of Vicos, and explicitly recalled the uprising of 1885. Lostaunao claimed that the rebellion of 1885 had originated in Vicos, but the lieutenant governor of Marcará denied the accusation, pointing out that it was an attempt to slander Germán Schreiber, who was then Huaraz's representative to the Peruvian National Congress. Prefect Huapaya ordered his subprefect, Agustín del Río, to take repressive action against the *vicosinos,* in effect imposing a settlement on them that favored Lostaunao. Subsequent events led to Huapaya's abolition of the *alcaldes*. Prefect Saldías turned the case into an *expediente judicial,* dismissing it as a judicial rather than a political matter. See AGN, Ministerio del Interior, Legajo 95, Mesa de Partes 443 and 374, 1904.

49   Rumors of rebellion in Chacas in 1903 probably contributed to Prefect Huapaya's

shrill discourse and attack on the *alcaldes* of Huaraz. The prefect had sent a small force to Chacas under the command of the subprefect, who captured the two *alcaldes* of Chacas and with them "the imposter Lenin Ynga who, pretending to be Jesus Christ, incited the Indian communities to rebellion and to the extermination of the white race." See AGN, Ministerio del Interior, Prefecturas Ancash, Legajo 89, Mesa de Partes 62, Subprefect of Huari to Prefect Huapaya, Chacas, 7 March 1903.

50 The *"vara* question" was so pressing that it prompted the initiation of a lengthy *expediente,* or documentary investigation, which unfortunately has not yet been recovered.

51 AGN, Archivo del Ministerio del Interior, Legajo 95, Mesa de Partes 73, Prefect Huapaya to the Ministry of Government, 11 March 1904.

52 Castilla's code of municipal government did recognize *alcaldes pedáneos, síndicos,* and *regidores,* however. See *El Comercio,* 17 February 1855. Apparently the Ministry of Government either did not recognize such municipal *alcaldes* as legitimate or considered the *alcaldes ordinarios* to be not municipal authorities but, rather, "political" authorities (i.e., state functionaries dependent on the prefecture).

53 AGN, Ministerio del Interior, Legajo 95, Mesa de Partes 424, Prefect Saldías to the Ministry of Government, 18 October 1904.

54 The repression of the Indian *alcaldes* was begun in earnest under the autocrat Augusto Leguía and his official indigenism in the 1920s. In the name of national integration, the "despotic" *varayoc* would be displaced by the "more democratic" *cabildos,* or communal councils, a reform supported by many *indigenistas* who saw nothing but vestiges of "feudal" oppression and the "colonial legacy" in these ostensibly traditional authorities. Still, some *varayoc* authorities in Ancash would persist until the agrarian reforms of the late 1960s.

55 Florencia Mallon, "Nationalist and Anti-State Coalitions in the War of the Pacific: Junín and Cajamarca, 1879-1902," in Steve J. Stern, ed., *Resistance, Rebellion, and Consciousness in the Andean Peasant World, 18th to 20th Centuries* (Madison, 1987), pp. 268-69.

56 George Kubler first recognized the remarkable Indianization trend in Huaylas (and Huanuco), although his contention that the 1826-54 period produced a new majority of Indians in Huaylas is mistaken and is contradicted by his own sources. Kubler claimed that "non-Indians" were a majority in Huaylas in 1791-95 (p. 40). But non-Indians were never a majority in Huaylas. The Census of 1791, reproduced in Kubler, clearly indicates that Indians were the slight majority in Huaylas, making up 51.28 percent of the total population. The years 1791-1848/50 were relatively stable, with no significant rise of the Indian percentage, which maintained its slight majority. The important Indianization trend does not take off until the century-long period between 1848/50 and 1940, with the largest leap occurring sometime after 1876. Kubler noticed this leap when he observed that in the period of 1876-1940, "from the Callejón de Huaylas eastward to Huamalíes, extremely sharp Indian increases in well-defined territory appear" (p. 47). Lack of statistics for intervals between 1876 and 1940 prevents specifying the critical moments in

this marked trend. Kubler is right, however, about the overall trend: "Surely the re-markable modern Indianization of the Callejón de Huaylas has antecedents in the steady if small Indian gains in Huaylas, continuous there from 1795 to the present" (p. 47). See Kubler, *The Indian Caste of Peru, 1795–1940* (Washington, D.C., 1952).

57 Gootenberg's insightful revision of the demographics exhibits one or two minor in-congruencies in the tabulation of Huaylas demographic trends. These are owing to shifting provincial boundaries, of which Gootenberg rightly warns his readers. For readers who will rely upon his tabulations, the provincial subtotals for the Depart-ment of Ancash given in table 1 (p. 112) of Gootenberg require some adjustment. For Huaylas, the figures for 1791, 1836, and 1850 are correct. The 1862 figure, how-ever, is not equivalent, since Huaylas was halved in 1857. The equivalent figure for 1862 (Huaylas and Huaraz) is 93,113. The provincial subtitle "Huari, Conchuco" should be read as "Huari, Conchucos Alto," and the 1862 figure for Conchucos Bajo (Pallasca and Pomabamba) should be 57,937. In addition, Cajatambo (now Lima) was part of Ancash in 1862. Paul Gootenberg, "Population and Ethnicity in Early Republican Peru: Some Revisions," *Latin American Research Review* 26:3 (1991), pp. 109–57.

58 Kubler, *The Indian Caste*, p. 59.

59 National trends from 1827 to 1940 were from 66 percent Indian and 34 percent *mestizo*-white (in 1827) to 58 percent Indian and 39 percent *mestizo*-white (in 1876) to 46 percent Indian and 53 percent *mestizo*-white (in 1940). If one were to hazard a guess, then perhaps sometime around 1900–1920 the "indigenous" ceased to be the official majority in Peru. See *Censo nacional de población—Resultados generales* (Lima, 1941), p. 62, for the 1876 and 1940 figures. For 1827, see Gootenberg, "Popu-lation and Ethnicity." National trends are also given in Kubler, *The Indian Caste*.

60 Of the forty-nine Peruvian provinces for which data were available, eleven high-land provinces exhibited this late indigenization trend. These eleven provinces were Abancay, Andahuaylas, Aimaraes, Conchucos, Huamalíes, Huari, Huaylas, Jauja, Paruro, Tayacaja, and La Unión. See Kubler, *The Indian Caste*, pp. 27–30.

61 See John Rowe, "The Distribution of Indians and Indian Languages in Peru," *Geo-graphical Review* 37:2 (1947), pp. 202–15. The nuances of census-taking in republi-can Peru are mostly undocumented. In Huaylas-Ancash, individuals and commu-nities often declared their "caste" choice to census-takers who, in disputed cases, checked these against previous registers and/or baptismal records. Cases where an entire community changed its collective classification are known, though. In 1940, Atun Huaylas declared itself to be 100 percent *mestizo*. Nineteenth-century ledgers indicate, however, that routinely one-third of the Atun Huaylas population de-clared itself to be *indígena originario*.

62 Kubler, *The Indian Caste*, p. 43.

63 Orin Starn's provocative argument about the advent of "Andeanism," or the es-sentialized concept of *lo andino*, in contemporary Anglo-American anthropology unfortunately neglects historical trends in Peruvian discourse on the Andes. See Starn, "Missing the Revolution: Anthropologists and the War in Peru," *Cultural*

Anthropology 6:1 (1991), pp. 63–91, and commentary in "La guerra en los Andes," *Allpanchis* (Cuzco) 39 (1992), pp. 5–129.

64   See Manrique, *Campesinado y nación,* pp. 105–9. Bolívar had done the same.

65   Paul Gootenberg, *Imagining Development: Economic Ideas in Peru's "Fictitious Prosperity" of Guano, 1840–1880* (Berkeley, 1993), p. 196.

66   *Ibid.,* p. 197.

67   Luis Carranza, *Colección de articulos publicados por Luis Carranza, médico* (Lima, 1887–88). Consulted in Manuscripts and Archives, Yale University Library, Call no. 16499–16500.

68   Manrique, *Campesinado y nación,* pp. 105–10.

69   Archivo Histórico Militar, Lima (AHM), Prefecturas Ancash, Prefect Iraola to the War Ministry, Huaraz, 11 June 1885.

70   In 1886 criminal suit was brought against Iraola, Callirgos, and other *iglesista* officers accused of "asesinatos, incendios y robos" perpetrated in 1885. This criminal suit was apparently abandoned in 1887. Callirgos was tried and convicted for complicity in the assassination of Puga in Huamachuco, however. Later, his conviction was overturned by the Superior Court of Cajamarca, then reinstated by the Supreme Court. The more general charge of mass murder of peasants and the destruction of their property was politically unsustainable, while the assassination of a *caudillo* of the stature of Puga was not. The conviction of Callirgos was largely owing (apparently) to the efforts of Puga's widow. Because I was unable to pick up the trail of these lost court cases, I here rely on the work of C. A. Alba Herrera, *Atusparia y la revolución campesina de 1885 en Ancash* (Lima, 1985), pp. 202–5.

71   Newspaper reports ranged from 1,000 to 3,000 Indian fatalities, although Iraola's official *partes* reported far fewer. See, for the upper estimate, *El Comercio,* 22 June 1885.

72   I thank Florencia Mallon for first suggesting to me the fruitful idea that the *indio manso* and *indio bravo* images might form a single continuum of racist imagery.

73   Fidel Olívas Escudero, "Sublevación indígena de 1885," in *Geografía del Perú* (Lima, 1887), pp. 123–28.

74   The Janus images of "indio manso" and "indio bravo" that were applied to the memory of the Atusparia insurgency were echoed in subsequent literary and historiographical characterizations of the personages of Atusparia and Cochachin. The indigenist writer Ernesto Reyna, picking up on newspaper accounts and local legend, would portray a Cochachin endowed with "the ferocity of the savage." Cochachin is the encarnate "indio bravo"—untamed, violent, anti-clerical; a rapist, "skull-crusher," and "drinker of [white] blood." Meanwhile, Atusparia, the "noble and timid," has much of the compromising "indio manso" in him, as he seeks peace with whites (the why of his supposed envenenation), but is also the wise Indian, and thus represents the future, spiritual *mestizaje* of Peru (realized in his son?).

75   In the parlance of the day, "capitalistas" referred to the landholding class of the coastal plantations, many of whom were identified with the Magdalena govern-

ment as "argollas" and, later, with the Iglesias regime as collaborators. Persons like Alonso Cartland would have fit this description, for example.

5. Republican Histories, Postcolonial Legacies

1   See Cecilia Méndez, "República sin indios: La comunidad imaginada del Perú," in Henrique Urbano, ed., *Tradición y modernidad en los Andes* (Lima, 1993), pp. 15–41.

2   Eric Hobsbawm, "Peasants and Politics," *Journal of Peasant Studies* 1:1 (1973), p. 5.

3   Ibid., p. 8.

4   Scholarly efforts to type and measure the scale of peasant uprisings in Peru include the following: Jürgen Golte, *Repartos y rebeliones: Tupac Amaru y las contradicciones de la economía colonial* (Lima, 1980); Scarlett O'Phelan, *Rebellions and Revolts in Eighteenth-Century Peru and Upper Peru* (Cologne, 1985); Wilfredo Kapsoli, ed., *Los movimientos campesinos en el Perú* (Lima, 1977); and Rodrigo Montoya, *Capitalismo y luchas campesinas en el Perú del siglo XX* (Lima, 1989). Golte and Montoya are particularly concerned with the scale of peasant uprisings.

5   See Steve J. Stern, "New Approaches to the Study of Peasant Rebellion and Consciousness: Implications of the Andean Experience," in Stern, ed., *Resistance, Rebellion, and Consciousness in the Andean Peasant World, 18th to 20th Centuries* (Madison, 1987), pp. 3–25.

6   Steve J. Stern, "The Age of Andean Insurrection, 1742–1782: A Reappraisal," in Stern, ed., *Resistance, Rebellion, and Consciousness*, pp. 34–93.

7   Ibid.; Sempat Assadourian, *El sistema colonial en los Andes* (Lima, 1982); Scarlett O'Phelan, "Comunidades campesinas y rebeliones en el siglo XVIII," in Alberto Flores Galindo, ed., *Comunidades campesinas: Cambios y permanencias* (Lima, 1987), pp. 95–114; and Jan Szeminski, "Why Kill the Spaniard? New Perspectives on Andean Insurrectionary Ideology in the 18th Century," in Stern, ed., *Resistance, Rebellion, and Consciousness*, pp. 166–92.

8   John Rowe, "El movimiento nacional inca del siglo XVIII," *Revista Universitaria* (Cuzco) 107 (1954), pp. 17–47.

9   See Florencia Mallon, *Peasant and Nation: The Making of Postcolonial Mexico and Peru* (Berkeley, 1995), pp. 327–28 and n. 18.

10 Rowe, "El movimiento nacional inca."

11 Heraclio Bonilla, "Continuidad y cambio en la organización política del estado en el Perú independiente," in Alberto Flores Galindo, ed., *Independencia y revolución, 1780–1840* (Lima, 1987), pp. 270–94, and "Comunidades indígenas y estado nación en el Perú," in Flores Galindo, ed., *Comunidades campesinas*, pp. 13–27.

12 In Peru the critical period spanned the years circa 1880–1900, with key events in 1883–85; in Bolivia the same two decades were critical, and events came to a head in 1899–1900. In Ecuador, the understudied civil war campaign of Eloy Alfaro in 1895 was of critical importance and included the participation of Andean peasants.

13 See Florencia Mallon, "Nationalist and Anti-State Coalitions in the War of the Pacific: Junín and Cajamarca, 1879–1902," and Tristan Platt, "The Andean Experience of Bolivian Liberalism, 1825–1900: Roots of Rebellion in 19th-Century

Chayanta (Potosí)," both in Stern, ed., *Resistance, Rebellion, and Consciousness,* pp. 232–79 and pp. 280–323.

14   See Antonia Moreno de Cáceres, *Recuerdos de la campaña de La Breña* (Lima, 1976) for image of Cáceres as a messianic "Inka."

15   Stern, "New Approaches," p. 9.

16   The elite *alcalde mayor* position was extinguished in Huaylas-Ancash by the eighteenth century.

17   On "intellectuals" in this sense of mediation, see Steven Feierman, *Peasant Intellectuals: Anthropology and History in Tanzania* (Madison, 1990), pp. 17–18.

18   Roger Rasnake, *Domination and Cultural Resistance: Authority and Power among an Andean People* (Durham and London, 1988).

19   Alberto Flores Galindo, *Buscando un inca: Identidad y Utopía en los Andes* (Lima, 1987) and "In Search of an Inca," in Stern, ed., *Resistance, Rebellion, and Consciousness,* pp. 193–210.

20   On the *tupamarista* vision, see Jan Szeminski, *La utopía tupamarista* (Lima, 1984) and "Why Kill the Spaniard?"

21   C. A. Alba Herrera made this interesting rhetorical claim in Peruvian newsprint.

22   On Andean leadership in the rebellions of 1780–83, see Szeminski, "Why Kill the Spaniard?"; O'Phelan, "Comunidades campesinas"; Flores Galindo, *Buscando un inca;* and Mark Thurner, "Guerra andina y política campesina en el sitio de La Paz, 1781," in Henrique Urbano, ed., *Poder y violencia en los Andes* (Lima, 1991), pp. 93–124. The La Paz case demonstrates that local *alcalde*-like peasant authorities, or *hilacatas,* also played a decisive role there. Moreover, "Tupac Katari" was not a hereditary *kuraka* but a purveyor of coca and cloth, and that was what counted most. He claimed to be a reincarnate "Inka king" and carried out what he and his followers imagined to be the symbolic and political roles of such a figure.

23   Szeminski, "Why Kill the Spaniard?"

24   Manuel Burga, *Nacimiento de una utopía: Muerte y resurrección de los incas* (Lima, 1988).

25   On the latter, see Flores Galindo, "In Search of an Inca," and David Brading, *The First America: The Spanish Monarchy, Creole Patriots, and the Liberal State, 1492–1867* (Cambridge, 1991).

26   The notion of native rebellion emerging in the logical political space of indirect rule is developed in Karen Fields, *Revival and Rebellion in Colonial Central Africa* (Princeton, 1988).

27   On the role of the *reparto,* see Stern, "The Age of Andean Insurrection," and Brooke Larson and Robert Wasserstrom, "Coerced Consumption in Colonial Bolivia and Guatemala," *Radical History Review* 27 (1983), pp. 49–78.

28   Szeminski, "Why Kill the Spaniard?" Also see Brooke Larson, "Caciques, Class Structure, and the Colonial State in Bolivia," *Nova Americana* 2 (1979), pp. 197–235, and Alberto Flores Galindo, ed., *Tupac Amaru II* (Lima, 1976).

29   Szeminski, "Why Kill the Spaniard?"

30   On the election of ritual "Ingas" in the fiestas of early republican Huaylas-Ancash,

see Archivo Departamental de Ancash, Huaraz (ADA), Fondo Documental Valerio, Causas Criminales, Legajo 01, Autos criminales seguidos de oficio contra los reos Francisco Castaneda, María Bernarda, y María Visitación por la muerte de José Espíritu, indígena de Caraz, 1826. Such customs were also observed in late eighteenth-century Huaylas, and they are still practiced in parts of Ancash today. See Burga, *Nacimiento*.

31   See ADA, Fondo Notarial Valerio, Civiles, Legajo 44, Don Pedro Pablo Atusparia con Don Francisco Huayané sobre propiedad de los terrenos de Huanchacpampa, 1879. Atusparia's shaky signature appears in ADA, Fondo Notarial Valerio, Civiles, Legajo 48, Juicios Verbales, fols. 1–iv, 4 February 1886.

32   William Stein, *El levantamiento de Atusparia* (Lima, 1988), pp. 300–307.

33   Ernesto Reyna, *El amauta Atusparia* (Lima, 1932), p. 1. The serialized "Amauta Atusparia" appeared in Mariátegui's review *Amauta* 26–28 (1929–30).

34   José Carlos Mariátegui, *Siete ensayos de interpretación de la realidad peruana* [1928] (Lima, 1989), pp. 204–5. My translation.

35   Fernand Braudel, *The Mediterranean World in the Age of Philip II* (New York, 1972), quoted in Rena Lederman, "Changing Times in Mendi: Notes toward Writing Highland New Guinea History," *Ethnohistory* 33:1 (1986), p. 23.

36   On the highland journey, see Miguel de Estete, "La relación del viaje que hizo el señor capitán Hernando Pizarro por mandado del señor gobernador, su hermano, desde el pueblo de Caxamalca a Parcama, y de allí a Jauja," in Francisco de Jérez, *La verdadera conquista del Perú* [1535] (Lima, 1938).

37   We may associate the influential indigenist Luis E. Valcárcel (an associate of Mariátegui) with the "two Perus" phrase, although it undoubtedly has an earlier coinage. See, for example, "Sobre peruanidad," *Amauta* 26 (1929), p. 100. The "Perú profundo" notion is probably Jorge Basadre's. Juan Martínez-Alier criticized the indigenist tendency to essentialize Indians in "Relations of Production in Andean Haciendas: Peru," in Kenneth Duncan and Ian Rutledge, eds., *Land and Labour in Latin America: Essays on the Development of Agrarian Capitalism in the Nineteenth and Twentieth Centuries* (Cambridge, 1977), p. 161. Nils Jacobsen's recent study, *Mirages of Transition: The Peruvian Altiplano, 1780–1930* (Berkeley, 1994), continues to cite the "colonial legacy" as the defining characteristic of rural life in the southern highlands of Peru during the nineteenth century.

38   María Rostworoski, *Doña Francisca Pizarro: Una ilustre Mestiza, 1534–1598* (Lima, 1989), pp. 20–21.

39   Although geographically inscribed perceptions of Peruvian dualism are relatively new, certain antecedents in colonial political geography were important for Peru's cultural formation. Unlike Mexico, which Spain governed from its precolonial highland center, Peru was administered from the lowland coastal enclave of Lima, which became Spanish South America's gilded "City of Kings." But sixteenth-century Lima, like nineteenth-century Bombay—in kind, not degree—could never have maintained colonial rule without regional nodes of control located in the densely populated agrarian hinterlands. Huaraz was one such regional node. And

rather than leave such hinterland regions untouched, Spain's colonial civilizing mission dramatically reconfigured Andean political formations in the interests of neo-Mediterranean state formation. See Mark Thurner, "From Two Nations to One Divided: The Contradictions of Nation-Building in Andean Peru" (Ph.D. diss., University of Wisconsin–Madison, 1993), chap. 2.

40   The revised notion that Peru's modern dualism stems from the nineteenth-century "guano age" is suggested in Paul Gootenberg, *Between Silver and Guano: Commercial Policy and the State in Postindependence Peru* (Princeton, 1989), p. 89, and *Imagining Development: Economic Ideas in Peru's "Fictitious Prosperity" of Guano, 1840–1880* (Berkeley, 1993), p. 198.

41   Peralta's synthetic claims seem problematic in light of the wealth of data he presents on Cuzco—most of which agrees with the general findings of the present book and, in my view, can be read to support the contrary assertion. See Víctor Peralta, *En pos del tributo* (Lima, 1991), p. 12.

42   Spivak's readings against the grain of the early work of subaltern studies exposed the liberal historicity of dependency narratives in Indian historiography. A similar critique could be leveled on the narratives of *dependentista* historiography concerning Latin America. See Gayatri Chakravorty Spivak, "Subaltern Studies: Deconstructing Historiography," in Spivak, *In Other Worlds: Essays in Cultural Politics* (New York and London, 1987), pp. 197-221.

43   See Marie-Danielle Demélas et al., "Informe preliminar al problema de los estados-naciones en los Andes," in Jean-Paul Deler and Yves Saint-Geours, *Estados y naciones en los Andes* (Lima, 1986), pp. 17-28.

44   Of course, closet monarchists, reactionary Hispanists, and some clerics were eager to critique republican misrule, but their arguments were easily dismissed or simply stamped out on nationalist political grounds. But the well-meaning criticism of liberal political economists like Del Río (or, after him, Emilio Dancuart), and the critical petitions of "patriotic" Indian spokespersons, raised more serious questions.

45   Biblioteca Nacional del Perú, Sala de Investigaciones (BNP/SI), D8075, Petición de los Alcaldes Ordinarios de Huaraz al Sor. General Cáceres, Presidente de la República, Huaraz, 24 March 1887.

46   Milan Kundera, *The Book of Laughter and Forgetting*, trans. M. Henry Heim (New York, 1980), quoted in Ana María Alonso, "Gender, Power, and Historical Memory: Discourses of Serrano Resistance," in Judith Butler and Joan W. Scott, eds., *Feminists Theorize the Political* (New York, 1992), p. 418.

47   Benedict Anderson, *Imagined Communities: Reflections on the Origins and Spread of Nationalism* (London and New York, 1991); Partha Chatterjee, *Nationalist Thought and the Colonial World: A Derivative Discourse?* (London, 1986) and *The Nation and Its Fragments: Colonial and Postcolonial Histories* (Princeton, 1993).

48   Alonso, "Gender, Power, and Historical Memory," p. 418.

49   Dipesh Chakrabarty, "Postcoloniality and the Artifice of History: Who Speaks for 'Indian' Pasts?" in H. Aram Veeser, ed., *The New Historicism Reader* (New York, 1994), pp. 342-69.

50 See Mark Thurner, "Historicizing 'the Postcolonial' from Nineteenth-Century Peru," *Journal of Historical Sociology* 9:1 (1996), pp. 1–18.

51 Mallon, "Nationalist and Anti-State Coalitions" and *Peasant and Nation;* Nelson Manrique, *Campesinado y nación: Las guerrillas indígenas en la guerra con Chile* (Lima, 1981).

INDEX

Mark Thurner is Assistant Professor of History
at the University of Florida.

Library of Congress Cataloging-in-Publication Data

Thurner, Mark.
From two republics to one divided : contradictions of postcolonial nationmaking
in Andean Peru / Mark Thurner.
p.   cm. — (Latin America Otherwise: Languages, Empires, Nations)
Includes index.
ISBN 0-8223-1805-9 (alk. paper). — ISBN 0-8223-1812-1 (pbk. : alk. paper)
1. Indians of South America—Peru—Ancash—Government relations.   2. Quechua
Indians—Government relations.   3. Huaylas (Peru : Province)—History.
4. Insurgency—Peru—Huaylas (Province)   5. Atusparia, Pedro Pablo, 1840–1887.
6. Peru—History—1812–1904.   I. Title.
F3429.1.A45T58   1997
985'.21—dc20   96-7813   CIP